Women's Guild of St. Mark's Church

Clever Cooking

Women's Guild of St. Mark's Church

Clever Cooking

ISBN/EAN: 9783744792417

Printed in Europe, USA, Canada, Australia, Japan

Cover: Foto ©Andreas Hilbeck / pixelio.de

More available books at **www.hansebooks.com**

He who eats what's cooked our way
Will live to eat some other day

CLEVER

COOKING

PUBLISHED BY THE

WOMEN'S GUILD OF ST. MARK'S CHURCH,

SEATTLE, WASHINGTON.

COMMITTEE:

Mrs. RICHARD C. STEVENS,

Mrs. HENRY C. COLVER,

Mrs. HORACE C. HENRY,

Mrs. JAMES D. LOWMAN,

Mrs. EDWIN A. STROUT,

Mrs. CHARLES E. SHEPARD,

Mrs. WINFIELD R. SMITH

SEATTLE, WASH.
METROPOLITAN PRINTING & BINDING CO.,
1896

A PREFACE usually both disappoints and aggravates—it says nothing, with a deal of words; and it holds the hungry reader from the feast before his eyes. But a cook-book's should more kindly speed on rather than hinder from that crowning banquet of literature. Yes, *crowning:* for is it not the essence of all things good? And does it not contain the very provender which goes to the making of all other books. and without which even our brains would evaporate? Epitome it is, too. of man's deep excogitations and indeed of life itself. Here you have mathematics, science, the philosopher's "cause and effect," the "high seriousness" of all great poetry—are not our cream-puffs soulful poems —the wit's spice and tartness, the artist's daintiest device. the arguments of state which make and unmake crowns. Nay, only look deeper, and find in that microcosm the kitchen. besides the object lessons which it fabricates, other most nutricious lessons of the Greek's golden moderation and other moralities. But of all to be learned there or to issue thence the preface cannot give you a first course or even a taste. That is not its part. It can only ask you to partake. It is like a lady who at evening welcomes her guests. Much agony hath gone to the morning's work ; and sundry costly viands too—else had not her art triumphed. Yet of all this not a hint in her voice or mien as she smilingly:

> " Madam, the dinner is served."
> "Ah, well then, ladies and gentlemen—
> 'Now, good digestion wait on appetite
> And health on both.' "

*" To be a good cook means the knowledge of all fruits,
herbs, balms and spices, and of all that is healing and meet in
fields and grove, savory in meat. It means carefulness, in-
ventiveness, watchfulness, willingness and readiness of appli-
ance. It means the economy of your great-grandmother and
the science of modern chemists; it means much tasting and no
wasting; it means English thoroughness, French art and
Arabian hospitality; it means in fine that you are to be perfectly and always ladies, and you are to see that everybody has
something nice to eat."—*RUSKIN.

ACKNOWLEDGMENT.

It would be a pleasure to thank by name each one who has assisted this book, but that is impossible. Primarily are we indebted to our advertisers. We have an added kindly feeling for them because from personal experience we know their trustworthiness and the merits of the articles they advertise.

In the compilation we have received especial courtesies from Mrs. Lincoln, Mrs. Rorer, and *The Household News;* and also from many a notable housekeeper outside the Parish of St. Mark's.

TABLE OF

WEIGHTS AND MEASURES

2 teaspoonfuls of dry ingredients..........	1 tablespoonful
4 teaspoonfuls of liquid......	= 1 tablespoonful
4 tablespoonfuls of liquid	= ¼ gill, ¼ cup or 1 wineglassful
1 tablespoonful of liquid................	= ½ ounce
1 pint of liquid......................	= 1 pound
2 gills of liquids..........................	= 1 cup or ½ pint
1 kitchen cup	= ½ pint
1 heaping quart of sifted flour....	= 1 pound
4 cups of flour...........................	= 1 quart or 1 pound
1 rounded tablespoonful of flour....	= ½ ounce
3 cups of cornmeal	= 1 pound
1½ pints of cornmeal......................	= 1 pound
1 cup of butter.......................... ...	= ½ pound
1 pint of butter	1 pound
1 tablespoonful of butter	= 1 ounce
Butter the size of an egg.................	= 2 ounces
Butter the size of a walnut...............	= 1 ounce
1 solid pint of chopped meat	= 1 pound
10 eggs	= 1 pound
A dash of pepper.........................	= ¼ teaspoonful, or 3 good shakes
2 cups of granulated sugar	= 1 pound
1 pint of granulated sugar	= 1 pound
1 pint of brown sugar	= 13 ounces
2¼ cups of powdered sugar..........	= 1 pound
An ordinary tumbler....................	= ½ pint
2 tablespoonfuls	= 1 fluid ounce

TABLE OF CONTENTS

L'ENVOI—TABLE TALK

For a Dinner Party of Thirteen.

(When making put in a thirteenth line according to taste.)

For soup, of books we'll have a rich extract.
  Fish, sallies caught from fancy's sparkling stream:
And oysters, our young folk in love, with tact
  For sauce to both. In fitting time 'twill seem
Mete we partake of dish of sage discourse.
  A salad of crisp shoots of gossip-vine
With char'ty's oil and just a dash (no worse)
  Of malice. But each guest must bring the wine
Of his own wit. Judgments of frozen sense
  On things of church and state shall be dessert.
While sweets the gracious hostess must dispense.
  Alas, too soon from feast to crusts we shall revert!
            M. TREIZE INCONNU.

ERRATA

Page 11. Tomato Soup No. 3—Read 1 *tablespoonful* of cornstarch.
Page 38. Venison Steak—Read 1 tablespoonful *butter* instead of water.
Page 57. Chicken Terrapin—Line 5, read *sauce* instead of same.
Page 67. Lobster Baskets—Line 7, read *heat* instead of beat.
Page 92. Lactiola Dressing—Line 8, read mustard instead of nutmeg.
Page 125. Omelette—Line 11, read *over* instead of once.
Page 192. Coffee Jelly—Line 1, insert *gelatine* after box.
Page 219. Scripture Cake—Line 3, read *22* instead of 24.
Page 219. Scripture Cake—Line 6, read *xliii* instead of iii.
Page 219. Scripture Cake—Line 11, read *teaspoonful* baking powder.
Page 225. Nut Cake No. 1—Line 1, read 1½ cups sugar and ½ cup butter
Page 228. Spice Cake No. 2—Line 11, read *flavored* instead of flavored.
Page 232. Chocolate Filling No. 2—Line 5, read *boil* instead of cool.
Page 240. Oatmeal Cookies—Line 1, read 1¼ cups Quaker Oats.
Page 255. Jelly—Line 8, read *skimming* instead of simmering.
Page 255. Jelly—Line 16, insert *not* after for.
Page 268. Maple Creams—Line 3, read *hairs* instead of is hard.
Page 270. Molasses Taffy—Line 2, read ¾ instead of ⅔.
Page 279. Soda Mint—Line 3, read *cork* instead of cook.

We are indebted to Dr. Sarah J. Dean for a large portion of our Sick Room recipes.

SOUPS

Bouillon

Will Serve Five Persons.

1 tablespoonful of butter
1½ pounds of finely chopped beef (from the round)
1 bay leaf
½ of an onion, sliced
1 stalk of celery
3 or 4 cloves
2 slices of carrot
2 sprigs of parsley
Shell and white of 1 egg

Melt the butter in a granite saucepan, add the onion and cook until thoroughly brown, when add the beef, celery, cloves, carrot, bay leaf and parsley and one quart of cold water. Cover the saucepan and stand on the back of the stove where it will heat slowly. Let it *simmer* gently for three hours; strain, return to the kettle and bring to a boil. Beat the white of an egg with one-half cup of cold water until thoroughly mixed. Crush the shell and add it to the egg; add this to the boiling bouillon. Boil four minutes, stand on the back of the stove one minute to settle, and strain through cheese cloth. Be sure to wring out the cloth from cold water before straining.

MRS. C. E. SHEPARD (from Table Talk).

(1)

Brown Soup Stock

Will Serve Eight or Ten Persons.

4 pounds hind shin of beef

8 whole cloves

4 teaspoonfuls mixed sweet herbs

1 small carrot

4 quarts cold water

8 whole peppercorns

1 tablespoonful salt

3 large onions

2 stalks celery

2 sprigs parsley

Wipe and cut the meat and bones in small pieces. Put the marrow, bones, half of the meat and the cold water into the kettle. Soak half an hour before heating. Add spices and herbs. Brown the onions and the remainder of the meat and add them to stock. Add the vegetables cut fine, *simmer* eight or ten hours and strain. When cold, take off the grease; it may be necessary to wring a cloth out of hot water and wipe off the stock—not a pinhead must be left. To clear it, allow the white and shell of one egg to every quart of soup, adding the egg when the soup is perfectly cold. Beat them well together, then set on the stove, stirring until hot. Let it boil ten minutes without stirring. Draw it back on the stove and add half a cup of cold water. Let it stand ten minutes. Wring a napkin out of hot water and lay it on the colander. Put the finest wire strainer on the napkin and pour the soup through, letting it take its own time to drain. When ready to serve, heat to the boiling point. You may serve with it in the tureen, thin slices of lemon, glass of sherry, or yolks of hard-boiled eggs, sliced.

MRS. C. E. SHEPARD.

Spice Soup

Good for Dinner Party.

Boil a large bone all day, and see that your stock measures when strained four quarts. Add 2 cups tomatoes, 1 teaspoonful cloves, ½ teaspoonful each of mace, cinnamon and allspice, pepper and salt to taste, grated peel and juice of 1 lemon, 1 teacup browned flour moistened in water and stirred in while your soup is boiling, ½ dozen hard-boiled eggs, the whites chopped fine and yolks added just before serving.

Mrs. R. W. EMMONS.
(From Webfoot Cook Book.)

Veal Soup (Excellent)

Put a knuckle of veal into three quarts of cold water, with a small quantity of salt, and one small tablespoonful of uncooked rice. Boil slowly, hardly above simmering, four hours, when the liquor should be reduced to half the quantity; remove from the fire. Into the tureen put the beaten egg and stir well into it a teacupful of cream or, in hot weather, new milk ; add a piece of butter the size of a hickory nut; on this strain the soup, boiling hot, stirring all the time. Just at the last, beat it well for a minute.

Mrs. ALBERT T. TIMMERMAN.
(From White House Cook Book.)

Cream of Mutton Soup

2½ pounds of mutton
½ cup of rice
1 tablespoonful of flour (scant)
¼ carrot
1 tablespoonful of salt
1 teaspoonful of catsup (mushroom, walnut or tomato)
1 cup of tomatoes
1½ quart of water
1 quart of milk
1 small onion
1 tablespoonful of butter
Black pepper and cayenne
Small bouquet of herbs
Tiny bit of mace
3 tablespoonfuls of sherry

Put the mutton (neck will do) with the vegetables, rice and cold water into the soup-pot. The meat should be free from fat and cut in small pieces. When it begins to boil, skim carefully, and let it *simmer* for three or four hours. (At the end of two hours add the herbs and mace.) Then cream the butter and flour together, add this, the seasoning and the catsup, and cook for five minutes longer. Put the milk into the double boiler.

HORSESHOE Soap will not *draw* your *hands*.

Put the soup into a colander, rubbing through as much as possible. Rinse out the kettle, return the soup to it, add the boiling milk, taste for seasoning, add sherry, more or less, as you like it, and serve *immediately*.

MRS. RICHARD C. STEVENS.

Cheese Soup

1 pint stock, heated	1 pint milk, boiling hot
1 tablespoonful corn starch	Yolks 2 or 3 eggs

1 cup grated cheese

Put the corn starch into the hot milk, pour into the stock, then gradually pour over the beaten yolks, beating all the time. Have the cheese in the tureen and pour the above mixture over it.

MRS. J. W. CLISE.

Mock Chicken Soup

Will Serve Six Persons.

2 tablespoonfuls of flour	2 tablespoonfuls of cream
1½ pints of beef stock	1 egg

Butter size of an egg

Put the butter and flour in a saucepan, stir until smooth; add stock little by little. Just before taking from the fire add the cream and egg well beaten together; salt and pepper to taste.

MRS. T. M. DAULTON.

Green Turtle Soup

Take the meat from a can of green turtle, add a quart of stock and put in a stew pan, add a bouquet of sweet herbs (in a muslin), a dozen peppercorns and a half dozen cloves. Put a piece of butter the size of an egg into the frying pan and add a small onion, a stalk of celery, a small slice of turnip and two slices of carrot, all minced fine. Fry until nicely browned, about ten minutes, and skim out into the soup. Put two tablespoonfuls of flour into the butter and stir into the

WEBB'S Extracts are triple strength. Use them.

soup; *simmer* for an hour; skim carefully, strain and return the soup to the kettle. Separate the meat as much as possible from the vegetables, cut in dice and return to the soup with mucilage and green fat (diced), which was laid aside in the beginning. Season with salt and pepper; boil up; add two hard-boiled eggs, chopped fine, three tablespoonfuls sherry and serve with thin slices of lemon cut in points. Do not boil after adding the eggs. Water may be used instead of stock.

MRS. RICHARD C. STEVENS.

Crab Soup

Will Serve Four Persons.

1 large or 2 small crabs   1 quart new milk
3 square crackers   1 teaspoonful salt
Dash of cayenne   2 tablespoonfuls sherry
1 piece butter size of an egg

Put the meat from the body of the crabs into a chopping bowl and chop coarsely; add the crackers, rolled fine, the salt, pepper and butter. Put the milk in a double boiler, and when just at the boiling point add the crab meat, etc., and the meat from the claws cut in nice bits. Taste for seasoning. Cover for one minute, stir well, add the sherry and serve *immediately*. The sherry may be omitted (it is not so nice though), or you may use more or less, according to your liking. A little whipped cream is an improvement.

MRS. RICHARD C. STEVENS.

Oyster Soup

100 oysters   1 large tablespoonful flour
¼ pound butter   1 pint cream.

Rub the flour and butter till perfectly smooth. Take the liquor from the oysters and let it come to a boil, skim well and pour it into a dish. Rinse out the kettle carefully. Pour back the liquor and into it put the

cream, oysters, butter and flour, salt, red pepper and a
little whole mace.   Boil, stirring constantly, until the
gills of the oysters begin to curl.   Serve immediately.

MRS. W. A. PETERS.

Claret Soup

Pour 1 pint of boiling water into a pint of claret ; add
a tablespoonful of lemon juice, and ½ cup of sugar;
moisten one tablespoonful of arrowroot with a little cold
water, add it to the hot soup, cook in double boiler just
a moment and stand aside to cool.   May be served
either hot or cold.   By permission of

MRS. S. T. RORER and THE HOUSEHOLD NEWS CO.

Split Pea Soup

Soak ½ cup of split peas for several hours, then boil
them two or three hours.   Have about a pint of water
on them when done.   Rub through a strainer.   Add 3
or 4 cups of milk, a little salt and pepper and 1 teaspoonful of butter.   Usually it is thick enough, but if
not, thicken with a large teaspoonful of flour, mixed to
a smooth paste in a little milk.   Serve with croûtons.

MRS. WINFIELD R. SMITH.

Split Pea Soup No. 2

4 cups split peas	2 onions
1 head celery	1 turnip
1 carrot	Salt and pepper
2 quarts stock or 2 quarts water and some fresh meat bones	

Soak the peas twelve hours, drain and put into a
kettle with the stock, or 2 quarts of water and some
fresh meat bones; add the vegetables and seasoning
and boil about three hours, or until the peas are very
tender, stirring occasionally.   Take out the bones and
rub the soup through a fine sieve.   Serve with dried
mint and croûtons.

MRS. BONE.

WEBB'S Ground Spices are perfectly pure.

Green Pea Soup

1 quart canned peas   1 teaspoonful of salt
1 quart of milk   ¼ teaspoonful of pepper
1 tablespoonful of butter   2 tablespoonfuls of flour
3 slices of dry bread

Put the peas, flour, salt and pepper in a saucepan, and cook till the peas are soft, then rub through a colander. Have the milk heated to boiling point in a separate saucepan, add to the strained peas with the butter and flour rubbed together, taste for seasoning and serve immediately with croûtons made of the three slices of bread.

Mrs. NINA C. SPENCER.

Vert Pré Soup

Take 1 pound of spinach, well washed, put into saucepan with enough water to cover, a tiny bit of soda and a little salt. Let it just come to the boil, then drain and press out the water. Put the spinach into a saucepan with

2 ounces of butter   ½ pint shelled peas
2 onions sliced fine   A spray of green mint
A small bunch of herbs

Simmer fifteen or twenty minutes, then add 2 tablespoonfuls of flour, or rice flour, and 3 pints of water. Cook all together one and a half hours. Rub the purée through a fine hair sieve and to each quart of the purée add ½ pint of cream or milk and yolks of 3 eggs. Stir in a double boiler till it thickens, strain into tureen and serve with small round croûtons.

Mrs. SILLITOE.

Spinach Soup

Boil 1 quart of spinach for ten minutes in salted water, drain and rinse in cold water, chop fine and rub through a strainer into three pints of boiling milk. Thicken with 2 tablespoonfuls of butter and one of flour.

Mrs. ANDREWS.

HORSESHOE Soap for economy and quality.

Purée Printanier Maigre

Vegetable Soup.

2 large carrots
2 potatoes (peeled)
2 leeks
2 bay leaves
1 good handful of lettuce
1 tablespoonful of flour
3 ounces butter

2 large onions
2 turnips
1 pound of asparagus (if in season)
1 sprig of thyme and parsley
3 pints of milk

Yolks of 3 eggs

Cut up the vegetables and fry well in 2 ounces of the butter, add the flour and milk, and *simmer* three-quarters of an hour, or until tender; rub through a purée sieve. Let it heat again in the bain Marie, or a double boiler, and to each quart of purée add ½ pint of warm cream, to which has been added the remaining ounce of butter and the eggs. Stir all well till it thickens. This soup may be prepared with stock or water instead of milk.

MRS. SILLITOE.

Asparagus Soup

2 bunches of asparagus
1 teaspoonful of salt
Butter, size of a walnut

3 cups of milk
A dash of pepper
1 tablespoonful of flour

½ cup of whipped cream

Cut off the tender portion of the stalks and lay aside to serve as a vegetable. Cut the remainder of the stalks into small pieces and boil until tender (it will take about three-quarters of an hour), and have a pint of water on them when done. Have the milk hot in the double boiler, mash the asparagus in the water and strain into the hot milk. Rub the butter and flour together, and add to the hot mixture; also add the seasoning. Put the whipped cream in the tureen and pour the soup over it, and serve *immediately*.

MRS. WINFIELD R. SMITH.

WEBB'S Extracts are triple strength. Use them.

Turtle Bean Soup

1 pint black turtle, or pink 1 onion
    Spanish beans   1 carrot
1 beef bone   1 turnip
5 quarts water   1 teaspoonful whole cloves
            Salt and pepper

Soak the beans over night; in the morning drain, add the water and bone and boil two hours, when add the vegetables and seasoning and boil two or three hours longer. Rub through a sieve and pour into tureen into which has been put ½ glass wine, 1 lemon and 1 hard boiled egg sliced.

Miss HOPKINS.

Black Bean Soup

1 pint black beans, soak over night; in the morning drain and put over to boil with enough water to cover, and cook until tender; mash and press through colander; put over the fire again, and add about 1 quart of water, 1 tablespoonful of flour, 1 tablespoonful butter. Rub flour and butter together, with 1 saltspoonful of mustard, 1 teaspoonful of salt, and a small pinch of red pepper. When soup is ready to serve add 1 sliced lemon and 2 cold boiled eggs sliced. Serve with soup dice. Wine may be added if desired.

MRS. CHARLES STIMSON.

Potato Soup

1 quart potatoes   4 quarts water
2 medium-sized onions minced Salt, pepper and butter
    fine, or 1 head celery minced

Boil the potatoes in the water till tender, drain (saving the water), mash fine, add the seasoning and the onion or celery. Cook in the same water one-quarter of an hour longer. Stand on the back of the stove and stir in two eggs well beaten with a cup of cream or milk. Let the soup get *hot* again, but not boiling.

MRS. ISAAC H. JENNINGS.

HORSESHOE Soap for Luck.

Celery Soup

1 bunch of celery	1 pint of boiling water
1 pint of milk	1 large slice of onion
1 large tablespoonful flour	1 cup of whipped cream
Pepper and salt	A small bit of mace

Boil the celery (cut up fine) in the water forty-five minutes. Let the milk, with the onion and mace, come to a boil, then skim these out and strain the celery into the milk; thicken with the flour, wet with a little cold milk, and cook eight minutes. Salt and pepper to taste. Pour into the tureen, and just before serving stir in the whipped cream. An egg may be substituted for the cream.

MRS. C. J. SMITH.

Vegetable Oyster Soup

1 pint of vegetable oysters cut fine	3 cups of milk
	1 teaspoonful salt
Butter size of a walnut	½ cup rolled crackers

Have the milk hot in the double boiler. Cook the vegetable oysters until very soft, and have about a pint of water on them when done. Rub the vegetable oysters through a strainer, using the water in which they were cooked, and add to the hot milk. Add the salt and butter. Just before serving add the rolled crackers.

MRS. WINFIELD R. SMITH.

Laura's Soup

1 pound can tomatoes	2 tablespoonfuls chopped carrots
2 tablespoonfuls chopped celery	4 tablespoonfuls chopped onions
2 cloves	1 bay leaf
Piece cinnamon 1 inch long	½ teaspoonful pepper
2 teaspoonsfuls salt	1 teaspoonful sugar
2 tablespoonfuls butter	
2 tablespoonfuls flour	

Fry (slowly) the vegetables in the butter for half an hour, add the other ingredients to the tomatoes, also

WEBB'S Ground Spices are perfectly pure.

one quart of water and boil slowly for half an hour; then put all together and boil half an hour longer; thicken with the flour; strain and serve. This is enough for six or eight persons.

MRS. L. G. BANNARD.

Tomato Soup No. 1

1 small onion chopped fine   Butter size of an egg
1 can tomatoes   1 pint boiling water
1 tablespoonful sugar   1 tablespoonful Worcester-
¼ teaspoonful cloves   shire sauce
Salt, pepper and a dash of   1 tablespoonful corn starch
  cayenne

Strain through a colander.

MRS. R. W. EMMONS.

Tomato Soup No. 2

1 can of tomatoes   1 quart of boiling water
  ½ of an onion

Boil these twenty minutes and thicken with :

2 tablespoonfuls of flour   1 tablespoonful of butter

Rubbed well together and melted with a few spoonfuls of hot tomato juice. Let come to a boil, strain and serve with fried bread dice.

MRS. CALVIN E. VILAS.

Tomato Soup No. 3

Will Serve Five or Six Persons.

1 can of tomatoes   1 quart of milk
1 teaspoonful of salt   Soda sufficient to cover end
1 scant teaspoonful of corn   of a teaspoon
  starch

Boil the tomatoes and boil the quart of milk each separately. Strain the tomatoes and throw into them while hot the pinch of soda. Make thickening of the tablespoonful of corn starch in same quantity of cold milk. Add this to boiling milk and let the mixture boil

HORSESHOE Soap will not ruin your clothes.

five minutes: then throw the tomato juice into the hot milk, stirring gently as you do so. Add teaspoonful of salt and serve immediately.

MRS. D. C. GARRETT.

Tomato Soup No. 4

Will serve Six or Eight Persons.

1 quart tomatoes   3 soda crackers
1 quart sweet milk   ½ teaspoonful soda
1 tablespoonful butter   Pepper and salt

Roll the crackers very fine; boil the tomatoes until thoroughly done (in using fresh tomatoes it is well to put on a little more than a quart, as they boil down), put through a strainer and return to the kettle to come to a boil again. Bring the milk to a boil, being careful not to burn it. Add to the tomatoes the crackers and soda, stir well to make smooth; then pour into the boiling milk, boil up once as quickly as possible, stirring constantly: put on a cooler part of the stove and add the seasoning. Pour into the tureen in which you have put the piece of butter. Be sure the *tomatoes and milk are both boiling* when you mix them. This may be made in the morning and reheated for dinner in a double boiler.

MRS. J. McB. SMITH. Victoria.

Noodles

Two eggs   Pinch of salt
Two tablespoonfuls of water

Mix well and add flour until very stiff. Roll out as thin as possible and cut with sharp knife in narrow strips. Have ready a kettle with plenty of boiling water, drop the noodles in and allow them to boil five minutes. Then drain and serve with butter as a vegetable. Or without butter in soup.

MRS. A. W. ENGLE.

WEBB'S Extracts are triple strength. Use them.

Croûtons for Soup

Cut slices of bread into squares, lay in a pan, drip good melted butter over them, place in the oven and toast until a light brown color. Use as desired for garnishing or for serving with soup.

Mrs. C. P. DAM.

FISH

The following general rules for fish will hold good for all kinds.

Selection of Fish

Great care should be taken to preserve the freshness of fish, as no other food deteriorates so rapidly in flavor. Fresh fish should be firm and the skin and scales bright. When it does not look so, do not buy it, as it will only be a disappointment. *Do not wash* the fish until *just before using.* An old fish-dealer is our authority for the statement that slimy coating always found on fish is a great factor in preserving its freshness, therefore if the fish is to be kept some hours before using, scale, clean and scrape it well, sprinkle a little salt on the inside, and just before using wash once quickly in cold water. Do not let the fish stand in the water or the best flavor will be lost.

Boiled Fish

There are three ways of boiling fish. The length of time required for a fish weighing four or five pounds is thirty minutes. A fish weighing more than six pounds

HORSESHOE Soap will not shrink your flannels.

should cook five minutes longer for every two pounds additional.

First Method—Pin the fish in a strong white cotton cloth, then plunge in kettle of boiling water and *simmer* gently for thirty minutes. *Hard boiling breaks the fish*.

Second Method—Lay the fish on a cloth or plate and place in steamer and simply steam until done, about the same length of time as for boiling.

Third Method—Put in a double boiler, or if one has not a double boiler large enough, put the fish in a lard pail and set in the large kettle of boiling water. The flavor of the fish is preserved best in the two latter methods.

MRS. R. W. EMMONS.

Baked Fish

1 fish weighing about 5 ℔s	1 pint of bread crumbs
Butter size of walnut	¼ teaspoonful of pepper
1 teaspoonful of salt	

Scrape and wash the fish clean if not already prepared, then rub into it a tablespoonful of salt. Mix together the bread crumbs, butter and seasoning for the stuffing and moisten with cold water. Put this into the body of the fish and fasten with skener. Cut gashes across the fish about two inches apart, one-half inch deep and two or more inches long and into each put a strip of salt pork, dust over pepper and salt and sprinkle thickly with bread crumbs or flour, according to taste. Put into the roasting pan and bake one hour, basting frequently; the bottom of the pan should be covered with hot water when the fish is first put in. Serve with drawn butter sauce, or any of the fancy sauces suitable for fish.

MRS. R. W. EMMONS.

Fried Fish

The best method for frying fish is to first prepare your fat by frying slices of salt pork a crisp brown, remove and place around the edge of your platter. Have your fish well covered or rolled in flour and Indian meal mixed and salted; then lay it in the frying pan and fry in the salt pork fat. Fry brown on one side, then turn and fry on the other. Be sure to have the fat smoking hot when the fish is put in and fry quickly. Serve very hot, garnished with the salt pork and parsley or lemon sliced.

Mrs. R. W. EMMONS.

Broiled Fish

Always use a double broiler to facilitate turning the fish. Before using rub the broiler with butter or a piece of salt pork to prevent the fish from sticking. The size of the fish will have to be the guide to the length of time required in cooking; a fish weighing four pounds requiring twenty minutes to half an hour. In broiling, the inside of the fish should be put over the coals first. Great care is required not to burn the skin. Mackerel will cook in from twelve to twenty minutes. After the fish is removed to the platter it should be spread generously with lumps of butter.

Mrs. R. W. EMMONS.

Smelts

Split the smelts down the back, take out the intestines and backbone; most of the side bones will come with it; wipe clean and salt the inside lightly. Roll in salted corn meal and fry quickly in *very hot* deep fat, or in butter. The fat must be very hot to brown quickly or the fish will become hard. Serve with tartare sauce.

Mrs. RICHARD C. STEVENS.

HORSESHOE Soap will not ruin your clothes.

C. C.—2

Fish Turbot

Steam until tender a white-meated fish. When done, remove the bones, pick up very fine, and season with pepper and salt.

Dressing

1 pint of milk	1 tablespoonful of flour
A large lump of butter	1 or 2 eggs
Onion and parsley	

Heat the milk, salt to taste, and thicken with the flour. When cool, add the butter (melted), eggs well beaten, and season with onion or parsley. Put in the baking dish a layer of fish, then a layer of sauce, until full; cover the top with bread crumbs, and bake half or three-quarters of an hour. Canned salmon, any cold boiled fish, or salt codfish freshened, can be prepared in the same way, and is very nice.

Fish Cream Cutlets

Chop, with a silver knife, 1 pound of uncooked halibut rather fine, add 1 teaspoonful of salt, two tablespoonfuls of minced almonds, a drop or two of onion juice, a dash of cayenne and the unbeaten white of 1 egg. Mix well, and stir in ½ pint of whipped cream. This cream must be stiff and fine. Put this mixture into small cutlet shaped moulds; stand them in a steamer and cook about ten minutes. Turn carefully from the moulds. Cover the bottom of the serving dish with cream sauce, arrange the cutlets, put a pretty sprig of double parsley in the "bone" end of each and serve very hot. Sightly and very good; quite new. By permission of

Mrs. S. T. RORER and THE HOUSEHOLD NEWS CO.

Flaked Fish Steamed

1 cup of cold fish	2 cups of mashed potatoes
½ cup of cream or milk	2 tablespoonfuls of melted
2 hard boiled eggs	butter
1 raw egg	1 teaspoonful lemon juice
1 teaspoonful of salt	½ saltspoonful of pepper
A dash of cayenne	
1 tablespoonful of chopped parsley	

Flake the fish carefully. To the hot mashed potato add the cream and melted butter, stir in the fish, then the hard boiled eggs chopped fine, followed by beaten egg and seasoning. Steam for one-half hour in buttered pudding mould. Serve with either cream or tomato sauce poured over it.

Mrs. GEORGE H. HEILBRON.

Creamed Fish

Take any nice, firm fleshed fish. Boil and remove the bones. Chop 1 small onion and a little parsley very fine and mix in with the fish, adding salt and pepper. Put it in a deep dish and cover with bread crumbs about two inches deep. Put small lumps of butter over it and add a little nutmeg (if you like it), and pour sweet cream over it until it, is all wet. Bake in a quick oven till nicely browned.

Miss MALTBY.

Baked Salmon

For Fish Weighing Four or Five Pounds.

Leave fish whole and fill with dressing made as follows :

2 cups of bread crumbs
1 tablespoonful of butter
1 scant teaspoonful of salt
1 teaspoonful of thyme or summer savory

Sew up fish and bake one hour; place slices of salt pork over fish ; baste often; enough water should be put in pan to keep it from burning. Serve with cream sauce made as follows :

Cream sauce (have ready in saucepan)
½ cup of hot water
½ teaspoonful of Worcestershire sauce
1 cup cream or rich milk
2 tablespoonfuls of butter
1 tablespoonful of flour or corn starch

Add drippings from pan in which fish was baked; flavor with parsley chopped fine.

Mrs. JAMES FIELDS.

HORSESHOE Soap for Luck.

Salmon in Mould

1 can salmon or 1 pound of cold boiled salmon	4 tablepsoonfuls of butter
	1 cup of bread crumbs
3 eggs	Milk, pepper and salt

Chop the fish and rub it in a bowl with a silver spoon with 4 tablespoonfuls of butter until it is a paste. Beat the bread crumbs with the well-beaten eggs and season with salt and pepper; adding this mixture to the salmon and working all together with a little milk or cream. Put in a covered buttered mould and boil one hour and a quarter. Turn out and serve with the following sauce:

1 cup of milk	1 tablespoonful corn starch
2 tablespoonfuls of butter	1 teaspoonful of catsup
Pinch of mace	Pepper
1 teaspoonful of chopped parsley	1 egg

Boil the milk and thicken with the corn starch and butter. Add the seasoning, pour all carefully over the beaten egg, cook one minute and pour over the form of salmon. Serve hot.

MRS. S. W. R. DALLY.

Escaloped Halibut

Will Serve Six Persons.

2 teacups halibut	1½ teacups milk
½ teacup fine bread crumbs	1 heaping tablespoonful
1 teaspoonful onion juice	flour
1 tablespoonful finely chopped parsley	1 tablespoonful butter
	Salt, cayenne

Take 2 cups of cold boiled halibut, pick into small pieces, removing all bone and skin. If a white or egg sauce was served with the fish and there is any left mix with the fish. As there is rarely enough left make a small quantity of white sauce. Mix one half of the sauce with the fish, the parsley, onion juice, salt if needed, and another *speck* of cayenne if needed. Butter a shallow pudding dish, put the fish in, smooth the top.

WEBB'S Extracts are triple strength. Use them.

cover with the remainder of the sauce (and also a sprinkle of parsley, so allow a little more than the tablespoonful), then the bread crumbs and ½ tablespoonful of butter scattered in bits over the bread crumbs.

Put the dish in a pan of boiling water and put in a rather quick oven for twenty minutes. Should brown nicely in that time.

Mrs. EDMUND BOWDEN.

Halibut à la Poulette

Sprinkle three slices of halibut with the juice of 1 lemon and salt and pepper. Put a slice of onion on each and set away for thirty minutes. Dip each piece in melted butter, roll up and fasten with a toothpick. Put in a pan and dredge with flour and bake twenty minutes. Remove picks, sprinkle with the yolks of 3 hard-boiled eggs, chopped very fine. Pour over the sauce and garnish with the whites of the eggs cut into rings.

Sauce.

Boil ¼ tablespoonful of onion and 2 teaspoonfuls of butter and 2 tablespoonfuls of flour together until done. Stir in slowly 1 cup of soup stock, 1 cup of cream, 1 teaspoonful salt, ¼ teaspoonful of pepper, boil up once and strain and add 1 tablespoonful of lemon juice.

Mrs. E. W. ANDREWS.

Fish Croquettes

Any fish may be used for croquettes, but the white meat is the best; for instance, halibut. After boiling, pick the fish into *small* pieces, taking out all the bones. Mix with a white sauce, season with salt and pepper, and a little chopped parsley, if desired. Shape into cylindrical balls, roll in crumbs, then egg, then crumbs again, and fry in deep lard. A nice way to use up cold fish.

Mrs. WINFIELD R. SMITH.

HORSESHOE Soap for economy and quality.

Steamed Clams

Wash the clams thoroughly with a stiff brush. Fit a steamer with a soup plate, or better a jellycake tin, so that there is a margin all around to allow the steam to come up freely. Pile the clams on the tin, put in the steamer and cover closely. The kettle should be boiling *hard* and there should be plenty of water when the clams are put in. It will take fifteen minutes, or longer, for the clams to open, according to size, and they should be as nearly one size as possible. Have prepared some nice rounds of toast, *hot*; quickly take out the clams and lay on the toast, squeeze the juice of half a lemon into the tin with the clam liquor, add a dash or two of cayenne and pour over the clams; then bathe in melted butter, so that each clam is moistened. If you are *quick* you can cut off the black heads with scissors, which will improve them, but you *must not* let them cool. Serve *immediately*. The clams should be in the steamer only *just long enough* to open.

MRS. RICHARD C. STEVENS.

Devilled Clams No. 1

Serve Eight Persons.

4 qt. pail of clams (with shells on)	1 cup of cream or milk
2 tablespoonfuls of flour	1 tablespoonful of butter
Yolks of 2 raw eggs	2 tablespoonfuls of dry bread crumbs
1 tablespoonful of chopped parsley	Salt and pepper to taste

Remove clams from their shells. Drain and rinse them. Chop very fine. Scald the cream (or milk). Rub the butter and flour together until smooth, add to the scalded cream and stir until it thickens. Then add bread crumbs, eggs and parsley. Take from the fire, mix well together, stir in the clams, add salt and pepper. Do not add salt until the clams are stirred in for they may flavor the mixture sufficiently. Fill clam, scollop

WEBB'S Ground Spices are perfectly pure.

or silver shells, brush over with the beaten yolk of an egg, sprinkle with bread crumbs and brown in a hot oven.

MRS. WM. H. DE WOLF.

Devilled Clams No. 2

25 good sized clams   1 small onion
3 crackers rolled fine   1 small piece of bacon
1 tablespoonful of butter

Chop together the clams, onion and bacon and dredge with the crackers. Wash some large shells, fill with the mixture which should be well seasoned with salt and pepper. On each shell put a small piece of butter and a sprig of parsley. Roast about fifteen minutes and serve hot.

MRS. DOUGLAS YOUNG.

Waldorf Clam Broth

1 quart "shucked" clams, boiled until perfectly tender, then squeezed until entirely dry. Season the juice thus obtained nicely with butter, pepper, salt and a hint of onion juice; thicken a little with flour. Serve in bouillon cups *very* hot. Just before sending to table put 1 tablespoonful of whipped cream on top of each cup (do not stir it in). If you cannot obtain fresh clams, you can get an excellent substitute in bottled clam juice. Very nice for luncheons and card parties.

MRS. NATHANIEL WALDO EMERSON, Boston.

Clam Pot Pie.

1 quart clams
1 dozen crackers pounded fine

Place a narrow rim of paste round the upper part of the baking dish. Then sprinkle a thin layer of the cracker over the bottom of the dish, then a layer of clams; over them place small pieces of butter, salt and

HORSESHOE Soap, *Big Cake, 5c.*

pepper. Repeat until the last two layers, when use soda crackers in place of the powdered. Moisten the whole with a little milk, cover with a nice paste and bake like a pie.

Mrs. V. A. RITON.

Clam Chowder

75 to 100 clams	Onions, chopped
4 slices of salt pork	Crackers

Clean the clams thoroughly, and if large, cut into small pieces. Fry the pork crisp, and chop. Sprinkle some of this in the bottom of the granite or porcelain kettle, lay upon them a stratum of clams, sprinkle with pepper and salt, and scatter bits of butter profusely over all. Next have a layer of chopped onions, then one of small crackers split and moistened with milk. On this pour a little of the fat in which the pork was fried. Repeat, beginning with the chopped pork. Proceed in this manner until all the clams are used. (The clams may be divided into two equal parts, making two complete layers.) Pour over all the liquid from the clams, and add enough water to cover all. Stew slowly, with the stew pan closely covered, three-quarters of an hour. If the chowder thickens too much while cooking, add more water.

Oyster Bouillon

Chop oysters finely, put into a double boiler and heat very slowly to draw out the juices. Put into a cheese cloth and press out the liquor. Return to the fire, clarify and strain as for beef bouillon, add an equal quantity of *hot* milk; season and serve. A little whipped cream improves it.

Mrs. RICHARD C. STEVENS.

Oyster Cocktail

Served in punch or champagne glasses or bouillon cups. To every glass allow:

1 tablespoonful of lemon juice
1 tablespoonful of strained tomato
2 tablespoonfuls of tomato catsup
¼ teaspoonful Worcestershire sauce
2 tablespoonfuls of Sound oysters
1 drop tobasco sauce   A little salt

If the tomato catsup is very mild, put in no strained tomato and proportionately more catsup.

MRS. WINFIELD R. SMITH.

Oyster Fricassee

Dry the oysters. Have some butter in a saucepan, and when it is brown add the oysters. Keep stirring them all the time in the hot butter, until they swell up; then add 1 pint of boiling cream, in which you have stirred 2 tablespoonfuls of flour; salt and pepper to taste. Have some large crackers warmed and on your meat platter, and pour your oysters over them.

Creamed Oysters

Put a bit of onion as large as a bean, and ¼ of a blade of mace, with a pint of cream, into a double boiler. Put 1 quart (or can) of Eastern oysters into a saucepan and let cook in their own liquor until they are plump and the edges begin to curl. Skim and set aside where they will keep *hot* but not cook. When the cream comes to a boil, thicken with a tablespoonful of flour mixed in a little cold cream or milk; let boil up, season with salt and cayenne, skim out the onion and mace. Drain the oysters and add to the cream. A dessert spoonful of sherry may be added if liked.

MRS. RICHARD C. STEVENS.

Frizzled Oysters

Have ready on a platter sufficient toast, which has been dipped quickly into hot, slightly salted water, and

HORSESHOE Soap will not *draw* your *hands*.

buttered. Turn the oysters. with only their own liquor.
into a very hot frying pan; season with salt and pepper.
Soon as their edges begin to curl. stir in a large spoonful of butter, and turn immediately over the toast.
Nice for breakfast.

Oysters en Beure Noir

1 pint of oysters   2 tablespoonfuls of butter
1½ tablespoonfuls of vinegar Salt. and a dash of cayenne

Drain and rinse the oysters. let stand a half hour and
cook in the liquor formed until plump. sprinkle with
salt. Brown the butter. but be careful not to burn; add
the pepper and vinegar. then the oysters. Fill Dresden
fritters and serve hot.

MRS. FRANK MITCHELL.

Oysters Served in Shells

Drain six large oysters and wash the shells. Marinate the oysters with melted butter. salt and pepper
and minced parsley. Fill the shells and cover with
rolled bread crumbs. Put bits of butter on top and
brown in a very hot oven.

MRS. FRANK MITCHELL.
(Mrs. Hinckley's Portland cooking class.)

To Fry Small Oysters

1 quart of oysters   3 eggs. well beaten
1 cup of corn meal

Drain the liquor from the oysters and wipe them
dry. Take three or four at a time and dip into the egg.
then in the meal. and again in the egg, keeping the oysters together. Put them on a platter until all are
treated in this way. and then fry a few at a time in equal
parts of hot butter and drippings. Olive oil may be
used instead of butter and makes them very rich. Season with red pepper and salt to taste. Cook until
brown. turning carefully to keep them in shape. and be

WEBB'S Ground Spices are perfectly pure.

sure they are well done. Serve very hot with slices of lemon.

Mrs. CHARLES J. RILEY.

Toasted Oysters

Wrap one large or two or three small oysters in very thin slices of bacon, having put a little cayenne and lemon juice on the oysters. Stick toothpicks through to hold in place, and broil or fry till bacon is crisp. Do not take out toothpicks. Serve *hot*.

Miss HOPKINS.

Olympia Oysters on Toast

1 quart of oysters	1 cup of cream or rich milk
2 tablespoonfuls of butter	2 tablespoonfuls of flour
1 teaspoonful of lemon juice	Salt and cayenne pepper

Drain the oysters and throw them into a hot pan and stir carefully until they look plump. Heat the butter, into which stir the flour, rubbing until smooth, and add gradually the cream. When thoroughly cooked pour over the oysters in the pan, heat through, put in the salt and pepper and lastly the lemon juice. Pour over crackers or nicely toasted bread.

Mrs. A. W. ENGLE.

WEBB'S Extracts are triple strength. Use them.

MEATS

"O! the roast beef of Old England."—*Fielding*.

" Venison's a Cæsar in the fiercest fray,
Turtle an Alexander in the way :
And in quarrels of a slighter nature,
Mutton's a most successful mediator."—*Pindar*.

Roast Beef

Buy a prime roast (first, second or third ribs). Have the butcher cut off the ends of the ribs, making a standing roast. Wipe clean with a damp cloth; *do not wash*. Put a heavy steel frying pan onto the range and let it get *very hot*, then put the roast in and sear over all the cut surfaces. This keeps the juices in, and if thoroughly done, a small roast can be made almost as juicy as a large one. Salt and pepper the meat, run a steel skewer through the fleshy part to keep it from bulging; put the meat rack in the pan, place the roast on it, cut side up, and dredge well with flour, not forgetting the pan. Put in the oven, and when the flour in the pan has browned, add enough hot water to just cover the bottom. The oven should be *very hot* at first, and should be diminished a little after the roast has browned. From this time baste every five minutes, keeping only

WEBB'S Ground Spices are perfectly pure.

enough water in the pan to prevent burning; any more makes too much steam and draws out the juices. An 8-pound roast will be well done on the outside and rare in middle in one hour. Save the ribs cut off, for braised short ribs.

Mrs RICHARD C. STEVENS.

Braised Short Ribs

2 or 3 short ribs   1 onion
5 slices salt pork

Put the salt pork on the stove in a braising or dripping pan and slice the onion in it. fry till a golden brown. dredge the ribs well with flour and brown also: then cover with a pint of hot water. set in the oven and cook for three hours. having the braising pan closely covered. Baste often and add more water if necessary. This is a very satisfactory way to treat any of the tougher cuts of meat. Sprinkle quite thickly with pepper and salt; it is impossible to give exact quantity as it would vary with weight of meat.

Mrs. R. W. EMMONS.

Leg of Lamb With Dressing.

Buy a hind quarter of spring lamb. have the leg cut off and boned the same as a fillet of veal. The remainder of the quarter may be cut into chops. Make dressing. using about 1½ cups of grated bread. 1 tablespoonful of minced mint. salt and pepper. soft butter sufficient to moisten slightly. and about half as many chopped pecans as bread crumbs. Rub the meat with salt and pepper inside and out. put in the dressing. taking care to fill the cavity so as to give shape to the leg. but do not press too tight or the dressing will be heavy. Roast about fifteen minutes to the pound; baste *very often*. or it will be dry. Put a bouquet of herbs. or a few sprigs of mint in the pan. and serve with a nice brown or mint sauce. or with a mint sorbet.

Mrs. RICHARD C. STEVENS.

WEBB'S Extracts are triple strength. Use them.

Leg of Mutton

Peel back the outside skin and with a sharp pointed knife make slits or gashes, into which force thin slices of salt pork which have been rolled in equal parts of ground cloves and allspices. Replace the skin and roast, basting frequently.

MRS. HELEN M. HUNT.

Boiled Dinner

If one will only take the trouble, it pays to *corn* the beef and thus avoid the use of saltpeter. To corn: Put a pint of rock salt to 1 gallon of cold water, let it come to a boil, skimming carefully. Cool before putting in the beef. A six pound piece of the flank is a good piece. Leave in brine four or five days. Cook in a kettle large enough to hold both meat and vegetables. Put the meat on in hot water and boil three hours before adding the vegetables. These can be used according to taste. The usual ones are potatoes, cabbage, turnips and beets; some, however, add carrots and parsnips. Put the first three into a wire basket on top of meat, keeping *all* covered with water and boil one hour, making four hours the entire time for boiling meat. The beets, on account of discoloring the other vegetables, should be boiled in a separate kettle, and unless very young will require two hours boiling.

A boiled dinner may be served in two ways. The meat on a large platter, with the vegetables placed around it, or the potatoes and turnips mashed separately or together, and beets and cabbage each in a vegetable dish.

MRS. SARAH CONANT.

Veal Cutlets

Dip the cutlets in egg, then in bread crumbs, and cook on top of the stove until brown on both sides.

HORSESHOE Soap will not shrink your flannels.

Then cover and cook in the oven about three-quarters of an hour. Make a brown thickened gravy, of the fat in the pan after the cutlets are removed, a good lump of butter, some flour and heated milk. Pour over the cutlets on the platter.

MRS. CHARLES E. SHEPARD.

To Fry Chicken

Joint the chicken as for frying; put into a dish and set into a steamer, which should be ready with the water boiling, and steam until tender. Take up and fry quickly in *very hot* fat, half butter and half beef suet, until lightly browned. Serve with a cream gravy. An onion and a stalk of celery cut up finely and put into the steamer with the chicken gives a good flavor. This method is for a chicken a year old.

MRS. HINCHLIFFE.

Roast Turkey or Chicken

Having prepared the fowls for roasting, make a thick dough of Graham flour and water and roll out one inch thick. Have it large enough to cover the fowl completely. Butter the fowl thoroughly, then place the rolled dough over, being careful to press down around the neck and legs. Pour boiling water into the pan about one inch deep. Have the oven *very hot*, keep just enough water in the bottom of pan to prevent burning. One-half hour before serving time remove the pan from the oven and lift off the dough blanket. The turkey will be tender, but white. Cool the oven and brown the turkey. There is no basting or opening of the oven door except to see that the water in the pan has not boiled out.

MRS. HINCHLIFFE.

Tongue With Sweet Gravy

Boil a fresh beef tongue in salt water until very tender, having about 1 quart of water when done. Roast

WEBB'S Ground Spices are perfectly pure.

as brown as possible without burning (in a large skillet). a large teacupful of flour, in half butter and half lard. Thin it out slowly with the liquid, stir till smooth, adding a few cloves. ½ teacupful of sugar and ½ teacupful of strong vinegar; also a teacup of raisins and a little more salt if necessary. Skin the tongue while hot, cut in slices and place while warm on a large meat dish, pouring the gravy over it and garnish with a few slices of lemon and blanched almonds.

L. M. THEDINGA.

Curried Mutton

1 cup of cold mutton cut 1 small onion
   in dice   1½ cups of new milk
         1 heaping teaspoonful of curry

Fry the mutton and onion together with a good lump of butter. When brown add the milk and thicken with flour, into which the curry has been stirred. Boil in a double boiler at least an hour. Serve with boiled rice, putting curry in the center of platter, arranging the boiled rice around it. When the curry is done it should be the consistency of thick cream.

Mrs. T. M. DAULTON.

Jellied Tongue

One cup of the liquor in which the tongue was cooked.

2 cups good stock of any ½ box of gelatine
   meat except mutton   1 gill of cold water
1 cup of boiling water   2 tablespoonfuls of vinegar
1 glass of sherry   1 cold boiled tongue, sliced

Soak the gelatine in the cold water for two hours, pour over it the boiling water, the stock and the tongue liquor, heated. Unless the stock is highly seasoned, boil a bay leaf, a sprig of parsley, slice of onion and a few sweet herbs in a cup of water and then strain this and pour it over the gelatine instead of using the

C. C.—3

plain boiling water. Flavor the jelly with the vinegar and sherry, pepper and salt, strain through a cloth. When the jelly begins to harden pour a little of it in a mould, first wetting the mould in a little cold water. Arrange slices of tongue on this, pour in more jelly, then another layer of tongue and so on until the materials are all used, having jelly on top. Set the mould on ice until hard, then turn it out and slice.

Mrs. ALBERT T. TIMMERMAN.

French Mutton Stew

Cut the mutton in pieces one-half the size of the hand. Place in a stew pan with 1 tablespoonful of hot fat and brown on both sides. Now add 1 tablespoonful of flour, mix well and add just enough stock or water to cover the meat. Skim while boiling one-quarter of an hour. Add two small onions sliced. Cook steady one hour more.

Mrs. L. H. GRAY.

Spiced Beef

Boil a three or four-pound pot roast slowly for three or four hours. Chop very fine. Add ½ teaspoonful of cloves, cinnamon and a pinch of nutmeg. Salt and pepper to taste and turn into a mould.

Mrs. BONE.

Egg Dumplings

1 egg	1 cup of milk
1 heaping teaspoonful of baking powder	Flour to make quite a thick batter

Drop into hot gravy, cover over and cook about ten minutes. These are nice with stewed chicken or with lamb or mutton stew.

Mrs. C. P. DAM.

WEBB'S Ground Spices are perfectly pure.

Sausages

1½ pounds of pork
¼ wineglass sage, rubbed
fine

1½ pounds of beef or veal
1½ tablespoonfuls of salt
1 tablespoonful of pepper

Use a patent meat chopper; mince thoroughly.

MRS. HELEN M. HUNT.

Veal Loaf No. 1

2 pounds veal
Six crackers, rolled
1 teaspoonful salt
½ nutmeg grated

¼ pound salt pork
2 eggs
½ teaspoonful pepper
Butter size of an egg

½ cup cream

Mince the meat together, add seasoning, eggs well beaten, butter and cream. Form into a long loaf, cover well with the cracker crumbs, and bake. Baste frequently with sweet milk.

MRS. CORWIN S. SHANK.

Veal Loaf No. 2

3 pounds veal
½ pound salt pork
1 pint milk

½ cup bread crumbs
3 eggs
2 tablespoonfuls salt

1 teaspoonful pepper

Mix well and put in tin, put cracker crumbs on top, and dot with butter. Bake three-quarters of an hour, basting with butter and water.

MRS. BENTON.

Jellied Veal

2 pounds breast of veal
1 teaspoonful of savory
Salt
Nutmeg
4 tablespoonfuls of parsley
chopped

1 teaspoonful of thyme
½ teaspoonful of marjoram
Pepper
2 bay leaves
½ lemon
3 eggs hard-boiled

Cut the veal into small pieces and put with the bones into boiling water. *Simmer* one hour. Remove the

HORSESHOE Soap for economy and quality.

meat and add to the bones and water, the herbs and seasoning. *Simmer* two hours, strain and pour over the other ingredients which have been arranged in a deep buttered dish as follows: A layer of small pieces of veal, over these sprinkle salt, pepper, a little lemon juice and grated rind; also a suspicion of nutmeg. Then a layer of hard-boiled eggs cut in thin slices, chopped parsley sprinkled between, another layer of veal, with seasoning as before; so on until all the veal and egg are used. Pour the hot soup over this; when cold turn out and cut in thin slices. Serve very cold.

MRS. S. W. R. DALLY.

Beef Loaf

4 pounds round of beef, chopped fine
4 soda crackers, rolled
6 eggs, well beaten
½ cup butter, melted
Salt and pepper to taste

Make in loaf and bake one hour.

MRS. H. C. HENRY.

Pressed Meat

Four pounds of beef (the part that is called the "thick flank") boiled until it is very tender, then remove from kettle and chop very fine, season with salt and pepper, then add the broth in which the meat was cooked until quite soft. Set away to cool and slice like beef or veal loaf. This is very nice for lunch.

MRS. ALBERT T. TIMMERMAN.

French Ragout

Will Serve Six Persons.

3 lbs lean beef   4 medium sized onions
1 tablespoonful of French coloring flour

Cut the meat in about two-inch squares, season and roll *well* in flour. Slash onions in quarters (do not cut

WEBB'S Extracts are triple strength. Use them.

apart), and stick a whole clove in each quarter. Sprinkle flour plentifully in bottom of baking pan or sauce pan, put in onions, then the floured meat and tablespoonful of caramel or French coloring, cover with water and *simmer* in oven four hours, putting on more water as it is needed.

MRS. EUGENE RICKSECKER.

Brains

. To Serve Six Persons.

1 quart of brains	2 eggs
6 soda crackers	

Beat the eggs well and roll the crackers very fine. Cover the brains with cold water, to which add a tablespoonful of salt, and let stand over night. In the morning put them into warm water for a few minutes, after which carefully remove all particles of the tissue which surround the solid part. Next put them into boiling water and let them *simmer* for ten minutes to make them firm. Take them up, drain and wipe, and dip, one at a time, first in the egg, then in the cracker, and lastly in the egg. Take equal parts of butter and drippings (lard or cottolene if preferred), and when very hot fry the brains. Turn them often and be careful that they are thoroughly cooked. When done they should be a rich brown color. Season with pepper and serve very hot.

MRS. CHARLES J. RILEY.

Creamed Frogs

Parboil the frogs, then make a rich cream sauce of 3 tablespoonfuls of butter, 1 tablespoonful of flour, 1 cup of cream and a tiny bit of mace, salt and cayenne. Add the frogs, cover closely for fifteen or twenty minutes, adding more cream if it becomes too thick. Skim out the mace and serve very hot on toast.

HORSESHOE Soap, *Big Cake, 5c.*

Venison Steak

Venison steak 1½ inches   1 tablespoonful water
   thick   1 saltspoonful salt
1 teaspoonful lemon juice   2 tablespoonfuls quince jelly
½ pint claret or Madeira   A bit of mace
      A pinch of cayenne

Melt the butter in a frying pan, put in steak, cover and cook three minutes; turn and cook three minutes longer. Add the other ingredients and *simmer* all together six minutes. Serve on *hot* plates.

Stewed Pigeons

Pick, draw and clean, then lay in cold salted water for one hour. Put to cook in a pot with cold water to cover them. Stew until quite tender, then add milk, butter, pepper and salt to taste. Thicken with flour and milk and serve. Doves may be treated in the same manner.

MRS. DOUGLAS YOUNG.

Native Wild Ducks

First in excellence is the mallard, then the teal, and the widgeon, during the winter months.

Dry pick the duck, singe, clean thoroughly and wipe dry with a clean towel. If badly shot wash in cold salt water or even soak half an hour in salt and water, wiping *well* before stuffing. The stuffing:

2 teacupfuls stale bread   1 tablespoonful of butter
   crumbs   ½ (scant) teaspoonful dried
Pepper and salt   thyme

Crumb the bread very fine, add the seasoning and the butter broken in bits. This quantity will stuff one mallard or two teal or other small ducks. Tie securely, rub the outside with pepper and salt and a little butter, *very* little if the duck is very fat, put in pan, breast side up in a moderate oven with *just* enough water to keep from burning. Cover with another pan and cook

WEBB'S Extracts are triple strength. Use them.

one hour or a *trifle* more for a mallard or large duck.
Do not baste as it makes the dressing wet. If not
brown enough remove the cover ten minutes before
serving. Skim the gravy in the pan, add more water
if necessary and thicken with flour. Season and serve
hot, with currant jelly.

MRS. J. W. EDWARDS.

Broiled Game Birds

Take any small birds, draw, clean and wipe quickly
with a damp cloth, split down the back, rub with salt
and pepper, and broil over hot coals. Put each bird on
a triangle of toast and pour over a sauce made as follows:

Bread Sauce for Game

1 cup of bread crumbs	1 slice of onion
1 cup of stock	Salt and pepper

Put in the double boiler, cook half an hour, strain
and add 1 large tablespoonful of butter. Serve *at once*
on a *hot* platter. Garnish with parsley.

MRS. FRANK MITCHELL.

Quail au Delire

¼ lb of bacon	¼ lb veal liver
1 bay leaf	1 shallot
½ carrot, chopped	A little chopped onion

Salt and pepper

Fry the bacon, add the liver cut in small pieces, the
vegetables and seasoning and stew until cooked.
Pound together with a few mushrooms, and rub
through a sieve. This force meat will stuff two birds.
Put a piece of butter on the breast of each and roast
half an hour, if liked rare, longer if to be well done,
baste every ten minutes. For the sauce, add 1 cup of
stock to the baking pan, thicken, add 2 tablespoonfuls
of currant jelly, season and serve *very hot*. Pigeon, reed
birds or any small tender birds cooked after this manner are delicious.

MRS. FRANK MITCHELL.

HORSESHOE Soap for Luck.

MEAT AND FISH SAUCES

Epicurean cooks sharpen with cloyless sauce his appetite.
—*Shakespeare.*

Drawn Butter

1 tablespoonful flour	1 tablespoonful butter
1 cup of boiling water	¼ teaspoonful of salt
Dash of pepper	

Melt the butter and stir in the flour; add carefully the water, then season.

Many other sauces are made with drawn butter as a foundation:

Caper Sauce—Add 3 tablespoonfuls of capers. (Boiled mutton.)

Egg Sauce—Add 1 egg, hard-boiled and chopped fine. (Fish.)

Sauce Piquant—Add 2 teaspoonfuls of lemon juice, 2 teaspoonfuls each of chopped olives, pickles, parsley and capers.

Brown Sauce

1 tablespoonful of butter	Salt
1 tablespoonful of flour	Pepper
1 tablespoonful of onion	1 teaspoonful of lemon juice
1 cup of stock	

Chop the onion and fry in butter; then add flour; then the stock and seasoning; strain.

HORSESHOE Soap will not shrink your flannels.

The following sauces can be made by using brown sauce as a foundation:

Mushroom Sauce—Add ½ cup mushrooms.

Olive Sauce—Add 8 olives chopped. (Game.)

Wine Sauce—Add ½ cup wine and 1 tablespoonful of currant jelly. Thicken a little with flour. (Venison.)

S. W. S.

Mint Sauce

For Lamb

1 cup fresh chopped mint ½ cup sugar
½ cup vinegar

Use only leaves and tender part of mint. Let it stand an hour before serving. Use more sugar if the vinegar is strong.

MRS. LINCOLN'S COOK BOOK.

Anchovy Sauce

For any kind of Fish

2 tablespoonfuls of butter   1 tablespoonful of chopped
1 tablespoonful of lemon   parsley
      juice   ¼ teaspoonful of salt
          3 tablespoonfuls of anchovy paste

Mix all the ingredients and knead well in a bowl. Should be perfectly smooth. By permission of

MRS. S. T. RORER and ARNOLD & CO.

Celery Sauce

For Boiled Fowl or Turkey

2 tablespoonfuls of flour   ½ cup of butter
1 pint of milk   3 heads of celery

Mix the flour and butter, add the milk hot. Cut the celery into small bits and boil a few minutes in water, which strain off. Put the celery into the butter and milk, and stir over the fire for five or ten minutes.

(The Home Cook Book.)

WEBB'S Ground spices are perfectly pure.

Parsley Butter

For Oysters, Fish and Vegetables.

Cream 1 heaping tablespoonful of butter, add ½ teaspoonful salt, ¼ saltspoonful pepper and 1 tablespoonful chopped parsley.

Mrs. LINCOLN (in the American Kitchen Magazine).

Bearnaise Sauce

Crab Chops, Steak or Fried Fish—French.

Beat the yolks of 4 eggs, add ¼ cup of best olive oil, and when well mixed add ¼ cup of hot water. Set the bowl over the tea kettle, or in a pan of boiling water, and cook till thick, stirring constantly. Take from the fire, beat well and add salt, a dash of cayenne, and a tablespoonful of vinegar; Tarragon is best; let cool.

Mrs. RICHARD C. STEVENS.

Hollandaise Sauce

For Fish.

Make a drawn butter sauce, remove from fire and add yolks of 2 raw eggs, juice of half a lemon, 1 tablespoonful of chopped parsley and 1 teaspoonful of onion juice. By permission of

Mrs. S. T. RORER and ARNOLD & CO.

Horse Radish Sauce

Potato Balls or Fish.

Chill 1 cup of thick cream and beat it until thick enough to hold in shape. Add ½ teaspoonful of salt, ½ saltspoonful of pepper, and 3 tablespoonfuls of prepared horse radish. If fresh grated horse radish is used, add 2 tablespoonfuls of vinegar and 1 teaspoonful of sugar to the radish. Keep this in a cold place, as it should be stiff and thick when used. If served on the dish with hot meat, put it in a shallow sauce dish, and cover the dish with a garnish of water cress.

Mrs. LINCOLN (in The American Kitchen Magazine).

WEBB'S Ground Spices are perfectly pure.

White Sauce

1 pint of milk	2 tablespoonfuls of butter
1 tablespoonful of flour	½ teaspoonful of salt
	½ saltspoonful of pepper

Heat the milk over hot water. Put the butter in a granite sauce pan and stir until it melts and bubbles. Be careful not to brown it. Add the flour dry and stir quickly till well mixed. Pour on one-third of the milk. Let it boil and stir well as it thickens; tip the sauce pan slightly to keep the sauce from sticking. Add another third of the milk, let it boil and thicken and stir until perfectly smooth. Be sure that all the lumps are rubbed out while it is in this thick state. Add the remainder of the milk; let it boil and when smooth put in the salt and pepper.

A richer sauce is made as follows:

Cream Sauce.

1 cup hot cream	1 heaping tablespoonful of
1 heaping tablespoonful	butter
of flour	½ teaspoonful of salt
	½ saltspoonful of pepper

Make in the same manner as the White Sauce.

MRS. LINCOLN'S Boston Cook Book.

Use the White Sauce for turnips or carrots cut in dice and for cauliflower. Use the Cream Sauce for fish, oysters, crabs and sweetbreads prepared in shells. Mix with the Cream Sauce, put in the shells, cover with bread crumbs and bits of butter and brown.

Sauce Allemande

French—For Fish.

2 ounces butter	2 ounces flour
1 pint clear soup stock	Salt and pepper
	Yolks of 3 eggs

Melt the butter and mix thoroughly with it the flour; add immediately the stock and seasoning, boil fifteen min-

WEBB'S Extracts are triple strength. Use them.

utes. remove from fire and carefully skim off the grease. When it has ceased boiling add the yolks mixed in a little water and stew in quickly with an egg beater so as to make the sauce light.

Mrs. ERASTUS BRAINERD.

Sauce

For Onions, Turnips, Carrots and Spinach.

1 ounce butter	1 ounce flour
1 pint milk	1 onion
½ ounce lean raw ham	Salt and pepper

Melt the butter, stir in the flour, add the onion sliced, the ham and seasoning. When beginning to color slightly moisten with the milk; stir well and boil ten minutes. Strain and serve.

Mrs. ERASTUS BRAINERD.

Lemon Sauce

For Boiled Chicken.

1 ounce butter	1 ounce flour
Salt, pepper	A little nutmeg
1 glass water	Juce of 1 lemon

Rub flour and butter together; season; add the water, stirring until it boils; then add another ounce of butter and the lemon. Strain and serve.

Mrs. ERASTUS BRAINERD.

Bread Sauce

For Game.

1 onion	4 ounces of bread crumbs
Salt and pepper	1 glass of milk
1 glass of cream	

Chop the onion fine, put in the saucepan with the bread crumbs which have been put through a sieve; add seasoning, and milk. Boil ten minutes, add cream and serve.

Mrs. ERASTUS BRAINERD.

HORSESHOE Soap will not ruin your clothes.

Sauce Bordelaise

Fish.

Peel and chop fine 4 cloves of garlic and put in saucepan with 3 tablespoonfuls of olive oil. When slightly colored add 1 tablespoonful of chopped parsley. This should not be made until just ready to serve.

Mrs. ERASTUS BRAINERD.

Tomato Sauce

For Beef.

Put into saucepan 1 ounce of raw ham, 1 carrot, 1 onion, a little thyme, 1 bay leaf, 2 cloves, 1 clove of garlic, ½ ounce of butter; *simmer* for ten minutes; add 1 ounce of flour well mixed in ½ pint of tomatoes, and 1 glass of consommé. Boil for one-half hour; season with salt, pepper and a mite of nutmeg. Strain and serve.

Mrs. ERASTUS BRAINERD.

Sauce Tartare

Fish.

Make a mayonnaise, but use double the quantity of mustard. Chop 1 pickle and 1 tablespoonful of capers and dry in a napkin. Chop some parsley, 1 green onion and a few Yarragon leaves. Mix all with the dressing.

Mrs. ERASTUS BRAINERD.

Meat Sauce

4 ripe tomatoes   1 large onion
1 tablespoonful of butter

Chop the onion, add the tomato and butter, season with salt, pepper, a little cayenne and stew gently for fifteen minutes. Serve hot with any meats.

Bechamel Sauce

For Vegetables, Eggs and Chicken.

1 tablespoonful of butter   ½ cup of stock
1 tablespoonful of flour   Yolk of 1 egg
½ cup of milk   Salt and pepper

Melt the butter in a sauce pan, but do not brown, add the flour and stir till smooth. Add the stock and milk and stir constantly till it boils. Take from the fire, add the salt and pepper and egg well beaten.

Mrs. NEUFELDER.

Chestnut Sauce

Roast Turkey.

Blanche the chestnuts. Cook in stock until soft. Mash fine in the stock. Thicken with flour and butter rubbed together. Salt and pepper. One-half cup of cream may be added.

A LITTLE DINNER

"Without good company, all dainties
Lose their true relish, and like painted grapes
Are only seen, not tasted."

The giving of a small dinner in a household where several trained servants are kept is a matter of little moment to the hostess, who has simply to notify her cook of the number of guests expected, give her orders as to menu, etc., and then dismiss from her mind all feeling of responsibility, and await with composure the arrival of her guests. In the ordinary home, however, where as a rule one, or at most, two maids are kept, the addition of several guests to the dinner table requires much thought and preparation which necessarily must devolve upon the mistress. Successful dinner-giving, like genius, implies an infinite capacity for taking pains. In giving a small dinner of, say, six guests in addition to the family, it is necessary to first consider the resources of the household in the way of dishes, silver, etc., as upon these will depend the number of courses in the menu. This inspection completed, the next step is the preparation of the menu, not forgetting in the consideration of each dish the possibilities of the cook in the way of losing her head at the prospect of guests. It is a good plan to select only those dishes which the cook has tried before, as even

HORSESHOE Soap for Luck.

the best of cooks frequently fails to succeed in the first trial of a new receipt.   As far as possible it is advisable to select dishes which may be prepared the preceding day, thus lessening the work and confusion on the day of the dinner.   Salted almonds, cheese sticks, patéshells and all kinds of blanc mange and jellies should be prepared the day before.   The question of menu settled, all orders should be given the day before, so that no harrowing non-arrival of some essential article shall mar the composure of the hostess.   On the morning of the day for the dinner the mistress should explain to the waitress which plates and other dishes are to be used for each course; it is a good plan to write on slips of paper the words, "Fish," "Roast," "Salad," "Entrée," etc., and put the paper on top of the pile of plates to be used for that purpose.   A menu should be prepared very plainly and distinctly written, giving the exact order in which the courses are to be served, stating what dishes are to be passed with each course and when to use the crumb knife.   The menu may be written thus :

MENU.

1. Raw Oysters.
2. Soup.   Pass crackers.
3. Fish.   Pass potatoes, then bread.
4. Roast.   Pass vegetables and celery.
5. Entrée.   Pass jelly.
6. Sorbet.
7. Game.   Pass olives.
8. Salad.   Pass cheese sticks.
9. Use crumb knife.
10. Pudding.
11. Ice Cream.
          Fruit.   Cake.   Nuts.
                    Cheese.
12. Coffee.

The menu should be pinned in a conspicuous place where the maids may refer to it readily.   After the

WEBB'S Extracts are triple strength.   Use them.

table is set the mistress should make a thorough inspection of the dining room, to see that the necessary extra silver and china is laid out upon the sideboard, that the arrangement of decorations and of lights is satisfactory and that the temperature is neither too high nor too low, as none but a thoroughly competent waitress could be trusted to attend to these details. It is better to err on the side of too low a temperature for the dining room than too high, as with the lights, the warm food and the number of people, the room is likely to become uncomfortably warm. With final admonitions to the maids in regard to the different viands, the warmth of the soup, the coolness of the water and other details, the mistress should try to slip up to her room in time to insure at least a few moments quiet and rest before dressing to receive her guests. At the appointed time the maid should throw open the doors of the dining room, and upon the signal "Dinner is served," the host should lead to the dining room, escorting the lady in whose honor the dinner is given, the other guests following, and the hostess last of all with the gentleman to be most honored. Confusion is avoided by having name cards at each place, the guests of honor of course being seated at the right of the host and hostess. If the first course consists of oysters these are upon the table when the guests enter the dining room, and as either a cube of bread or a roll has previously been placed in a fold of the napkin for each guest, no dishes are to be passed during this course. The maid stations herself back of the chair of the host and after the oysters are eaten, at a look from the mistress she removes the plates. The dishes should always be served at the left side and removed from the right side. Taking care not to pile too many dishes upon her tray at once, the maid swiftly and noiselessly transfers the oyster plates to a table in the kitchen assigned to that purpose. After the oysters follow soup, with which crackers are usually passed: then fish with its accompanying cucumbers or other relish; then roast entrées. sorbet. game and salad. each in turn served with its accompanying dishes in strict accordance with the written menu. When the salad is finished. all side dishes. and salts and peppers, should be taken away and all crumbs removed neatly with a crumb knife or napkin and the maid should see that the necessary dessert forks and spoons are at each cover. If preferred the dessert may be placed before either the host or hostess, who will serve her guests, the maid standing ready to pass each plate as it is served. After the pudding course has been removed comes either the pastry or ice. When this course is finished finger bowls may be placed at each plate, and at the same time come fruits. nuts. and raisins. Last of all the coffee in small cups. which should be served fresh and very hot. When dinner is over, the hostess gives the signal to arise and the host leads to the drawing room, after which the gentlemen. if they wish, may retire to smoke.

MENU

▼▼▼▼▼▼▼▼

Oysters on a Block of Ice

Potage à la Reine

Celery   Salted Almonds   Olives

Smelts à la Tartare

Parisienne Potatoes

Roast Chicken, Chestnut Stuffing and Sauce

Green Peas   Potato Timbale

Crûstades of Asparagus

Tomato Salad

Water Crackers   Neufchatel Cheese

Custard Soufflé   Cream Sauce

Strawberry Ice Cream   Cake

Fruit   Nuts

Coffee

ENTRÉES.

A genial savour
Of certain stews and roast meats and pilaus,
Things which in hungry mortal's eyes find favor.—*Byron.*

When art and nature join th' effect will be
Some nice ragout or charming fricassee.

Curry Hawaiian

Will Serve About Eight People.

1 small cocoanut, or 1 cup dessicated cocoanut	1 quart of milk
	½ teaspoonful of salt
2 tablespoonfuls of curry powder	1 teaspoonful of butter
	A few shreds of onion

Put on the stove and stew for half an hour or longer. Thicken with a tablespoonful of corn starch mixed in a little milk. For shrimp curry add the shrimps. heat through and serve. For oyster curry put them into the mixture and boil up once. For chicken, mutton. beef or veal curry. cut the meat in small pieces. place in a sauce pan with a tablespoonful of butter and fry a nice brown. add to the curry mixture and set back to cook slowly an hour if uncooked meat is used. Serve with rice.

MRS. NINA C. SPENCER.

Russian Entree

Boil fresh tongue. When nearly done pour off the water and add fresh water in which put 1 pound of prunes, previously soaked ten hours, and 1 lemon sliced very thin. *Simmer* until prunes are done. When ready to serve throw in 2 wine glasses of Madeira.

Mrs. ERASTUS BRAINERD.

Veal Olives

6 large slices veal   3 slices salt pork
2 cups bread crumbs

Trim uniformly the veal, spread with chopped pork and bread crumbs well seasoned with salt, pepper and butter; roll up and bind with small skewers—small wooden toothpicks do very well. Lay in pan; add 1 cup boiling water and roast, basting often with melted butter. When done remove the skewers carefully and make a brown gravy to pour over the olives. Serve with tart jelly.

Mrs. DOUGLAS YOUNG.

Macaroni Stufato

Italian.

½ pound macaroni   1 pound lean beef, chopped
½ pint cooking sherry   fine
½ pound cheese, grated   Spices

Cook macaroni until tender in boiling water. Put the chopped beef in water enough to cover it, with 2 cloves of garlic, 3 cloves, 2 allspice, 2 tablespoonfuls tomato catsup, 1 tablespoonful walnut catsup, 1 tablespoonful Worcestershire sauce, salt to taste, 1 teaspoonful of jelly or sugar. Cook slowly; when done add sherry. Put in a baking dish first a layer of the cooked macaroni, then a layer of the stew, then one of grated cheese, alternating until the dish is filled. Put pieces of butter on the top and brown in oven. Any stew left

when the dish is filled may be served as a dressing for
the dish.

Mrs. ERASTUS BRAINERD.

Macaroni

Turkish Way.

Break macaroni into pieces, throw it into boiling
water; boil rapidly for thirty minutes; drain and throw
into cold water; strain ½ pint stewed tomatoes, put it
over the fire while macaroni is boiling, let it stew until
reduced one-half. Add 1 tablespoonful of butter and ¼
cup of chopped almonds; let it remain fifteen minutes
longer. Add 1 teaspoonful of beef extract. Drain
macaroni, throw it into the tomato, pull it to the back
of the fire. where it may *simmer* for ten minutes. Add
1 teaspoonful of salt. ½ teaspoonful of paprica and turn
into a dish. Pass with a dish of grated Parmesau. By
permission of

Mrs. S. T. RORER and THE HOUSEHOLD NEWS.

Veal and Macaroni

1½ pounds veal   1½ pounds macaroni
2 eggs

Cook the veal and chop fine, mixing thoroughly with
macaroni. also cooked and chopped fine. Season well
with salt, pepper and butter; add the eggs, well beaten.
Put in a baking dish, and pour over this the broth in
which the veal was cooked. It must be very moist.
Bake one-half hour.

Cold Weather Dish

Take the largest size bologna sausage (four or five
inches in diameter), cut in thin slices without skinning.
Put a piece of butter the size of a large walnut in the
frying pan. When melted drop in a few slices of the
sausage and let them crisp as bacon does. They will
curl into a cup about like half an orange. In a stewpan

put three or four muffin rings and boiling water
enough to cover nearly to the top of the rings. Into
each ring break a fresh egg; season with pepper and
salt. When cooked take out of the ring and lay on the
slice of prepared sausage. Serve hot on hot plates.
The sausage "cup" with the egg may be laid on lettuce
leaves if desired.

Mrs. NATHANIEL WALDO EMERSON, Boston.

Veal or Chicken, as Terrapin

1 chicken, or same quantity of veal
4 eggs yolks, hard-boiled
½ teaspoonful of mixed mustard, salt, pepper
½ teaspoonful of cloves, ground
1 teaspoonful of browned flour
1 wineglass of wine
Piece of butter

Cut meat in small pieces; make gravy of other ingredients stirred into enough of the water in which the
meat was cooked; add meat; stir well together and
serve hot with a little more wine.

MISS HOPKINS.

Mock Terrapin

1 quart of cold diced veal
½ pint of stock
2 tablespoonfuls of butter
1 tablespoonful of flour
¼ blade of mace
1 clove
Small bit of cinnamon
1 tablespoonful of mush-
 room or walnut cat-
 sup
3 hard boiled eggs
½ pint of cream
1 small slice of onion,
 minced fine
Juice of half a small lemon
½ cup of chopped mush-
 rooms
2 tablespoonfuls of tomato
 catsup
3 tablespoonfuls of sherry
Salt, pepper and cayenne

Put the butter and onion into a sauce pan and cook
till light brown, add the veal, cut in dice, (raw meat
may be used, but is not as nice as cold roast), put the
pan where it is quite hot and let the meat brown, care-

WEBB'S Ground Spices are perfectly pure.

fully stirring. then add the flour and stir well for a
moment or two. Pour in the stock, or water will do, (a
little gravy left from the roast may be added to the
water). Add to this all the seasoning except the lemon
and wine. Tie the spices in a muslin bag and let *simmer* for two hours, covered tightly. At the end of the
time take out the spices, add the cream, eggs and
mushrooms chopped fine. Taste for seasoning, let boil
up hard for a minute, then add the lemon and sherry
and serve *immediately* in a very hot dish. Nice for a
luncheon dish, an entrée or patties, and tastes very
much like terrapin.

MRS. RICHARD C. STEVENS.

Chicken Terrapin

1 cold roast chicken   1 parboiled sweet bread

Sauce.

1 cup rich, hot cream   ½ cup of butter
2 tablespoonfuls of flour   Salt and pepper to taste

Chop the chicken and sweet bread moderately fine;
add to the same and heat over hot water fifteen minutes.
Just before serving add the yolks of 2 eggs, well beaten
and 1 wineglass of sherry.

MRS. STROUT, from Mrs. Lincoln.

Chicken Jelly

Joint a chicken, put it into a saucepan, with 2 slices
of onion, a stalk of celery, a couple of slices of carrot,
a couple of cloves and ¼ bay leaf; cover with hot water
and cook *slowly* till the meat will come from the bones.
When about half cooked, add salt, pepper and a light
dash of cayenne. When thoroughly cooked take out
the meat and set both meat and liquor away to cool.
Soak 2 tablespoonfuls of gelatine in a little cold water.
Take every bit of fat off the liquor, and put it into a
saucepan. Add a sprig of parsley, and if you have no
celery, a little celery salt. Taste for seasoning and

HORSESHOE Soap will not shrink your flannels.

simmer about fifteen or twenty minutes, then add the gelatine, and when it is dissolved, a tablespoonful of sherry or more to your taste. There should be about 1½ pints of the liquor. Take the skin and bones from the chicken and pull apart lengthwise in small pieces. Put a little of the liquor in a mould: a narrow bread tin is good; then a layer of hard-boiled eggs sliced; then the chicken laid lengthwise of the tin; then more of the liquor and another layer of eggs, and cover all with the liquor. If you like, a layer of chopped mushrooms may be put through the center of the chicken, making two layers of chicken. Set aside to harden. Turn out of the mould and cut in thin slices.

MRS. RICHARD C. STEVENS.

Cream Chicken

1 chicken, 4½ pounds	4 sweetbreads
1 can of mushrooms	1 quart of cream
5 spoonfuls of flour or cracker	4 tablespoonfuls of butter

Boil the chicken and sweetbreads, and when cold cut up as for salad. Put the cream in a saucepan with the butter; add the flour or cracker crumbs; stir until well melted, and put the hot cream over, stirring all the time until it thickens; season highly with black and red pepper. Put all in the baking dish and cover with bread crumbs and pieces of butter. Bake twenty minutes.

Blanquette of Chicken

Will Serve Six or Eight Persons.

1 quart cooked chicken cut in small pieces	1 large cup white stock
	1 cup cream
3 tablespoonfuls butter	2 heaping tablespoonfuls flour
Yolks of 4 eggs	
1 saltspoonful salt	½ saltspoonful pepper

Beat the butter in a saucepan; add flour, stirring until smooth, but not brown; add stock and cook two minutes, then seasoning and cream. As soon as this boils

add chicken and cook ten minutes. Beat the yolks of
eggs with 4 tablespoonfuls of milk, add to other ingredients and cook about one-half minute. Serve on
hot dish with rice or potato border, or on toast.

Mrs. WEBSTER BROWN.

Cold Venison

A good way to utilize bits of cold venison is to chop
them fine, then heat with some of the gravy left from
dinner or some water and a generous lump of butter,
season with pepper and salt, then fill some patty pans
with the venison and cover the top with crust; bake until the crust is "done brown."

Mrs. JOSEPH SHIPPEN.

Bread Croquettes

1 pint bread crumbs, rubbed fine; add to them 1 teaspoonful of cinnamon, grated rind of 1 lemon, whites of
2 eggs, unbeaten; add ½ cup chopped English walnuts,
mix and form into croquettes; dip in egg, then in
crumbs, and fry. Serve with a liquid pudding sauce.
By permission of

Mrs. S. T. RORER and THE HOUSEHOLD NEWS.

Turkey Croquettes

Chop very fine the remnants, freed from fat or bone,
of a roast or boiled turkey. Heat a piece of butter the
size of an egg; chop together a little onion and a sprig
of parsley and add to the butter with a large tablespoonful of flour. When well cooked put in a cupful of
strong stock and seasoning of pepper, salt, a little
lemon juice and sherry, and the turkey. Set away to
cool, and when cold mould into small rolls, dip into a
beaten egg, then into cracker crumbs and fry in hot
lard. Serve heaped around a pile of peas, made very
hot and seasoned with butter.

Mrs. M. A. KELLOGG.

Veal Croquettes With String Beans

Chop 2 pounds of cold roast veal, and 2 sweetbreads. Moisten them with a little clear stock and bind together with the yolks of 2 eggs. Season with salt and pepper and a teaspoonful of chopped parsley. Roll into cones, dip in beaten egg, then in fine crumbs, then in egg and again in crumbs and fry in smoking hot lard. Arrange neatly on a dish with small end upright, and put around them a border of string beans, which have been boiled very tender and nicely seasoned.

Mrs. HATFIELD.

Chestnut Croquettes

Shell and blanch 1 quart of chestnuts, cover with boiling water, boil until tender, drain and sprinkle over a teaspoonful of salt. When dry, mash, add 1 teaspoonful of butter, a saltspoonful of salt and beat until light and smooth. Form into croquettes, dip in beaten egg, then in crumbs and fry in smoking fat. By permission of

Mrs. S. T. RORER and THE HOUSEHOLD NEWS.

Kidneys

1 tablespoonful of butter	1 onion
1 dozen lamb kidneys	½ cup of stock
1 lemon	Salt and pepper
Mushrooms	Sherry
Worcestershire sauce	

Put the butter in a saucepan and add the onion slices, and when brown add the kidneys sliced thin and cook five minutes. Dredge with flour, add stock, boil up, then mushrooms, sherry, salt, pepper and sauce, and serve on toast.

Mrs. NEUFELDER.

WEBB'S Ground Spices are perfectly pure.

Steak and Kidney Pudding

Will Serve Six Persons.

1 heaping cup chopped suet	1½ cups of flour
1 level teaspoonful of baking powder	2 pounds round steak
	2 veal kidneys
Pepper and salt	1 large onion

Chop the suet very fine, put in the flour, salt and baking powder; then mix to a stiff dough with cold water. Roll out, not too thin, line a basin holding about two quarts with part of it. Cut the steak into pieces about an inch square, rejecting all bones, gristle and fat; have salt and pepper mixed, in the proportion of 1 small teaspoonful of pepper to 2 large ones of salt, in a small dish. Now dip your pieces of steak and kidney on one side in the mixed salt and pepper, lay evenly on the crust in the bottom of the basin. When the bottom is covered put a layer of the onion very thinly sliced and finish with the seasoned meat, making three layers. Wet the edges of the crust, put on the top crust, press the edges closely together and leave no holes in the top. Wring a cloth out of hot water, flour well and tie very tightly over the basin, put in a kettle of boiling water and boil for three hours. Serve in the dish in which it is cooked.

The kidneys may be omitted and more steak used in place of them.

In using the kidneys cut out the centers well.

MRS. EDMUND BOWDEN.

Sweetbreads

In whatever manner sweetbreads are to be served they must first be parboiled and blanched. The following is a good way to do this:

As soon as received they should be put into cold water, and this should be changed two or three times, if they are bloody, until they are quite white; then put

HORSESHOE Soap for economy and quality.

them in a saucepan, cover with boiling water, add ⅓ teaspoonful of salt, and let them *simmer* on the back of the
range for twenty minutes.   If to this water you add ⅓ a
blade of mace, a couple of cloves, a bit of stick cinnamon, ⅓ a bay leaf and a very slight grating of onion
they will be much finer flavored in whatever way they
are prepared.   After simmering, drain and throw them
into icewater and let them stand for an hour.   Drain,
free from fat and membrane, and they are ready to be
cooked by any of the various methods.

MRS. RICHARD C. STEVENS.

Creamed Sweetbreads

Will Serve Four Persons.

2 sweetbreads	½ cup cream
6 slices bread	1 tablespoonful butter
Small teaspoonful flour	Pepper and salt

If milk must be used instead of cream add:

½ cup milk	1 heaping teaspoonful flour
1 teaspoonful butter	

Cut the sweetbreads into small pieces, put in a small
saucepan, pour over them the cream, and when boiling,
add the flour (previously mixed with a little of the
cream): boil three minutes, being careful not to burn,
and add the pepper and salt.   Have the six slices of
bread nicely toasted, cut into rounds with a large-sized
biscuit cutter, butter, dip the lower side in hot salted
water, arrange on a small platter and heap the sweetbreads on them.

MRS. EDMUND BOWDEN.

Sweetbread Patties

Cut the sweetbreads in small dice and mix with an
equal amount of boiled mushrooms.   Make dressing of:

1 cup sweet cream	2 tablespoonfuls of butter
3 teaspoonfuls of flour	

Boil until it thickens, add sweetbreads and mushrooms and put in patty shells.

MRS. JAMES FIELDS.

Sweetbread Fritters

Cut some previously parboiled sweetbreads into thin slices, scatter over these slices a little lemon juice, chopped parsley, pepper, salt and nutmeg. Dip them into batter and fry in hot lard. Drain all grease from them, arrange them on a napkin on a platter and serve garnished with parsley.

MRS. HATFIELD.

Breaded Sweetbreads.

For Five Persons.

After boiling six sweetbreads, split them, dip in beaten egg, season with salt, roll in cracker crumbs, dip in egg again, fry in hot butter, being careful not to scorch. Serve with sliced lemon.

MRS. JAMES FIELDS.

Mock Sweetbreads

1 pound of uncooked lean veal, cut into half-inch cubes, and cooked with 1 slice of onion in boiling salted water till tender, then put into cold water to whiten. Make 1 cup of white sauce, and season with 1 saltspoonful of salt, 1 saltspoonful of celery salt and ½ saltspoonful of pepper. Put the veal and ½ a cup of mushrooms cut into quarters into the sauce; heat over hot water five minutes, or till hot; remove from fire, add quickly 1 teaspoonful lemon juice and 1 well beaten egg. Serve inside a potato border, or on toast garnished with toast points.

MRS. LINCOLN'S Boston Cook Book.

Potato Patties

Rub cold potatoes through a sieve, add a little clarified butter and 1 egg; mould them into balls with a little flour to keep them smooth; take them in your hands, and with your thumbs in the middle, work it round to form

---

HORSESHOE Soap for Good Luck.
C. C.—5

the shell. Fry them in hot fat and fill with any kind of minced meat or fish. Mackerel with parsley sauce is very good.

Mrs. BEATRICE GREEN.

Baked Mushrooms

Peel the mushrooms, then cut the tops and upper portion of the stems into pieces of uniform size. Place in a buttered pan, with salt, pepper and bits of butter, and bake until the mushrooms seem tender, or about fifteen to twenty minutes. When almost ready to serve pour over them enough sweet cream to cover them; let all heat up together and serve very hot. In the absence of cream, milk may be used, but more butter must then be added.

Mrs. C. P. DAM.

Mushroom Entrée

1 cup of mushrooms
1 cup of chicken, or sweetbreads

Cut the chicken into dice, or if you use sweetbreads, which are even more delicate than chicken, boil and cut into small pieces. Cut the mushrooms in halves and mix with the meat. Make a white sauce, and season with salt, pepper, a dash of onion juice and a hint of bayleaf. Stir the mixture into this sauce, and serve *very hot* in small entrée dishes. Just before sending to the table put a tablespoonful of whipped cream on each dish.

Mrs. NATHANIEL WALDO EMERSON, Boston.

Croûstades of Asparagus

Cup off the tops of rolls or biscuits, scrape out the inside and set, with the tops in the oven to crisp. Make a white sauce, add the tips of 2 bunches of cooked asparagus; fill the rolls with this, put on the tops and serve very hot.

Mrs. FRANK MITCHELL.
(Mrs. Hinckley's Portland Cooking Class.

Fruit Entrée

Take equal quantities of white grapes skinned, small pieces of oranges picked with a fork, small pieces of bananas; use the juice also. Sweeten to taste. Keep several hours in icebox. Serve in glass lemonade cups, or bouillon cups, and just before serving add fine sherry to taste and 2 or 3 candied cherries to each glass.

Mrs. NATHANIEL WALDO EMERSON, Boston.

Lobster Baskets.

Get fresh lobsters if possible, if not canned will do. Cut fresh bread into slices a full inch thick, then cut with a large biscuit cutter into round pieces (without crust), scoop out of the center of the bread circle, a hole half way down to the bottom, drop them into boiling lard and fry a delicate golden brown. Meanwhile prepare a white sauce, beat it and stir in while hot *small* pieces of lobster. Fill the holes in the bread circles with this creamed lobster preparation, grate a little of the coral over the top and put small claws in like handles to the baskets, tied at the top with red baby ribbon, if you can get fresh lobsters, if not, lay each filled basket on a lettuce leaf and serve on an individual plate. The baskets and "filling" must be served very hot. Add a little sherry to the lobster if desired.

Mrs. NATHANIEL WALDO EMERSON, Boston.

Celeried Oysters

For 1 dozen large oysters, put 1 teaspoonful of butter in a stewpan, add 1 tablespoonful of minced celery and the oysters; cover and cook till the oysters are plump and the edges begin to curl; add the seasoning and the sherry; let it boil once, and serve *very hot* on toast.

WEBB'S Extracts are triple strength. Use them.

Oyster Kabobs

Put 1 large tablespoonful of butter in a stewpan, add a small onion, chopped *very fine*, a dessert spoonful of parsley and a dozen mushrooms chopped; let these fry one minute; add 1 dessert spoonful (scant) of flour, stir well together; then drop in as many oysters as required, which have previously been blanched and bearded. Stir and add the beaten yolks of three eggs, one at a time, taking care they do not curdle but get just thick enough to adhere to the oysters. Take skewers and string 6 oysters onto each one, basting with the sauce wherever it does not adhere. Let these cool, then roll in beaten egg and abundant cracker meal, so that it looks like a sausage with a skewer run through lengthwise. Fry, in deep fat, two minutes. Great care must be taken to have the fat hot enough, about 380 to 400 degrees, so that the oysters will become a pale brown in that time, as they would become hard and tough if cooked longer. Serve on a napkin, allowing one skewer to each person.

ADELAIDE M. BLACKFELL.

Oysters à la Poulette.

Put 2 tablespoonfuls of butter in a hot saucepan, melt and add 2 tablespoonfuls of chopped onion and 1 of parsley, 1 bay leaf and a sprig of thyme. *Simmer* for ten minutes, then add 2 tablespoonfuls of flour. Have 1 cup of stock hot and pour gradually over the ingredients in the saucepan; strain into a double boiler; season; add 1 cup of hot cream, and stir well until thick.

Drain 1 pint of oysters, pour cold water over them and drain again, then squeeze lemon juice over them and cook till plump, and add to the sauce.

Have ready shells prepared as follows: Cut slices of bread an inch and a quarter thick, and with a biscuit cutter cut rounds from each slice. With a smaller cutter cut nearly through the round and remove the center, leaving a cup. Roll these in beaten egg, then in

bread crumbs and fry in deep fat. to a delicate brown.
Fill with the prepared oysters and serve hot. garnished
with a sprig of parsley.

MRS. FRANK MITCHELL.

Olympia Oysters and Fresh Mushrooms

2 cups of mushrooms (a   1 pint of oysters
   few more or less will   2 tablespoonfuls of butter
   not matter)   2 tablespoonfuls of flour
¼ cup of sherry

Peel and break into small pieces the mushrooms and
put them in a stewpan with a little water: cook until
tender. stirring frequently. Heat the butter and stir
into it the flour, rubbing smooth, add the cream gradually and let it boil up once. Add to this the mushrooms
and oysters, season with salt and cayenne pepper and
add the wine. Serve on toast.

MRS. A. W. ENGLE.

Oyster Patties No. 1

1 can oysters   3 ounces butter
Yolks of 2 eggs   Salt. pepper and celery tops

Bake some tarts made of Puff Paste; keep warm;
drain the oysters. put in a stewpan with only enough of
their own liquor to keep them from burning; add the
butter laid in pieces among the oysters. To enrich the
gravy stir in the beaten yolks of 2 eggs and ¼ cup of
sweet cream. Season with pepper. salt and tops of
celery finely minced. Let stand about five minutes to
heat thoroughly, then fill the tarts with the oysters,
and pour gravy over and serve at once.

L. M. THEDINGA.

Oyster Patties No. 2

1 pint solid native oysters   1 large tablespoonful butter
1 saltspoonful salt   1 saltspoonful pepper
2 small tablespoonfuls flour 2 small cups milk
Yolks of 2 eggs

Stir your flour, pepper and salt in a little cold milk, then stir this into your boiling milk and add butter. When this is the consistency of cream, have a quart of boiling water and pour your oysters into it, and give them a shake or a stir with a spoon; then turn immediately into a colander, drain well, and stir them into your cream. Set over a slow fire for five minutes for oysters to finish cooking. Beat the yolks of the 2 eggs in a little milk and stir into your cream, then fill your shell. This will serve eight persons.

CHARLES MULCAHEY (Chef Rainier-Grand).

Chicken Patties

1 chicken, 4 pounds
A little parsley, celery, and onion (if you like)

Cut chicken into dice-shaped pieces, and stir into cream sauce as for oyster patties. Use lamb or sweetbreads in the same way.

CHARLES MULCAHEY (Chef Rainier-Grand).

Devilled Crabs

Make 1 pint of cream sauce and add:

¼ teaspoonful cayenne   1 teaspoonful made mustard
1 teaspoonful lemon juice   1 tablespoonful wine
                1 pint crab meat

Make the sauce thick, as the crabs liquify it.

MRS. CHARLES SHEPARD.

Crab Chops No. 1.

Take the meat from two good-sized crabs. Put in sauce pan 1 teacupful of cream, 1 teaspoonful of grated onion, 1 teaspoonful of finely chopped parsley. When mixture comes to a boil stir into it 2 tablespoonfuls of flour rubbed smooth in a little milk. Put in crab, season with pepper, salt, a little cayenne pepper, a tablespoonful of Worcestershire sauce, take from the fire, slightly cool, then stir in the beaten yolks of 2 eggs; add

HORSESHOE Soap will not *draw* your *hands*.

a small glass of sherry wine; replace on stove and cook long enough to set the egg. Turn the mixture on a platter to cool. When cold form into shape of chops, pointed at one end; roll in egg and bread crumbs; fry in boiling fat; stick a claw into the pointed end of each chop, after they are cooked. Garnish with parsley and serve with tartare sauce.

MRS J. C. HAINES.

Crab Chops No. 2

1 quart of crab meat
2 tablespoonfuls of flour
1 tablespoonful of Worces-
    tershire sauce
1 glass of sherry (small)
A dash of mace
Salt and pepper

¾ cup of cream
1 teaspoonful of grated
    onion
1 teaspoonful of chopped
    parsley
Yolks of 2 eggs
A dash of cayenne

Mix flour and part of the cream, add the onion and parsley and cook until thick, then add the remainder of the cream, eggs and other ingredients, the sherry last. When cold shape into chops, dip in eggs and bread crumbs, fry in *hot* deep lard, and serve with tartare sauce.

MRS. NEUFELDER.

Crab Cutlets

1 pint milk
2 tablespoonfuls butter
¼ teaspoonful salt

2 heaping tablespoonfuls of
    corn starch
¼ teaspoonful celery salt

Little bit of cayenne pepper

Heat the milk; put the butter in a pan, and when it commences to bubble, stir in cornstarch slowly and cook till *thick*, then stir in the crab meat; pour on a large flat dish. When cool, form into cutlets; dip in crumbs, then egg, then crumbs, and cook like griddle cakes. Serve on a lettuce leaf, with a claw stuck on one side.

MRS. TAYLOR (from Mrs. Harrington).

WEBB'S Extracts are triple strength. Use them.

Salmon Cutlets

1 pound canned salmon	½ pound crackers, rolled fine
1 ounce butter	1 teaspoonful salt
½ teaspoonful pepper	1 egg

Pour the oil off the salmon, pick out the bones and the skin, beat it; add a few tablespoonfuls of crackers, then the butter, salt and pepper and mix it all together. Form it into cutlet shape; dip into the beaten egg and then into the rolled crackers. Fry in very hot lard until brown, and garnish the dish with parsley.

L. M. THEDINGA.

Crab à la Roi

1 can of tomatoes	1 slice of onion
2 cups of crab meat	1 cup of cream
1 pinch of salt	1 red pepper
1 lump of butter size of an egg	

Cook the tomatoes with a pinch of salt, red pepper and slice of onion at least two hours. Then strain through a colander. Shred the crabs very fine, add the cream, then mix the crab with the tomatoes and just let it come to a boil; put in the butter but do not cook. Serve on small pieces of buttered toast on a warm dish.

This will serve six people for a luncheon course.

MRS. HOMER F. MORTON.

Crab Patés à la Creole

This Will Make Nine Patés

1 large Dungeness crab	1 cup rice
2 eggs	¾ cup milk
4 tablespoonfuls of melted butter	1 small pinch of cayenne pepper
Salt and pepper to taste	

Crack the shells of the crab, remove all of the white meat from the claws and body, also the yellow "fat" next the back shell, as this fat is the richest portion of the crab. Mince fine and set aside until the rice is ready. Wash the rice in several waters, then boil in double boiler, covering the rice with 1 quart of boiling water. Do not stir at all, but let boil until dry and tender. Stir the hot rice into the minced crab, add the butter, milk and seasoning, then last of all the beaten eggs. Drop into well buttered granite or iron gem pans, heap up as full as possible, brush over the top with beaten egg and bake in a hot oven until of a rich golden brown color, or it may be baked in an earthen baking dish.

Mrs. C. P. DAM.

Banana or Apricot Fritters

Will Serve Four Persons.

4 bananas	1 tablespoonful of flour
2 eggs	1 teaspoonful of sugar
½ teaspoonful of melted butter	

Remove the skins from 4 bananas, split them and cut in two. Beat the yolks of the eggs well, add 1 large teaspoonful of sugar. Mix the flour with 3 large tablespoonfuls of cold water and put in the eggs, then add the melted butter. Pour the mixture into the stiffly beaten whites, stirring constantly. Dip the bananas separately into the batter, drop them into hot fat and fry to a fine golden color. Serve at once. Canned apricots are even better than fresh ones if well drained.

Sauce.

1 small tablespoonful of corn starch
1 tablespoonful of butter
2 tablespoonfuls of sugar
1 teaspoonful of vanilla extract or nutmeg grated
1½ cups of boiling water

Mix the corn starch with 2 tablespoonfuls of cold water, add the boiling water, the sugar and boil three or four minutes, then put in the butter and flavoring.

Mrs. BOWDEN.

HORSESHOE Soap will not ruin your clothes.

Salted Almonds

Blanch the almonds; put them, with 1 tablespoonful of melted butter and 1 teaspoonful of salt to each cup of almonds, into a bowl and let stand an hour or more: then put them in a moderate oven in a large pan, and stir frequently till a light brown. More salt may be added as they come from the oven if not salted enough.

Mrs. RICHARD C. STEVENS.

CHEESE DISHES

Welsh Rarebit No. 1

1½ pounds of rich American cheese, grated or cut up in fine pieces: season with mixed mustard and cayenne pepper: melt this together, then add ale or beer to make the mixture the consistency of drawn butter. Serve on squares of toast. An egg broken into the mixture and well stirred through just before serving makes rarebit more creamy.

Mrs. J. C. HAINES.

Welsh Rarebit No. 2

½ pound rich cream cheese, broken in very small pieces
A little cayenne
½ cup lager beer (or milk)
2 teaspoonfuls mustard
1 teaspoonful salt
8 slices toast

Put cheese and beer together in kettle and melt; mix mustard, salt and cayenne together dry, and add; cook till it thickens, but does not curdle; pour over toast, serve at once.

Mrs. BAKER.

Genoa Ramaquins

Fit the bottom of a buttered pudding dish, with bread, sliced one-half inch thick. Beat 2 eggs, add ½ pint of milk and a saltspoonful of salt and pour over the bread and let it soak one hour. Then pour off any custard which may not be absorbed, and cover with the cheese mixture. There should be as much grated cheese as would cover the bread an inch thick. Put this in a double boiler, add ½ cup of cream and stir over the fire until dissolved; add salt and pepper, pour over the bread and bake half an hour or until brown.

ADELAIDE M. BLACKWELL, Brookmead.

Cheese Crackers

Take ordinary square crackers, butter them; cut a square piece of the common dairy cheese (fresh) the size of the cracker, and place on it. Spread the cheese with a little prepared mustard. Lay them in a dripping pan, put in the oven until the butter and cheese melt together. Serve *very* hot with salad.

MRS. NATHANIEL WALDO EMERSON, Boston.

Cheese Sticks No. 1

1 pound cheese, grated   1 cup of flour
1 tablespoonful of butter   1 full saltspoonful of salt
  5 drops of tobasco sauce or pinch of cayenne pepper

Mix as pie crust with cold water, roll thin, cut in strips and bake in a quick oven.

MRS. EUGENE RICKSECKER.

Cheese Straws No. 2

3 heaping tablespoonfuls   3 heaping tablespoonfuls of
  sifted flour   grated cheese
1 tablespoonful butter   Yolk of 1 egg
½ saltspoonful salt   ½ saltspoonful pepper
    1 tablespoonful milk and a little nutmeg

Stir cheese and butter in a bowl; add yolks, salt and

HORSESHOE Soap will not shrink your flannels.

pepper; stir well.   Pour in milk, then add flour; roll out
thin and cut in narrow strips and bake in buttered pan
fifteen minutes.

MRS. M. J. CARTER.

Cheese Fondu No. 1

Will Serve Five Persons.

¼ pound good rich cheese,   ½ teaspoonful salt
    grated   2 tablespoonfuls of melted
1 pinch cayenne pepper   butter
           6 eggs

Place the grated cheese in a bowl, add the salt,
cayenne, melted butter and beaten yolks, stirring in last
of all the whites of eggs, which have been beaten to a
stiff froth.   Pour into a buttered dish or into individual
moulds, bake in a hot oven for twenty minutes and
serve at once in the dish in which it has been cooked.
This makes a good entrée for dinner or an appetizing
supper dish.

MRS C. P. DAM.

Cheese Fondu No. 2

1 cup bread crumbs   2 small cups fresh milk
½ pound grated cheese   3 well beaten eggs
1 small tablespoonful of   A pinch of soda dissolved in
    melted butter   hot water and stirred
Pepper and salt   into the milk

Soak the crumbs in the milk and beat into these the
eggs, the butter, the seasoning, lastly the cheese.   Pour
the mixture into a buttered baking dish, strew dry
breadcrumbs on top, bake in a quick oven and serve immediately.

MRS. S. W. R. DALLY.

Cheese Souffle

2 tablespoonfuls of butter 1 heaping tablespoonful of
½ cupful of milk   flour
1 cupful of grated cheese   3 eggs
½ teaspoonful of salt   A speck of cayenne pepper

Put the butter in a saucepan and when hot add flour

and stir until smooth, but not browned; add milk and seasoning. Cook two minutes, then add the yolks of the eggs well beaten and the cheese. Set away to cool. When cold add the whites beaten to a stiff froth. Turn into a buttered dish and bake from twenty to twenty-five minutes. Serve the moment it comes from the oven.

MRS. H. R. CLISE

CHAFING DISH

A true epicure can dine well on one dish, provided it is excellent of its kind.

While the use of the chafing dish is said to date from the days of Homer, its present popularity is due to a revival of the past few years, and although the possession of one is a thing to be desired by the "gude wife" in her housekeeping, it is equally popular in the bachelor apartments, the artists' quarters in modern Bohemia, the light housekeeping of flats, the summer outing in a houseboat or to put in one's canoe, for a dainty tidbit on shore, after an evening's paddle. The modern chafing dish when complete consists of the stand and lamp, dish proper, cutlet dish, and hot water pan, and while preferable in sterling silver, just as good results have been made with a granite iron one, especially if to the delights of the palate there is added "A congenial group who make possible the feast of reason and flow of soul." Some objection has been made on account of the expense of fuel. In the Gorham Manufacturing Company's Chafing Dish book they claim ten of the recipes were prepared in one of their dishes and less than a pint of alcohol used. Wood alcohol we recommend as cheaper and just as good as grain alcohol. Except for coffee and tea, which can be made over another spirit lamp, almost any light breakfast or luncheon can be prepared on a chafing dish, and for late suppers for a few, no other way is as practicable. It

HORSESHOE Soap for Good Luck.

is also an attractive way of serving an entrée at dinner.

Always use a wooden spoon to avoid scratching the dish. Most of these recipes are improved by serving on fresh toasted bread or crackers.

Any ordinary cooking done in a saucepan on the range can be done in a chafing dish. Chops and steak can be daintily done by using a scant amount of butter. Chicken. trout. frogs legs. crab chops, liver and bacon can all be done equally well. The limits of the chafing dish include most breakfast and luncheon dishes and the majority of entrées. For a quick meal on a chafing dish nothing equals one of the many preparations of eggs. boiled. poached. fried with bacon. scrambled or in one of the many omelettes.

Scramble

Put a walnut of butter in chafing dish and drop eggs in whole. When they begin to set. stir lightly so when cooked the mixture is even white and yellow in appearance. Some add a tablespoonful or two of cream or milk.

Omelette

Some go so far as to make a fine omelette the test of a good cook, but once the knack is learned it is so simple and there are so many happy combinations it is quite worth the effort to do it well.

Plain Omelette

Is the foundation for all. The number of eggs depends on size of the chafing dish as well as the number to serve. Five eggs makes a good omelette. Beat whites and yolks separately. the former very stiff. Give the yolks about twelve good beats; add a large tablespoonfuls of milk to every two yolks. or if you find after making once. you prefer it more moist. take a small tablespoonful of milk to *each* egg, add pepper and salt to yolks, then put yolks and beaten whites together, mixing quickly. Have ready the hot chafing dish with a walnut of butter sizzling hot and pour in your mixture. Do *not* stir. This is perhaps the only chafing dish preparation that requires the use of a knife, but for the success of an omelette a broad-bladed knife must be slipped about the edges and under the omelette to lift it just a little all the time, to keep from burning. When it is set, run the knife under one edge and slip on a hot platter, deftly folding over one-half of the omelette on the other.

Cheese Omelette

Is made as above with the addition of grated cheese according to taste.

Oyster Omelette

When a plain omelette is prepared to serve, have ready a small oyster stew, and before folding the omelette lift several spoonfuls of oysters into the center of the omelette and fold over.

Peas Omelette

Peas left from dinner may be heated over and folded in plain omelette. Asparagus heads, corn, tomatoes, minced ham and other combinations will suggest themselves, and a little ingenuity can develop original omelettes.

Sweetbreads

There are many excellent ways of cooking sweetbreads in a chafing dish, but whether cooked at table or on the kitchen range, they must first stand in cold water an hour or two, then they should be parboiled, cooled, and all rough edges, membranes and sinews removed. They should then be put in cold water and kept on ice

WEBB'S Extracts are triple strength. Use them.

until wanted for the chafing dish. Calf's brains are prepared in the same way and may be cooked in any style sweetbreads are.

Creamed Sweetbreads

Put into the chafing dish a walnut of butter; when it melts put in slices of sweetbread or brains, cut not too thin nor yet too thick. or if preferred, cut in dice, and saute in butter. Open a can of French mushrooms, rinse in cold water. cut half of them into quarters, add them to sweetbread with 1 pint of cream; season with salt and pepper. Dissolve 1 heaping tablespoonful of flour, add it and *simmer* until the sauce is thick and smooth.

(Gorham Chafing Dish Recipes.)

Sweetbreads With Peas

Put into the hot water dish a teaspoonful of butter; toss about in the dish the three small sweetbreads which have been prepared as in the foregoing recipe. They may be larded also. When they have absorbed the butter and are in danger of burning. add ½ pint of strong beef or veal broth or gravy, 1 celery leaf chopped fine. salt. pepper and ½ teaspoonful of browned flour. Turn the sweetbreads. and when the sauce is reduced one-half the dish is ready.

Open a can of best green peas. or cooked fresh ones are better; put them into cutlet dish with 1 tablespoonful of butter. salt and pepper. When the peas are warmed through they are done. Serve both together.

(Gorham Chafing Dish Recipes.)

Lobster or Crab à la Newburg

Take 1 large cup of meat. cut into pieces about one inch long. Put an ounce of butter in the pan and add meat. tossing it about. Season with salt and pepper to suit and add 1 cup of heavy cream sauce. When well

heated add the yolk of 1 raw egg and 3 tablespoonfuls
of sherry. Serve on small pieces of dry toast.

RECTOR, Chicago.

Corned Beef Hash à la Murrey

The first important step is to select the proper cut
of corned beef; the second is to be positive that raw
potatoes only are used. cold boiled potatoes will spoil
the dish.

Select a very fine piece of navel corned beef, weighing about 3 pounds; boil it half an hour in hot water,
then take it out. throw the water away and cover the
meat with tepid water. *Simmer* on back of the range
two and a half hours; remove the pot from the range
and allow the meat to cool in the water. Skim off the
fat and remove the meat. placing it in ice box until
next day. Cut into small pieces 2 pounds of the beef;
peel. slice and cut into dice enough *raw* potatoes. which
when cut up will equal in quantity the cut meat. Peel
and cut up fine 1 large sour apple; chop these ingredients together in a chopping bowl. Cut up fine 2
medium sized onions; also a large sweet Spanish pepper, not the hot variety; now put into a large frying
pan a scant tablespoonful of beef drippings—butter
will not do. When hot add the onion and fry a delicate
brown. Next add the pepper, toss about for a few
moments. then add a gill of strong beef stock, after
which the other chopped ingredients, with a pint of
beef stock, or strong broth; mix well, cover and *simmer*
thirty minutes. Should the moisture evaporate too
quickly add more of the broth; stir to prevent sticking
to the pan and also to assist in evaporating the moisture
finally. Taste for seasoning and put away until next
day. when it should be warmed in the chafing dish with
the hot water dish underneath it.

(Gorham Chafing Dish Recipes.)

Welsh Rarebit No. 1

Grate 1 pound of full-cream mild American cheese, no other will give satisfaction. Melt a walnut of butter in the cutlet dish; when the butter is melted add the cheese, and as it melts, stir with a wooden spoon; add 1 tablespoonful of ale every few minutes until four or five are used. Cook six minutes; serve on toast. Do not make the mistake of putting large pieces of cheese into the dish or the rarebit will be lumpy.

Welsh Rarebit No. 2

1 egg beaten together	5 ounces domestic cheese
1 level tablespoonful butter	¼ teaspoonful salt
Pinch of cayenne	Level teaspoonful of dry
5 tablespoonfuls milk	mustard

To make a Golden Buck drop a poached egg on each piece of toast, covered with rarebit.

Fricassee of Oysters

Butter size of an egg	Sherry, wineglassful
Oyster juice, 1 cup	Cream, ½ cup
Good pinch cayenne	Yolks of 4 eggs
Puget Sound oysters, 1 pint	Lemon juice

Put into chafing dish butter the size of an egg; when hot add 1 wineglassful of sherry, reduce, add 1 cup of oyster juice, ½ cup of cream, a pinch of cayenne, yolks of 4 eggs. When like custard put in 1 pint of strained Puget Sound oysters which have been seasoned, and the juice of ½ of a lemon squeezed over them. Cook until plump.

MRS. HINCKLEY.

Oysters à la Creme

2 tablespoonfuls of butter	1 pint of cream
Saltspoonful of salt	Saltspoonful of pepper
Grating of nutmeg	Bay leaf
2 tablespoonfuls of bread crumbs	1 pint of California oysters

Put the butter in the chafing dish, when hot add

cream, pepper, salt, a grating of nutmeg, and a bay leaf. Stir in 2 tablespoonfuls of very stale fine bread crumbs. Blanch a pint of Puget Sound oysters by pouring boiling water over them, drain, and add to the sauce. Cook two minutes.

MRS. HINCKLEY.

Curried Oysters or Clams

1 small onion
1 teaspoonful of curry powder
1 pint of California oysters or 1 dozen of Eastern

2 tablespoonfuls of butter
2 teaspoonfuls of flour
1 pint of milk

Chop the onion fine. Put butter in the chafing dish when hot, add the onion; fry. Mix the curry powder with flour and stir into the butter; add 1 pint of hot milk gradually, strain the oysters and add, cooking them only until the leaves curl.

MRS. HINCKLEY.

Oyster Toast.

1 dozen Eastern oysters or
1 pint of Puget Sound oysters

1 teaspoonful of butter
Yolks of 2 eggs
Gill of cream
Salt, pepper and nutmeg

Chop the oysters moderately fine, season with salt, pepper, and a trace of nutmeg. Put into the chafing dish a teaspoonful of butter; add the oyster mince. Beat up the yolks of eggs with the cream, stir it into the dish, when the egg is firm. Serve on buttered toast.

(Gorham Chafing Dish Recipes.)

Oysters Maitre d' Hotel

½ dozen large oysters
¼ lemon

1 teaspoonful of butter
Chopped parsley
Season with salt and pepper

Dry the oysters in a napkin. Put butter in chafing dish. When it is very hot add the oysters, saute them

WEBB'S Extracts are triple strength. Use them.

on one side, then on the other, season with salt and pepper; put out light under dish, then squeeze the juice of ½ lemon over the oysters, strew over them a little chopped parsley and serve with or without toast.

(Gorham Chafing Dish Recipes.)

Shrimps à la Poulette

Squeeze over a cup of shrimps a little lemon juice, put into chafing dish 1 tablespoonful of butter; when hot, add 1 tablespoonful of flour; pour gradually over 1 cup of hot cream, season, stir in the yolks of 2 eggs; add the shrimps. When hot serve.

(Gorham Chafing Dish Recipes.)

Shrimps à la Creole

Take a pint of shelled shrimps, fresh or canned, and place them in a chafing dish in which you have 2 ounces of butter, ½ of a very small onion grated. Braise the shrimps in this preparation; add ½ a pint of canned tomatoes; season very highly with salt and Chili pepper; add 2 tablespoonfuls of French peas. Cook for about ten minutes and serve.

CHARLES E. RECTOR, Chicago.

Cheese Fondu

1 tablespoonful of butter	1 cup of milk
1 cup stale bread crumbs	½ teaspoonful dry mustard
Speck of cayenne pepper	1 cup grated English dairy cheese

Put the butter in the chafing dish; when melted add cup of milk, then cup of stale bread crumbs which have ·been seasoned with a ½ teaspoonful of dry mustard, a spec of cayenne, the beaten yolks and the cup of cheese. Stir all the time. Just before serving add the well beaten whites. Serve on toast. Twice as much cheese can be used if preferred without changing the other proportions.

MRS. HINCKLEY (recommended by Mrs. M. F. Backus).

HORSESHOE Soap for economy and quality.

Fresh Mushrooms

Peel 1 dozen medium-sized mushrooms, remove the stems. melt ½ a teaspoonful of butter in the cutlet dish. and before it gets hot lift the dish off and put it on a plate; cover the bottom of the dish with mushrooms; on top of each mushroom put a bit of butter the size of a marble; season each with a little salt and pepper. Return the dish to the flame. and cook from two to three minutes according to the size of the mushrooms.

(Gorham Chafing Dish Recipes)

SALADS

Mayonnaise No. 1

2 eggs (yolks only)	1 teaspoonful dry mustard
1 teaspoonful sugar	1 teaspoonful salt
2 tablespoonfuls vinegar	Juice of 1 lemon
1 pint best olive oil	A dash of cayenne

Rub the inside of a bowl with a slice of onion; beat the yolks of the eggs with the dry ingredients and with a silver fork beat in the oil, pouring in only a drop or two at a time. Always stir one way, and always be sure that the last drops of oil are stirred in thoroughly before adding more. After the mixture becomes thick and ropy the oil may be added in a little larger quantities, but it is better to be too careful rather than not enough so. If the mixture separates it is probably because it is not chilled enough or because the oil has been added too rapidly. Set the bowl on the ice in the refrigerator for fifteen or twenty minutes, then try again; if it still will not mix, add the yolk (very cold) of another egg, and perhaps a second one may be added. If it is still obstinate, and it is necessary to finish the dressing at once, it will be best to set this away and begin over again, taking great care that all the materials and utensils are well chilled, and in warm weather, or a warm room, set the bowl in a dish of cracked ice while beating. Sometimes two or three hours' chilling will bring the old dressing out all right; sometimes a few drops of lemon juice or a little unbeaten white of egg will restore consistency.

After the dressing becomes quite stiff and hard to stir, a few drops of lemon or vinegar may be added, then more oil and so on till all of the oil has been used. It is impossible to give exact quantities of vinegar and seasoning for a salad dressing, so much depends upon the strength of the materials; so that much must be left to the taste. But lemon juice is better than all vinegar, and tarragon vinegar is a great improvement upon cider vinegar.

To keep, this dressing should be thick enough to cut with a knife, put into a fruit jar and kept in the ice chest. The quantity needed may be thinned to the proper consistency by adding whipped cream, thick sweet cream, or sour cream. The white of an egg beaten to a stiff froth and added at the last makes it very light and delicate.

MRS. RICHARD C. STEVENS.

Mayonnaise No. 2

3 eggs   Saltspoonful of ground mus-
Saltspoonful of salt   tard
½ teaspoonful of Worces- Pinch of cayenne pepper
    tershire sauce

Beat the eggs and slowly drop in pure olive oil until it becomes a stiff paste; add the condiments and slowly thin with vinegar or lemon juice until the consistency of thick cream.

MRS. EUGENE RICKSECKER.

HORSESHOE Soap for Luck.

Cream Salad Dressing

Mixture for Seasoning.

8 teaspoonfuls of salt   4 teaspoonfuls of mustard
1 even teaspoonful of red pepper

Mix well together and place in a tin or glass can for future use.

Dressing.

To 5 tablespoonfuls of boiling vinegar add the well beaten yolks of 5 eggs. piece of butter size of an egg. and boil until it thickens, then remove from the stove and beat until cool; add 1 teaspoonful of the mixture to this and the juice of 1 lemon. Beat ½ pint of cream stiff and stir into the paste when ready to serve.

MRS. CHARLES STIMSON.

Sour Cream Salad Dressing

5 tablespoonfuls of vinegar   Yolks of 5 eggs
½ cup of butter or salad oil   1 teaspoonful of salt
1 saltspoonful of pepper   1 tablespoonful of sugar
1 teaspoonful of prepared   1 cup of sour cream
    mustard

Heat vinegar to boiling point and pour gradually into beaten yolks, stir until thick, then add butter gradually until all is dissolved, and lastly other ingredients.

C. HOWELL KIRBY.

Cooked Salad Dressing

4 eggs   ¼ teaspoonful of red pepper
1 teaspoonful of dry mus-   1 cup of best salad oil
    tard   1¼ teaspoonfuls of sugar
¾ cup of vinegar   1½ teaspoonfuls of salt

Beat the yolks and add the dry ingredients, then *very slowly* add the oil. This if rightly done will become waxey and thick. Add the vinegar a little at a time; then the beaten whites of the eggs. Put into the double boiler and stir from the edges and bottom carefully till it thickens.

HORSESHOE Soap will not shrink your flannels.

Lemon juice is much nicer than vinegar, or more lemon juice than vinegar. Put in a glass jar, keep in a cool place and use as required.

MRS. GEO. OSGOOD, Tacoma.

Lactiola Dressing

4 tablespoonfuls of butter
1 tablespoonful of salt
1 large teaspoonful of mustard
3 eggs

1 tablespoonful of flour
1 ounce of sugar
1 cup of milk
½ cup of vinegar
A pinch of cayenne

Heat the butter in custard kettle; add flour, stirring until smooth, being careful not to brown. Add the milk and boil up. Beat the eggs, salt, pepper, nutmeg and sugar together, and add vinegar. Mix with the boiling mixture and stir until it thickens like soft custard. Let cool and bottle, and it will keep in a cool place for weeks. Yolks of eggs may be used, requiring six yolks for this quantity.

MRS. CORWIN S. SHANK.

Salad Dressing

2 medium-sized boiled potatoes. While hot pass through a sieve; add well beaten yolks of 2 raw eggs, mixed mustard and salt to taste, and when well mixed and cold, beat in gradually and thoroughly as much oil as it will bear until stiff enough to bear up a fork. Put in vinegar, using your judgment as to quantity, and a dash of red pepper. If the oil does not mix readily, add a drop or two of vinegar or cold water. It needs a deal of beating and should be quite thick and creamy when done.

MRS. B. W. BAKER.

Salad Dressing

Yolks of 3 eggs
3 tablespoonfuls vinegar

6 tablespoonfuls of oil
Pepper and salt

Put into a bottle and shake till like cream.

MRS. ISAAC H. JENNINGS.

WEBB'S Extracts are triple strength. Use them.

Fruit Salad Dressing

4 tablespoonfuls sugar   ½ teaspoonful cinnamon
1 gill sherry   2 tablespoonfuls Madeira

Mix sugar and cinnamon together. add the wine and stir constantly until sugar is dissolved.

By Permission of

MRS. S. T. RORER and ARNOLD & CO.

Egg Salad

1 tablespoonful of butter   3 raw eggs
1 cup of cream   ¾ cup of vinegar
1 teaspoonful of pepper   1 teaspoonful of salt
     2 teaspoonfuls of dry mustard

Beat the eggs separately. then mix and to them add pepper, vinegar, salt and mustard and stir all in a saucepan in which is the tablespoonful of butter melted. Let it come to a boil. then cool before adding the cream. Cut the celery as for chicken salad and cut hard-boiled eggs in quarters or slices. having equal quantities of celery and eggs. Mix all together and stir in dressing.

MRS. R. C. WASHBURN.

Veal Salad With Nuts

Two pounds of cold veal. cut small: 1 head of celery. 1 pound of nuts (almonds. filberts and English walnuts). blanched and halved: marinate with French dressing. and at serving time place on tender lettuce leaves and add mayonnaise dressing.

MRS. RICHARD C. STEVENS.

Lobster Salad

2 raw eggs well beaten   1 teaspoonful of mustard
1 teaspoonful of salt   ¼ teaspoonful of pepper
1 tablespoonful of sugar   2 tablespoonfuls of olive oil

Remove the coral for the dressing. then chop the lobster with 1 bunch of celery. Heat the vinegar. add the seasoning except the oil and stir constantly until of

HORSESHOE Soap for economy and quality.

the consistency of thick cream. Add the oil and work
in gradually the coral which has been rubbed to a paste.
Pour over the hot mixture and set aside to cool.

MRS. DOUGLAS YOUNG.

Salmon Salad No. 1

1 quart cooked salmon	2 heads of lettuce
2 tablespoonfuls of lemon	1 tablespoonful of vinegar
juice	1 teaspoonful of salt
2 tablespoonfuls of capers	1 cup mayonnaise dressing

Break up the salmon with a fork, add to it the salt,
pepper, vinegar, lemon juice and capers. Place on ice
for two hours, and just before serving add the dressing,
tossing the fish lightly with a silver fork and spoon.

MRS. J. S. LOWMAN.

Salmon Salad No. 2

For Five Persons.

1 pound boiled salmon	1 head celery
1 teaspoonful white pepper	½ teaspoonful salt

Break salmon into small pieces, chop celery and
mix with a mayonnaise dressing. Garnish the dish
with white leaves of celery and serve.

MRS. NINA C. SPENCER.

Herring Salad

8 herrings	Cold roast veal
Raw apples	Pickled red beets
Cucumber pickles	2 onions
6 hard boiled eggs	

Soak the 8 herrings for twelve hours, pick out bones
and skin, cut in small pieces; add the same quantity of
finely cut cold roast veal, almost as much of apples and
red beets, and 1 saucerful of chopped pickles and 2
chopped onions. Shortly before using cut the whites
of 6 hard boiled eggs into it, and stir the yolks into the
milt of the herrings, which has been previously beaten

with vinegar; then add thereto pepper. salt. a little
mustard and more vinegar. Pour over the rest, and
when ready to use. ornament with beets, pickles, hard
boiled eggs (each chopped separately) and some capers.
Enough olive oil and vinegar to moisten.

L. M. THEDINGA.

Asparagus and Chicken Salad

Marinate cold boiled asparagus tips in French dressing and place on top of chicken or veal mayonnaise.
Garnish with mayonnaise.

MRS. RICHARD C. STEVENS.

Macedoine Salad

Vegetables which are ordinarily cooked before serving should be cooked before using for salad.   Mayonnaise should be added *just* before serving. as it liquifies
as soon as mixed with vegetables.

1 head celery	1 tablespoonful green peas
¼ cauliflower	1 tablespoonful string beans
	1 small beet

Cut into small pieces, cover with mayonnaise and
serve at once.   Any combination of vegetables may be
used.

MRS. WINFIELD R. SMITH.

Potato Salad

Boil 4 good sized potatoes in their jackets, peel, cut
in dice, put into a colander and marinate with French
dressing in which has been grated a few drops of onion.
When cold moisten slightly with mayonnaise which has
had 1 teaspoonful of minced cucumber pickles and one
of minced capers mixed with it.   Put a layer in the
salad bowl. a thin layer of sliced and salted cucumbers.
a spoonful or two of mayonnaise on this. then more
potatoes, etc., until all are used. putting potatoes last.
and mayonnaise liberally on top.   Garnish with pitted
olives, cold boiled beets cut in any shape desired, hard-

boiled eggs or capers. It is hardly possible to put too many good things into potato salad.

MRS. RICHARD C. STEVENS.

Potato Salad With Apple

Will Serve Six Persons.

6 potatoes boiled with skins 2 apples
on $\frac{1}{4}$ teaspoonful of celery seed
            4 tablespoonfuls of vinegar

When the potatoes are thoroughly cold cut in small cubes; prepare apples in the same way. Mix with them the celery seed and pour over all the vinegar. Let stand two or three hours. stirring occasionally. Serve with mayonnaise dressing.

MRS. EUGENE RICKSECKER.

Apple and Celery Salad

Select several ripe mealy apples and about half as much celery. Make a mayonnaise dressing. using lemon juice instead of vinegar. Add to this the well beaten white of 1 egg. Peel and slice the apples thin. Cut the celery fine. Stir these into the dressing. Garnish with celery tips and serve.

MRS. PETERS.

Apple Salad No. 1

1 cup of apples   2 cups of celery
2 tablespoonfuls of chopped walnuts

Cut the apples and celery into one-half inch pieces. Chop the nuts very fine. Mix with mayonnaise *just* before serving. and garnish with halves of walnuts. Serve very cold.

MRS. E. A. STOUT.

Apple Salad No. 2

A good salad for the spring months is made by com-

---

bining tart, juicy apples with celery. Cut the celery as for chicken salad, peel the apples, cut them as fine as the celery and cover with lemon juice to keep from turning dark. Cover with a French dressing and serve on lettuce leaves.

Mrs. WM. H. DE WOLF.

Tomato Jelly Salad

1 can tomatoes · · · · · · · ½ box gelatine
Pepper and salt

Put the tomatoes in a saucepan and let them come to a boil; season high with pepper and salt, particularly the latter. Strain through a fine sieve, add the gelatine (dissolved) and fill a mould. Set in icebox until cold. Cut in thin slices and serve on lettuce leaves with mayonnaise. Cucumbers sliced very thin may be added if desired.

Mrs. NATHANIEL WALDO EMERSON, Boston.

Tomato Salad

1. Select fine large tomatoes that have been in the ice-chest and are very cold; remove the skins without the use of hot water, arrange on a dish garnished with lettuce or parsley, and put a generous spoonful of mayonnaise on each tomato.

Beet Salad

2. Cut cold boiled beets into dice and mix with an equal quantity of celery cut into pieces not too small. French or mayonnaise dressing.

Asparagus Salad

3. Serve a spoonful of mayonnaise on the plate with boiled asparagus.

Mrs. CHARLES E. SHEPARD.

C. C.— 7

Cucumber and Sweetbread Salad

Sliced cucumbers on sweetbreads with French dressing.

Mrs. H. C. HENRY.

Fruit Macedoine

2 bananas, cut in quarters lengthwise and then in
inch long pieces; 2 oranges, having the pulp separated
as nearly whole as possible; a small pineapple, shreded;
a bunch of grapes, seeded, and ¾ cupful of nuts (pecans
are best, but almonds or walnuts may be used, or a
mixture). Have the fruit thoroughly chilled; moisten
lightly with French dressing. Serve at once on lettuce
leaves with mayonnaise on top. A great many combinations of fruits can be prepared in this way. Oranges alone, or oranges with nuts are good.

Mrs. RICHARD C. STEVENS.

Golden Chestnut Salad

Shell, blanch and boil until tender 1 pint of chestnuts; drain, dust with salt and stand aside to cool;
hard-boil 2 eggs. At serving time arrange the lettuce
in a salad bowl, put the chestnuts over, and moisten
with a nice French dressing, using lemon juice instead
of vinegar. Hold a small sieve over the bowl, and rub
the yolks through it, with which cover the salad lightly.
By permission of

Mrs. S. T. RORER and THE HOUSEHOLD NEWS.

Celery as a Garnish Salad

Take a large cork, as from a wide-mouthed bottle,
drive in needles head first quite close and regularly.
Have nice white celery cut about two inches long, draw
over the needles from the center (nearly) to one end,
then turn and draw to the other end, making the celery
into fringes, held together in the center. Throw into
ice water for a half hour, and it will curl and crisp

WEBB'S Extracts are triple strength. Use them.

beautifully. This is also a pretty way to prepare celery
for a salad.

Mrs. RICHARD C. STEVENS.

Truffle Salad

Russian.

4 dozen truffles	1 wineglass of sherry
1 tablespoonful of oil	1 teaspoonful of chopped
1 teaspoonful of chopped	tarragon
parsley	Salt and pepper

Chop the truffles and put over the fire with the sherry
for five minutes. When cold put in a bowl with the other
ingredients. Mix well and cover with mayonnaise.

Mrs. ERASTUS BRAINERD.

Cauliflower Salad

Boil a cauliflower until tender. Cool. Pick into
small pieces. or serve whole. Cover with mayonnaise.
Garnish with lettuce and hard-boiled eggs, sliced.

Mrs. ERASTUS BRAINERD.

Orange Salad

For Roast Game.

Slice oranges thin; free from seeds; and mix with a
dressing made of 3 tablespoonfuls of oil. 1 tablespoonful of lemon juice, salt. cayenne. Delicious.

Mrs. ERASTUS BRAINERD.

A Dainty Way to Serve Chicken Salad

Cut out the stem end of tomatoes and remove the
pulp. moisten the inside slightly with French dressing
and chill thoroughly. At serving time fill with chicken
mayonnaise (chicken salad. without the celery). put a
spoonful of mayonnaise on top. garnish with capers or
chopped pickles and serve on lettuce leaves.

HORSESHOE Soap, *Big Cake, 5c.*

Tomato Baskets

Select fine large tomatoes, carefully peel and put on ice. Leave a strip of the tomato in the middle to serve as the handle of basket. Prepare celery by splitting lengthwise the thickness of a straw and cut in half inch pieces. Mix with mayonnaise and fill the baskets. Mayonnaise of sweetbreads is very nice in these baskets.

Oyster Salad

Drain the liquor from a pint of Sound oysters, pour boiling water over them and let them stand until they plump. Set away until perfectly cold, then mix with $\frac{1}{2}$ cup of mayonnaise, and serve on crisp lettuce.

Pecan Salad

1 cup pecans, shelled $\frac{3}{4}$ cup celery, cut fine

Marinate with French dressing; chill well, and arrange on lettuce leaves, and garnish with mayonnaise.

MRS. RICHARD C. STEVENS.

A COLD LUNCH FOR A HOT DAY

Iced Bouillon

Halibut (cold boiled) with Mayonnaise   Cucumbers

Olives   Radishes   Small onions

Salted Almonds

Boned Capon, stuffed with Truffled Sausage

Cold Asparagus   Cold Cauliflower

Served with French Dressing

Roman Punch

Whole Tomatoes, filled with Sweetbreads and Celery.

Served with Cream Dressing

Peach Ice Cream   Cake

Fruit in Season

Iced Coffee   Maraschino

MRS. ERASTUS BRAINERD.

VEGETABLES

"Nor lacked our table small parade of garden fruits."

"What, and how great the virtue and the art
To live on little with a cheerful heart."

New Potatoes à la Crême.

Select new potatoes about the size of apricots. Boil in salted water till tender, drain them and when dry pour over a little drawn butter sauce. Serve very hot.

MRS. M. A. KELLOGG.

Potato au Gratin

Slice cold boiled potatoes, stew in milk, season with salt and pepper, sprinkle with grated cheese and bread crumbs mixed, and brown in oven.

MRS. V. A. RITON.

Potato Puff

To 1½ cups of seasoned mashed potatoes allow 1 egg and beat well. Yolks should be added first, then the whites, previously beaten stiff with a pinch of salt in them. Place the mixture in a well buttered dish and bake until light brown on top. A little minced parsley may be added, or a little finely chopped cooked meat of any kind or white fish minced fine. Serve *immediately* in the dish in which it is baked.

ANNA BEACH.

Duchesse Potatoes

5 cold boiled potatoes 5 heaping dessert spoon-
1 teaspoonful of baking   fuls of flour
 powder   2 eggs
    A little salt

Grate potatoes; add, lightly stirring with a fork, the other ingredients. Drop with a spoon into boiling lard, and fry until balls are a rich brown.

MRS. BURNSIDE.

Potatoes on the Half Shell

Wash, scrub and bake 3 smooth potatoes. Cut in halves lengthwise, and without breaking the skin scoop out the potato into a hot bowl. Mash and add 1 tablespoonful of butter, 2 tablespoonfuls of hot cream, 1 tablespoonful of chopped parsley, salt and pepper to taste. Beat the whites of 2 eggs stiff and mix with the potato. Fill the skins with the potato mixture, heaping it lightly on the top. Brown slightly. One tablespoonful of grated cheese may be used instead of the parsley.

MRS. CHARLES SHEPARD.

Potato Croquettes

Boil 6 large potatoes, mash fine, season with pepper and salt and 2 tablespoonfuls of melted butter. Beat separately the yolks of 2 eggs and the white of 1; first beat the yolks thoroughly into the potato, then add the white, beating all very light. Form into balls and roll, first in beaten egg, then into cracker crumbs, and fry in hot lard.

MRS. J. C. HAINES.

Scalloped Potatoes No. 1

Slice raw potatoes fine, put a layer in a baking dish; put over them a dust of flour, small pieces of butter, salt and pepper and celery salt, and a little milk (cream

is better if you have it); fill the dish in this way. Roll
3 crackers fine, sprinkle over the top, and bake one
hour in a moderate oven.

MRS. J. C. HAINES.

Scalloped Potatoes No. 2

Cut cold boiled potatoes into dice and alternate them
in a baking dish with layers of cream sauce, to which
may have been added a little onion juice or parsley.
Strew bread crumbs and bits of butter on top and bake
about thirty minutes.

MRS. CALVIN VILAS.

French Fried Potatoes

Pare the potatoes and cut into three-cornered pieces.
Fry as doughnuts in boiling lard; when brown add pepper and salt.

H. VAUGHAN HOWELL.

Potatoes and Eggs

Eight or 10 potatoes, 6 hard-boiled eggs. Boil and
mash potatoes, season with cream, butter and salt.
Put a layer of this in buttered baking dish. Separate
yolks from whites; mash the yolks, adding teaspoonful
of mustard, *very* little cayenne, tablespoonful of butter,
dessert spoonful of vinegar, cream sufficient to soften.
Mix this with the chopped whites; add a layer of this,
then the potatoes till the dish is filled, putting bits of
butter on top. Put in the oven and brown twenty minutes or a half hour.

MRS. LOUISE A. THOMPSON.

Potato Timbale.

Pare 8 good sized potatoes, cover them with boiling
water, let them cook until soft, drain water from them,
and mash smooth and light. Add 3 tablespoonfuls of
butter, two of finely chopped parsley; season with pep-

HORSESHOE Soap will not ruin your clothes.

per, salt and celery salt, and then gradually beat in 1 teacupful of hot milk, stirring hard; beat the yolks of 3 eggs and stir into mixture; butter baking dish and cover it thickly with fine crumbs; lastly beat the whites of the 3 eggs very stiff; beat well into prepared potato; turn all into dish and bake in a moderate oven for half an hour. Let the dish stand a few minutes after it comes from the oven; then place a heated platter over the top and turn them over together. If the timbale does not readily come from the dish, loosen with a thin bladed knife.

Mrs. J. C. HAINES.

Moulded Potato

Boil until mealy half a dozen large potatoes; mash smooth and light; stir into them 2 generous tablespoonfuls of butter and 3 tablespoonfuls of cream, and 2 tablespoonfuls of finely chopped parsley; season with pepper and salt. Beat very light the whites of 3 eggs, stir into potato, beating all well together. Have a quart tin jelly mould well buttered, pour the mixture into it, pressing down well into form; let stand a few minutes, then reverse mould on a buttered baking tin. Brush the moulded potato over with the beaten yolks of the 3 eggs, place in oven and brown lightly. This makes a sightly dish placed in the center of hot platter and French mutton chops piled around it. Garnish with lemon and parsley.

Mrs. J. C. HAINES.

Creamed Potatoes au Gratin

Put in saucepan 1 cup of thin cream, 1 small tablespoonful of butter, season with salt and pepper; cut into rather fine dice half a dozen cold boiled potatoes. When the cream mixture comes to a boil add the potatoes, let them boil up once and remove from fire. Place a layer of potatoes in a buttered baking dish and scatter over

---

WEBB'S Ground Spices are perfectly pure.

them some grated cheese, and then layers of potatoes and cheese until the dish is filled. Sprinkle over the top a layer of crumbs and bits of butter over all. Put dish in oven and bake until crumbs are brown, which will be in fifteen or twenty minutes.

MRS. J. C. HAINES.

Sweet Potatoes With Sugar

Boil the potatoes, then slice them. Put them in a baking dish, make a syrup by adding water and a little butter to the sugar; do not cook the syrup, but pour it over the potatoes and bake them in the oven. A very little while will suffice for the syrup to permeate the potatoes. A crust of sugar will form on the top potatoes.

MRS. THOMAS GREEN.

Spinach With Cream

Boil spinach and chop fine. In a saucepan over the fire put 4 ounces butter, 1 tablespoonful flour, salt, nutmeg and ½ pint of cream. Stir well until it boils; add spinach, and when hot serve with bread fried in butter.

MRS. ERASTUS BRAINERD.

Boiled Cabbage

Prepare the cabbage by cutting as for cold slaw and allow it to lie in cold water at least half an hour before cooking. Cover with cold water and cook *slowly* until tender, changing the water three times during the process in order to remove the strong cabbage taste and odor. When tender, drain off all water and add ½ cup of milk (this amount for about half a head of cabbage), butter, pepper and salt. Heat the milk through and serve at once. Cabbage cooked in this way is as delicate as cauliflower.

MRS. J. D. LOWMAN.

HORSESHOE Soap for Good Luck.

French Cabbage

Wash cabbage in salt water, cut in quarters and boil twenty minutes. Drain the water from it, but do not squeeze. Brown ¼ pound of butter in pan, put in cabbage and a teacup of cream and let *simmer* another twenty minutes. Good.

MRS. CHARLOTTE B. CHURCH.

Winter Succotash

Boil ½ pint of dry lima beans until tender; add 1 can of corn, season with butter, salt and pepper and add 1 cup of cream or milk.

MRS. FRANK BEACH.

Creamed Carrots

Will Serve Five Persons.

Scrape and wash 6 medium-sized carrots, quarter them and boil in salt water until soft. Drain and mash, season with salt, pepper, and butter the size of a walnut; add a cup of rich milk and serve.

MRS. JAMES FIELDS.

Mushrooms on Toast

For Six Persons.

Peel and rinse 1 dozen mushrooms, cut in pieces and stew in 1 cupful of water until tender; add 2 tablespoonfuls cream or a little butter; season with salt and pepper. Serve on slices of buttered toast.

MRS. JAMES FIELDS.

Salsify or Oyster Plant Patties

Will Serve Six Persons.

12 medium-sized salsify roots	2 tablespoonfuls butter
	1 egg
4 rolled soda crackers	Pepper and salt

Scrape the salsify and cut crosswise in half inch pieces, throwing at once into cold water to keep from

turning dark; a good deal more than cover with boiling
water; add 1 teaspoonful salt and boil until tender,
which will be an hour or longer; mash very fine, put
in ½ tablespoonful butter. pepper and a little salt if
needed, and let cool. In the meantime beat 1 egg lightly.
put in a *little* salt and pepper, roll the crackers very
fine, season with a *little* salt and pepper. Take a dessert
spoon and mould the salsify into little cakes, dip them
into the egg. handling carefully so as not to break them;
roll them in the cracker crumbs. Fry a light brown in
good hot beef dripping. or butter. The patties may be
prepared some hours before frying.

Mrs. EDMUND BOWDEN.

Fricassee of Rice

2 onions, chopped fine	1 cup rice
1 teaspoonful butter	1½ cups boiling water
4 tomatoes	5 green sweet peppers,
Salt	chopped fine

Boil rice, water and peppers an hour, stirring well;
put onions. butter and tomatoes in frying pan and fry
fifteen minutes; add to the cooked mixture, stirring
well. without breaking the rice.

Mrs. B. W. BAKER.

Rice and Cheese

Put 3 or 4 tablespoonfuls of rice into a saucepan of
boiling salt and water (use a good deal of water) and
keep it boiling *hard* twenty minutes. Strain. Butter a
baking dish, and put in a layer of rice. then bits of butter, salt and pepper: then a layer of grated cheese.
Repeat to the top, cover with a layer of bread crumbs
and pour in milk until you can see it at the top. Bake
a half hour. This is much more delicate than macaroni
and cheese.

Mrs. GEORGE OSGOOD, Tacoma.

HORSESHOE Soap will not *draw* your *hands*.

Baked Onions

Boil until well done and put whole into a baking dish. Pour over a small dishful ½ cup of cream or milk, add 3 tablespoonfuls of butter (less if cream is used), pepper and salt. Sprinkle bread crumbs over the top and bake half an hour.

MRS. CHARLES E. SHEPARD.

Fried Onions

Will Serve Five Persons.

Peel 6 large onions, slice, place in pan containing hot fat and fry until brown; leaving them uncovered and stirring often to prevent burning. Season with salt and pepper.

MRS. JAMES FIELDS.

Onion Tart

This is a very appetizing dish to all onion lovers. Place sliced onions in a dish lined with paste, seasoning with butter, pepper and salt and baking until the onions are tender.

If Spanish onions are used and a little cream is added, dredging each layer with a little flour, it makes a delightful accompaniment to baked meats. It must be eaten piping hot.

MRS. L. H. GRAY.

Celery

Cut the tender stalks into inch pieces and boil in water and a little salt three-quarters of an hour. The white root may be boiled with it. Pour over it a white sauce.

MRS. M A. KELLOGG.

WEBB'S Extracts are triple strength. Use them.

Creamed Celery

2 cups of cut celery
1 teaspoonful of butter
Bread crumbs

1½ cups of milk
1 teaspoonful of flour
Salt. cayenne pepper

Boil the celery not quite tender; add milk. flour. butter and seasoning; put in layers in a baking dish with alternate layers of soft bread crumbs; sprinkle fine. dry crumbs on top, with bits of butter.

MRS. CALVIN VILAS.

Catachis

2 rather small crooked-neck squashes
1 bell-pepper (from which seeds have been extracted)

4 medium-sized ripe tomatoes
1 large onion

Chop fine; melt 1 tablespoonful of butter in hot frying pan, put in vegetables, season, cover and cook one hour, stirring often.   Good warmed over.

Papas Rellenas

Spanish.

Boil some potatoes, mash smooth. put in salt and butter and line your dish with them; cut fine some cold roast beef, add some chopped onion. red peppers. thyme and parsley.   Put in a pan with some lard and fry a little; add some soaked bread, and if too dry a little water.   When nicely fried put in your potato dish. Slice some hard boiled eggs over it. cover with mashed potato and brown in oven.

Fried Cucumbers

Slice cucumbers lengthwise in thin slices after paring carefully, salt well and place on tilted board to drain thirty minutes to an hour; dry on towel, dredge with flour seasoned with pepper and fry on hot griddle.

MRS. EUGENE RICKSECKER.

HORSESHOE Soap will not shrink your flannels.

Boiled Cucumbers

6 cucumbers	6 slices of toast
1 cup of milk	1 tablespoonful of butter

Pepper and salt

Pare the cucumbers and slice lengthwise of the vegetable into long strips about the size of asparagus. Boil about twenty minutes until tender, drain and serve on toast. Cover with milk heated to boiling point; seasoned with butter, pepper and salt; if preferred the milk may be thickened with a little flour. This tastes very much like asparagus on toast and is an excellent substitute.

Mrs. R. W. EMMONS.

Stuffed Egg Plant

Will Serve Four Persons.

1 egg plant	1 teacup of chopped cold
1 teacup of bread crumbs	roast beef or steak, or
1½ tablespoonfuls of butter	½ pound round steak
1 teaspoonful of cracker	cooked and chopped
dust	Pepper and salt

Buy a good shaped egg plant weighing about a pound; cut the blossom end so that it will stand upright. Cut the stem end off about two inches from the top and peel the piece cut off. Now carefully remove the inside of the egg plant leaving the shell about a quarter of an inch thick. Stew the egg plant in just enough water to keep from burning until tender, about an hour, stirring often; mash, season with salt and pepper and 1 tablespoonful of butter and beat well. It will be dark in color. Mix the egg plant, bread crumbs and meat thoroughly, put back in the shell, dust the cracker crumbs on the top and dot it with the ½ tablespoonful of butter. Put it in a pan, without water, but slightly greased, in a hot oven and bake until the top is brown—about twenty minutes.

Mrs. BOWDEN.

Corn Dodgers

Will Serve Five or Six Persons.

6 ears green corn (grated)   1 pint of milk
2 eggs   Salt
2 teaspoonfuls of baking   2 tablespoonfuls of sugar
  powder

Flour sufficient to make a stiff batter. Drop in hot lard and fry as you do doughnuts.

MRS. C. P. DAM.

Stewed Tomatoes

Stew the tomatoes a few minutes, sweeten them; then add crumbled crackers, biscuit or light bread. Set the dish inside the oven until a crust forms.

MRS. THOMAS GREEN.

Stuffed Tomatoes

Select firm, large and ripe tomatoes; with a sharp knife cut a deep piece from the stem end of each; press them between the palms to extract as many of the seeds as possible without injury to the shape of the fruit; stuff them with any kind of chopped meat—ham, sausage or beef. Place them side by side in a dish well buttered. Sift bread crumbs thickly over the top, dot it with bits of butter, a teaspoonful in each. Bake in hot oven thirty minutes. They should be a light brown when properly cooked.

EMMA I. McLOGAN.

Fried Tomatoes

Cut tomatoes in half, sprinkle with flour and a little salt. Fry in butter with cut side down. When fried brown put into a dish. Put a piece of butter and some milk in the frying pan. When it boils pour over the tomatoes. Serve very hot.

MRS. V. A. RITON.

HORSESHOE Soap for economy and quality.
C. C.—8

Creamed Tomatoes

½ can of tomatoes
1 tablespoonful of butter
1 tablespoonful of onion, chopped
1 teaspoonful of parsley, chopped
1 teaspoonful of corn starch
5 eggs

Stew tomatoes, butter, onions and parsley together, adding corn starch after mixing it with a little of the tomato juice. Beat the eggs until very light and add to other ingredients, stirring all until thick and creamy. Serve on buttered toast. Nice with anchovies.

MRS. S. W. R. DALLY.

Escallopped Tomatoes

Put a layer of sliced tomatoes in the bottom of an earthen pudding dish; then a layer of fine bread or cracker crumbs. Season each layer with salt, pepper, sugar and bits of butter. Make three layers of each, having the top one crumbs with plenty of butter. Cover and bake one-half hour in a moderate oven or until nicely browned.

Pilaf

An Egyptian Dish.

½ cupful of rice   1½ cupfuls of water
1 cupful of boiled tomatoes   2 tablespoonfuls of butter

Boil the rice and water until soft, then add 1 cup of boiled tomatoes and season with salt, pepper and 2 tablespoonfuls of butter; mix thoroughly and serve hot. This is an especially nice dish for lunch.

Cauliflower With Cream Dressing

Pick over a good firm head of cauliflower, soak in cold salt water for at least half an hour before cooking. Cook until tender, then lift into the vegetable dish and pour over the following sauce: Rub 1 tablespoonful of butter and one of flour together. Into this beat the yolk of an egg. Dip up some of the cauliflower liquor into this until quite thin. Then pour all into the saucepan and boil up once and pour over the cauliflower. Some add a little lemon juice.

Mrs. T. M. DAULTON.

Cauliflower au Gratin

Boil a cauliflower until tender. Put in a baking dish and pour over it a rich cream dressing. Grate cheese on top and bake. Serve very hot.

Mrs. H. F. WHITNEY.

Corn Fritters

1 cup of cold sweet corn	1 beaten egg
2 tablespoonfuls of flour	Pepper and salt

Chop the corn, stir in the egg and seasoning and flour, and, if necessary, add a little milk to make consistency of batter. Fry by spoonfuls in butter. When brown, turn and brown on the other side.

BREAKFAST AND LUNCHEON

I like breakfast time better than any other moment in the day. No dust settles on one's mind then, and it presents a clear mirror to the rays of things.—*George Elliott.*

Escalloped Mutton.

Will Serve Four Persons.

1 cup of cooked mutton, chopped	1 tablespoonful of butter
1 cup of tomatoes	1 cup of bread crumbs
	Pepper and salt

Butter a shallow pudding dish, sprinkle it with a part of the crumbs, then the meat, then add the stewed seasoned tomatoes, and put the remainder of the crumbs on top, using the pepper and salt sparingly on the crumbs and tomato. Put a heaping teaspoonful of butter, broken in bits on the top and bake twenty minutes or half an hour.

The mutton should be chopped fine and all stringy and very fatty parts picked out. A nice breakfast or luncheon dish.

MRS. E. A. BOWDEN.

Hegerée for Breakfast

One large cupful of rice, boiled till tender and drained. The remains of cold fish from dinner picked up and freed from bones and skin; 2 hard-boiled eggs cut up; a good lump of butter, salt and pepper. Heat all together very hot.   Heap on a platter and serve very hot.

MRS. BEATRICE GREEN.

Ham Patties

Two cups of cold boiled ham chopped rather fine. 1 cup of bread crumbs moistened with 1 tablespoonful of milk.   Mix together with 1 beaten egg. form into oval shapes and fry in hot frying pan.

MRS. L. H. GRAY.

English Pasty

¼ pound of suet   ¼ pound of lard
1 quart of flour

Make a stiff paste. roll thin. and cut into as many pieces as you wish.   Take one piece and slice potatoes small to cover one-half of it; on this put a layer of chopped meat. or steak cut in small pieces sliced; on this put a layer of onions.   Parsley or turnip may be used in place of onions. Season to suit taste. Close the other half of the paste over these ingredients and pinch into a roll.   Make small hole in the top and pour in a little water; close again with small pieces of paste. Bake for one hour.   Pork or chicken can be used in place of steak.

MRS. S. CARKEEK.

Tomato Toast With Fish

Cut cold buttered toast in squares or rounds. lay a ring of tomatoes on this and some flakes of cold cooked codfish on the top.   Cover with a plentiful supply of parsley sauce. put it in the oven to warm and serve hot. The dish is very economical and serves to use up any stale bread or bits of fish or sauce.   Garnish with parsley.

MRS. V. A. RITON.

GERMEA—The Delightful Breakfast Dish.

Hash

Use equal quantities of chopped meat and fresh grated bread; moisten well with milk, stock or gravy; season well with salt, pepper, and a little tomato, walnut or mushroom catsup. Let cook slowly about fifteen minutes; add a good lump of butter and serve very hot. Half potatoes may be used instead of all bread if desired.

MRS. RICHARD C. STEVENS.

Corned Beef Hash

Equal quantities of cold corned beef, chopped, and cold boiled potatoes, chopped (mashed potatoes may be used but are not so nice); put into a stew pan, and moisten with stock, water or milk; a little left-over gravy is a nice addition. Let *simmer*, season with salt, cayenne and butter, and any sauce or catsup that is liked. Have an omelette pan very hot, put in a bit of butter sufficient to moisten the bottom thoroughly, put the hash in and spread evenly. Draw onto the back of the stove and let brown without stirring. Fold like an omelette, toss onto a *hot* platter and serve with tartare sauce. A few tablespoonfuls of chopped beets make a pleasant change.

MRS. RICHARD C. STEVENS.

Minced Ham

1 slice of bread and 1 pint of milk boiled together; 1 cup of fried or boiled ham chopped very fine, 1 egg. Pour the bread and milk over the ham and egg and beat all together. Bake a light brown.

ANNA BEACH.

Mock Minced Calf's Head

Original.

2 pounds lean veal   1 pound liver

Boil tender, chop fine, mix and make *very* moist with

rich drawn butter sauce; season highly with sage, salt and pepper.   Serve with baked potatoes.

MRS. M. H. YOUNG.

Lancashire Pie

Take cold beef. veal or mutton. chop and season as for hash; have ready hot mashed potatoes. seasoned as if for table.   Put in a shallow baking dish alternate layers of meat and potatoes till the dish is heaping full; smooth over top of potatoes and drop bits of butter over it; bake until a nice brown.

MRS. JOSEPH SHIPPEN.

Chicken Timbales

Chop uncooked lean chicken. freed from skin and bones. very fine; pound with a potato masher and rub through a sieve.   There should be a half pint of meat. Cook 1 cup of cream, ½ cup of grated bread, and a tiny bit of mace for fifteen minutes.   Take out the mace, and beat and mash the mixture till it is a smooth paste; add 3 ounces of butter. salt and pepper to taste. and the chopped meat; beat well. and add the stiffly beaten whites of 2 eggs.   Set away to cool.   When cold butter the timbale moulds and line with the paste.   This must be done very evenly and great care must be taken that there are no thin places.   When this is done fill with creamed chicken made as follows:

    1 cup of cold diced chicken
    3 tablespoonfuls of mushrooms (chopped). or
    2 tablespoonfuls of mushrooms and 1 of hard-
        boiled eggs (chopped)
    1 dessert spoonful of flour
    ¾ cup of cream

Mix the flour with a little of the cream. put the remainder on to cook in the double boiler.   When this boils add the flour and cook for a minute to thicken the flour; add the chicken and the mushrooms, salt and pepper to taste.   Mix thoroughly and cook about five

GERMEA—The Delightful Breakfast Dish.

minutes; take from the fire, grate in a hint of onion, and if you use it, a tablespoonful of sherry, in which case omit a tablespoonful of cream. Fill the lined moulds with this mixture, putting in a little at a time that there may be no air bubbles. Fill almost to the top and cover with paste, being careful to cover every part of the filling and not to heap it, but to have the top perfectly level with the edges of the mould. Put the moulds into a bain marie, or a deep pan, fill nearly to the top of the mould with warm water and bake a half hour. The oven should be about right for custards, so that the mixture will never bubble. Cover the moulds with buttered paper. They may be served on a napkin or on a hot dish with cream mushroom, Suprême or Béchamel sauce. Nice for luncheons, card parties or entrées.

Mrs. RICHARD C. STEVENS.

Sweetbread Timbales

These are prepared almost the same as chicken timbales, substituting sweetbreads for chicken in the filling, or part sweetbreads and part breast of chicken. Use the same paste for lining the moulds. If you wish them very elaborate, after buttering the moulds stick slices of mushrooms around the sides and bottom of the moulds; then line with the paste very carefully, so as not to displace them; hard-boiled eggs chopped, or almonds blanched, browned a little and chopped, may be used in the same manner.

Mrs. RICHARD C. STEVENS.

Scrapple

8 pounds of fresh pork	4 gallons of water
1 quart of cornmeal	Cayenne, black pepper
Mustard, summer savory	Sage, sweet marjoram
Buckwheat or entire wheat	Thyme, salt

Boil the pork in the water till very tender, then remove and chop fine. Return to the kettle and add seasoning to taste. When boiling add the cornmeal and let it *simmer* a few minutes, then *thicken* with the buckwheat or entire wheat. Let it stand on the back of the stove for a half hour, taking care that it does not burn, then pour into dishes and set away to cool. To serve, turn out of dishes, slice thin and fry in hot butter. Serve with baked potatoes.

MRS. TAYLOR.

Savory Pyramids

Will Serve Six Persons.

¾ pounds finely chopped meat (previously cooked meat
    may be used)
3 eggs
6 heaping tablespoonfuls fine bread crumbs
3 ounces butter, melted
1 tablespoonful finely chopped parsley
1 pinch cayenne, and salt
1 teaspoonful grated lemon peel (this may be omitted)

Mix the ingredients, then moisten the whole with gravy, cream or milk; stir together, form into small pyramids, dip in beaten egg, roll in bread crumbs and bake on a greased baking tin in a hot oven for about half an hour.

MRS. C. P. DAM.

Codfish

Pick very fine a small bowl of codfish, put into a saucepan and cover with cold water. Let it come to a boil and drain. Rub together a tablespoonful of sifted flour and one of butter. Return the fish to the pan, and add a half pint of cream. When this comes to the boiling point, stir in the creamed butter and flour and let boil a few minutes. Serve on slices of toast.

MRS. JOS. SHIPPEN.

GERMEA—The Delightful Breakfast Dish.

Codfish Balls

1 pint of fish, picked very   2 well beaten eggs
   fine   1 quart of raw potatoes
1 large tablespoonful of   A little pepper
   butter

Put the potatoes and fish into the kettle with cold
water and cook till potatoes are done. Drain off the
water; mash till very smooth, add butter, eggs and
pepper, and beat well. Drop by spoonfuls into deep
fat, *boiling* hot and cook till brown.

MRS. JOS. S IPPEN.

Mackerel Balls

Soak a mackerel over night. In the morning pour
cold water over it and let it come just to the boiling
point. Shred it carefully, carefully rejecting all bones
and skin. Add an equal quantity of cold mashed potatoes, 2 well beaten eggs, season with pepper and a few
drops of lemon juice. Make into small balls, and fry in
very hot deep fat. Serve very hot on a napkin.

Anchovy Toast

2 eggs   1 tablespoonful of cream
Anchovies   Minced tongue

Beat the eggs, add the milk and put into a saucepan.
Add the anchovies and some minced tongue. Let boil
up, spread on hot toast and serve immediately.

MRS. M. A. KELLOGG.

Prune Toast

Boil prunes until you can remove the pits, sweeten,
and if desired add a little sherry. Pour over toasted
bread and serve with cream.

Cream Toast

1 quart milk	3 tablespoonfuls butter
Whites of 3 eggs	2 even tablespoonfuls flour
Salt to taste	or cornstarch

Dip the toast into boiling water into which 1 table-spoonful of the butter has been dissolved; scald the milk, thicken with the flour, and let it *simmer* until cooked. Put in the rest of the butter, salt, and the beaten whites of eggs. Boil up once, pour over the toast, and set in the oven, closely covered, two or three minutes. Serve at once.

MRS. CHARLES SHEPARD.

Wheat Flakes

For Six People.

1 pint wheat flakes	1½ pints boiling water
	1 teaspoonful salt

Put the wheat into the double boiler, add the boiling water and salt; stir well; let cook for fifteen minutes. Longer cooking will not hurt it.

MRS. RICHARD C. STEVENS.

EGGS

Plain Omelette

The fire should be quite hot. Put a sauté pan or smooth iron spider on the stove, break the eggs into a basin, sprinkle over them pepper and salt, and give them twelve vigorous beats with a spoon. Put butter the size of an egg (this is enough for *five eggs*) in the heated pan, turn it around so that it will moisten all the bottom of the pan. When it is well melted and begins to *boil*, pour in the eggs. Holding the handle of the omelette pan in the left hand, carefully and lightly with a spoon draw up the whitened egg from the bottom, so that all the eggs may be equally cooked to a soft creamy substance. Now still with the left hand shake the pan forward and backward, which will disengage the eggs from the bottom; turn with a knife half of one side over the other, and allowing it to remain a moment to harden at the bottom, gently shaking it all the time, toss it once on to a warm platter held in the right hand. If unsuccessful in the tossing operation, one can lift the omelette to the platter with a pancake turner. It should be creamy and light in the center and firmer on the outside. A variety of omelettes may be made in the same way by adding boiled tongue cut into dice, sliced truffles, cooked and sliced kidneys with the gravy poured around.

MRS. D. C. GARRETT.

Omelette With Tomatoes

Just before folding the omelette place in the center three or four whole tomatoes boiled and seasoned. When the omelette is turned of course the tomatoes will be enveloped. Serve with tomato sauce.

MRS. D. C. GARRETT.

Omelette

Crumb 1 slice of bread and soak in hot milk. Beat the whites of 4 eggs to a high froth. Beat the bread, with all the milk it will *absorb, no more,* add beaten yolks and a little salt. Put one ounce of butter in frying pan. When *hot* pour in omelette; when set put in the oven for five minutes. This will never fall.

S. E. W.

JOHNSON'S Columbian Brand Pine Apples.

Quaking Omelette

Four eggs. ½ cup of milk. a rounded tablespoonful of flour and a teaspoonful of salt. Beat together the yolks of eggs. flour and salt; add them to milk. Then whip whites to a froth and stir into mixture. Put 1 tablespoonful of butter into a hot frying pan; turn mixture in. In about one minute put the pan into the oven; remain six minutes. Have a hot platter ready and a cup of cream sauce well seasoned. Turn the omelette on the platter. but do not try to fold it. Pour sauce around it. Serve at once; will fall if let stand.

Mrs. L. H. GRAY.

Savory Omelette

4 eggs
1 teaspoonful of grated onion
1 tablespoonful of chopped ham

1 tablespoonful of butter
1 teaspoonful of chopped parsley
Salt and pepper

Melt the butter in *hot* omelette pan. Beat the eggs lightly. just enough to mix. stir in the other ingredients. and pour in the hot pan. As soon as the edges begin to set. fold over half. cook one minute longer. turn on a hot dish and serve immediately.

These same ingredients. omitting the eggs. cooked with the butter until very hot. and spread on buttered toast. make a breakfast or luncheon dish which is excellent.

Mrs. BONE.

Oyster Omelette

6 eggs. beaten separately
6 tablespoonfuls of cream

6 tablespoonfuls of flour
Oysters

Chop the oysters fine and sprinkle with flour. Place where they will keep warm. Beat yolks of eggs. flour and cream together. then add well beaten whites of eggs. Fry on a griddle in butter. When omelette is firmly set put in some chopped oyster. and double the omelette over it. Serve at once.

Fricasseed Eggs

Boil 6 eggs hard. Remove the shells and slice them. Cook 1 cup of milk, 1 tablespoonful of flour, 2 tablespoonfuls of butter, 1 teaspoonful of chopped onion, 1 teaspoonful or more of chopped parsley, pepper and salt to taste. Pour this over the eggs and serve hot.

Mrs. M. H. YOUNG.

Egg Patties

For four people take four pieces of bread, three inches in diameter, three also in height. Make in the middle of each a hole two inches deep and one or two inches across; fry these toasts in butter. Put them on a buttered dish, break a fresh egg in every hole, sprinkle over salt and pepper, and about a teaspoonful of butter in each egg. Bake five minutes.

Another way: Butter the gem pan, drop an egg in each, salt; take from oven when the whites set.

Mrs. L. H. GRAY.

Golden Rod Pie

Boil 12 eggs hard, make a white sauce; line a deep dish with toast, put a layer of white sauce, then a layer of white rings of eggs sliced thin, then some of the grated or lightly mashed yolks, repeating until the dish is full, seasoning with salt and pepper to taste; a few bread crumbs on top. Bake about fifteen minutes, but do not let it get brown.

Mrs. MAURICE McMICKEN.

Stuffed Eggs

Boil good fresh eggs twenty minutes; when cold remove shells and carefully cut through the middle, removing the yolks into a dish by themselves. Mash the yolks well and add sufficient soft butter, vinegar, pep-

GERMEA—The Delightful Breakfast Dish.

per and salt to taste quite sharp. Refill the whites evenly. For picnics wrap in tissue paper to keep moist.

Mrs. CORWIN S. SHANK.

Deviled Eggs

Boil half a dozen eggs hard, remove the shell and cut in half lengthwise; take out the yolks and mash them fine; add some finely minced tongue, season well with salt, pepper and mustard. Mould in balls about the size of egg yolks and put one in each half of the whites. Serve on lettuce leaves.

Mrs. M. A. KELLOGG.

Curried Eggs

Boil 3 eggs 20 minutes, then remove shells and cut in slices; fry a bit of onion in a little butter and add 1 teaspoonful of cornstarch mixed with a saltspoonful of curry powder; add slowly ¾ cup of milk, season with salt and butter to taste, and *simmer* until the onion is soft. Add the eggs and serve when they are thoroughly heated.

Mrs. HATFIELD

" Egg Nests on Toast "

Will Serve Six Persons.

6 eggs   ½ teaspoonful salt
1½ tablespoonfuls butter   6 slices toast

Separate the eggs and keep the yolks whole by letting them remain in the half-shell until ready for use; beat the whites with the salt to a stiff froth; toast the bread and dip the edges in hot water, then butter, and heap the whites high on the toast. Make a depression in the center of each mound, add a little butter and the whole yolk of the egg. Place the nests on a pan in a moderate oven and cook for three minutes, or until the whites are a light brown. Serve on a warm dish.

Mrs. MOORE.

Baked Eggs

Butter small patty pans. line them with fine crumbs. drop an egg into each. cover lightly with crumbs which have been peppered. salted and moistened with melted butter. Bake until crumbs are brown.

BREAD

"Here is bread which strengthens men's hearts,
And therefore is called The Staff of Life."

"The bread of life is love; the salt of life is work; the water
of life is faith."

Irish Potato Yeast

6 medium sized potatoes   ¼ cup of sugar
2 tablespoonfuls of salt   1 "magic yeast" cake

Boil potatoes in 3 pints of water. When done mash
in the remaining water, and add sufficient cold water
to make the consistency of thick cream. When lukewarm add sugar, salt and yeast cake. Press out carefully all of the lumps, using the hands in doing so. Set
in a moderately warm place to rise, then remove to a
cold place and the yeast will keep sweet until consumed.
One small teacupful is sufficient for a quart of flour.

Mrs. W. H. H. GREEN.

Mary's Bread and Rolls

Put 3 quarts of flour in a pan and make a hollow in
the middle of it, into which pour a pint of lukewarm
water in which half a yeast cake has been dissolved.
Let this stand over night where it will not become
chilled. In the morning, to ½ pint of lukewarm water
and the same of milk add a tablespoonful each of salt,
sugar and shortening, and stir this into the sponge.

HORSESHOE Soap, *Big Cake, 5c.*

Let it rise for about an hour and a half, then add flour until stiff, kneading well. Let it stand again from one and a half to two hours or until light; then make into loaves.

For rolls—Save out 1 quart of the bread dough and add to it 1 tablespoonful each of sugar, lard and butter. Mix well and let it rise again, then make it into rolls.

This quantity makes three loaves of bread and about three dozen rolls.

MRS. CHARLES E. SHEPARD.

Bread

3 quarts of sifted flour   1 handful of salt
1 handful of sugar   2 small potatoes
1 cake of compressed yeast

Mix flour, sugar and salt. Mash the potatoes in 1 quart of potato water (taken after boiling potatoes for a meal). Dissolve the yeast in a little cold water. Pour warm potato water into the flour mixture; add yeast; mix stiff and knead thoroughly; cover and let rise over night. In the morning knead thoroughly again and form into loaves. Place in well greased pans, and butter the top of loaves also to make the crust moist. Let rise, and bake in an even oven about forty-five minutes. When done remove from pans, rub over the crust with butter, cover carefully with towels or napkins, then wrap well in woolen goods—for instance, an old clean small blanket.

MRS. CORWIN S. SHANK.

Whole Wheat Bread

Two or Three Loaves.

Take of the sponge set the night before for white bread 1 quart, 2 tablespoonfuls of molasses and enough of the whole wheat flour to make a stiff dough. Let it rise, knead down and let rise again. Shape into loaves, and when light bake one hour.

MRS. LEWIS H. SULLIVAN.

WEBB'S Extracts are triple strength. Use them.

Parker House Rolls

1 quart of flour
1 heaped tablespoonful of sugar
¼ ounce of compressed yeast

1 teaspoonful of salt
2 tablespoonfuls of butter
1 pint of boiling milk

Measure flour in bread bowl, make a well in the middle, into which put salt, sugar, butter and hot milk. Let stand *without stirring* until lukewarm, when add the yeast dissolved in ¼ cup of warm water, stir all together to make a soft batter, still leaving a little flour around the edges, cover closely and set to rise. When very light mix in the rest of the flour in the bowl, together with enough more to make a soft dough; knead well and set to rise again. If there is time after the second rising to cut down with a knife a few times the rolls will be much more delicate. About an hour before tea, roll out with as little flour as possible, to one-half inch thickness, cut out with large biscuit cutter, and spread with melted butter, fold over and place close together in pan. Let them rise until twice their original size. Bake in a *hot* oven.

Mrs. GEO. NEWLANDS.

Rolls

¼ cup of yeast
1½ cups of scalded sweet milk
Salt

1 tablespoonful of sugar
2 eggs
1¼ cups of water
Flour

1½ cups of melted butter

Mix with enough flour to make soft bread dough. Let rise three times. Bake in moderately quick oven about thirty minutes.

Mrs. H. R. CLISE.

Boston Brown Bread

"The Bostonians, you know, are most cultured 'tis said.
And it's greatly on account of their Boston brown bread.
The secret of making, I'm privileged to tell.
So one cup of corn meal, dear sister, sift well.

HORSESHOE Soap will not ruin your clothes.

Then add to the same one cup of *graham.
And a cup and a half of white flour,
Of molasses a cup, and an egg beaten up,
And one cup of milk that is sour,
One teaspoon and a half of soda to raise it,
And one of salt, or none would praise it,
Stir it up well, and four hours steam it,
And rest assured, all will deem it
A greater treat than finest cake
That one could eat, or cook could bake."

---

* A cup of rye flour in place of the graham makes a darker and more moist bread. A half cup of seeded raisins is a great addition.

MRS. E. A. BOWDEN.

Brown Bread No. 1

2 cups sour milk
2 cups flour
½ cup corn meal
Pinch of salt

¾ cup New Orleans molasses
1 cup Graham flour
½ cup rye flour
Even teaspoonful soda dissolved in boiling water

Steam four hours.

MRS. MORGAN CARKEEK.

Brown Bread No. 2

2½ cups sour milk
1 heaping teaspoonful soda in tablespoonful of boiling water

½ cup molasses
2 cups corn meal
1 cup whole wheat flour
1 teaspoonful salt

Steam three hours and afterwards brown in the oven.

MRS. LEWIS H. SULLIVAN.

Brown Bread No. 3

2 cups corn meal
1 cup flour
2 cups sweet milk
1 teaspoonful soda

1 cup rye meal
½ cup molasses
1 cup sour milk
1 teaspoonful salt

Steam three hours.

MRS. F. A. BUCK.

WEBB'S Ground Spices are perfectly pure.

Mrs. Manning's Recipe for Brown Bread

¾ cup corn meal
1 cup molasses
2 cups sweet milk

3 cups Graham flour
1 cup sour milk
2 even teaspoonfuls soda

A little salt

Steam three hours.

MRS. MARY M. MILLER.

Graham Bread

1 cup New Orleans molasses
⅔ cup butter and lard

3 cups sour milk
1 teaspoonful soda

Graham flour to make moderately stiff

Bake in bread tin in moderate oven.

MRS. C. H. FAIRBANKS.

Tea Biscuits

To 1 quart of flour and 2 teaspoonfuls of baking powder, salted, add 4 tablespoonfuls of lard; thoroughly mix, then moisten with sweet milk (using knife and not hand or spoon) sufficiently to roll out, but as soft as possible. Handle very little. Roll out about one-third inch in thickness, cut out, then place a small piece of butter on each biscuit, fold over and press down. Bake in quick oven.

MRS. JOSEPH SHIPPEN.

Virginia Beaten Biscuits

1 quart of flour
1 teaspoonful of salt
1 heaping tablespoonful of lard

Sift flour, add salt, and rub in the lard thoroughly with the hand; mix with milk or water, or half and half, into a *very stiff* dough. Lay on breadboard and beat with rolling-pin until it is thoroughly smooth and pliant. When it is beaten sufficiently it will blister. Divide into equal parts the size of a small egg; with the hands mould into biscuits, stick through with a fork three times, and bake in an oven, hot oven.

MRS. W. H. H. GREEN.

Maryland Biscuit

1 quart flour
2 scant tablespoonfuls cottolene

2 scant teaspoonfuls baking powder
Pinch of salt

Sift flour, salt and baking powder together; rub through this the cottolene; add enough sweet milk to make a stiff dough, knead until the dough is perfectly smooth. Roll out, cut, and prick with fork, and bake a light brown.

MRS. T. M. DAULTON.

Ragmuffins

Make a dough as for biscuit, roll one-half inch thick; spread with butter, cinnamon and sugar, roll up and cut off from the end the size of biscuit. *Bake quickly*.

MRS. HATFIELD.

Sally Lunn

1½ pounds flour
1 pint new milk
3 eggs

2 ounces butter
1 teaspoonful salt
3 tablespoonfuls yeast
1 dessert spoonful sugar

Warm the milk and butter together over water until the latter is melted; beat eggs and pour over the lukewarm milk; stir in the flour and add salt and yeast. After mixing well put the whole into a well-greased tin pan and set to rise all night. Bake an almond brown in a quick oven. A delicious southern breakfast dish.

MRS. W. H. H. GREEN.

Jenny Lind Bread

1 quart flour
¼ cup sugar
1 tablespoonful butter
Salt

2 cups milk
2 eggs
1 teaspoonful soda
2 teaspoonfuls cream tartar

Sift the salt, soda, cream tartar and sugar with the

WEBB'S Extracts are triple strength. Use them.

flour twice; add the eggs, well beaten, and the milk, also the butter which has been melted. Bake in a buttered dripping pan until golden brown; cut in squares and serve hot.

MRS. S. W. R. DALLY.

Blueberry Cake

1 cup sugar
2 large spoonfuls melted butter
3 cups of flour

2 eggs
1 cup sweet milk
2 teaspoonfuls baking powder
2 cups blueberries

Cut this in squares, serve hot with butter. A fine breakfast cake.

MRS. M. H. YOUNG.

Blueberry Muffins

1 cup blueberries
2 eggs
1 cup milk
1 cup sugar

½ cup butter
3 cups flour
2 teaspoonfuls baking powder

Some prefer less sugar.

Martha Washington Corn Bread

Authentic

1 pint Indian meal
1 cup boiled rice
1 tablespoonful butter

1 gill wheat flour
1 egg
½ teaspoonful salt

1½ pints of milk, or more, until it is a thin batter

Bake in tin pan greased: serve *hot.*

Mount Vernon, Va.

Southern Corn Bread

1 cup corn meal (white)
2 eggs
1 cup milk

1 cup cold cooked rice or hominy
1 even tablespoonful butter

Sift a teaspoonful of salt into the meal, then pour boiling water over it, scalding it thoroughly. Soften the rice or hominy with boiling water and then beat into

HORSESHOE Soap will not ruin your clothes.

the meal; add the butter, then half of the milk, next the
eggs beaten light and the remainder of the milk. The
mixture should be as thin as for batter cakes. Pour into
a well buttered pan and place at once in the oven. Bake
for half an hour.

MRS W. A. PETERS.

Spoon Corn Bread

1 cup white corn meal	1 quart milk
3 eggs well beaten	2 tablespoonfuls of flour,
3 tablespoonfuls sugar	rounded
1 teaspoonful salt	

Heat the milk and gradually stir in the corn meal;
boil about ten minutes. Take from the fire and let cool
a little before stirring in the rest of the ingredients.
Bake thirty-five minutes in a well buttered baking dish.

MRS. HELEN M. HUNT.

Johnny Cake

1 cup sour milk	1 cup white flour
1 cup sour cream	2 cups sugar
2 cups corn meal	2 eggs
1 teaspoonful soda	

If you have no sour cream use 2 cups sour milk and
2 tablespoonfuls melted butter, and a little less meal
and flour.

MRS. GEORGE OSGOOD, Tacoma.

Lenten Graham Gems

1 egg	2 cups of cold water
2 tablespoonfuls of melted	2 tablespoonfuls of sugar
butter	1 tablespoonful of baking
1 cup of white flour	powder (scant)

Graham flour enough to make batter. Beat the egg
thoroughly, add water, sugar, white flour with baking
powder mixed in it, the melted butter and graham

HORSESHOE Soap for economy and quality.

enough to make like ordinary cake. Drop in buttered gem pans and bake in brisk oven. Will make 12 gems.

NELLIE BEACH.

Graham Gems

1 egg	1 teaspoonful of baking
2 teaspoonfuls of sugar	powder
1 cup of milk	1 cup of graham flour
Pinch of salt	

Stir thoroughly. Bake in hot oven fifteen minutes. This amount makes eight gems.

MRS. M. A. KELLOGG.

Graham Muffins

1 cup of graham flour	1 cup of wheat flour
1 egg, beaten very light	3 tablespoonfuls of melted
2 small teaspoonfuls of	butter
baking powder	$\frac{3}{4}$ cup of milk
A pinch of salt	

Stir the milk in flour and then the egg and butter. Beat hard before putting in pans.

MRS. W. F. BROOKES (by Mrs. H. C. Henry).

Muffins

2 cups of sour milk	1 egg
3 tablespoonfuls of melted	2 tablespoonfuls of sugar
butter	1 teaspoonful of soda

Flour enough to make as stiff as soft cake.

MRS. R. B. LANGDON (by Mrs. H. C. Henry).

World's Fair Muffins

Will Make About Fifteen.

2 heaping tablespoonfuls	Scant $\frac{1}{2}$ cup of butter
of sugar	1 cup of milk
1½ cups of flour	3 teaspoonfuls of baking
2 eggs	powder

Cream the sugar and butter, add the beaten yolks,

WEBB'S Extracts are triple strength. Use them.

and then the milk and flour (sifted with the baking powder). Beat well and stir in the beaten whites last of all. Bake in a moderate oven.

MRS. C. P. DAM.

Raised Muffins

2 cups of potato water   ¾ cup of yeast
2 tablespoonfuls of lard   Flour to make stiff batter
2 eggs   ¼ cup of sugar

Stir the lard into the potato water while hot. When cool add the eggs, sugar, yeast and flour. When light bake in gem pans, or muffin rings.

MRS. H. R. CLISE.

English Muffins

Take a quart of flour (if California flour is used a little more will be needed); add a tablespoonful of salt and make a dough with 1 pint of lukewarm water, in which has been dissolved ½ cake of compressed yeast, or ¼ cup of liquid yeast, in which case omit ½ cup of the water. Mix and beat very thoroughly for fifteen or twenty minutes. Let rise till *very* light, then with well floured hands make into balls about as great in diameter as ordinary muffin rings. Put these onto the bread board and roll down to about one-half inch in thickness. Have the cake griddle greased slightly (the muffins should be pretty well floured), place the muffins on this and put on the back of the range. In a half hour they should be very light and spongy. Draw the griddle forward and bake; turning over whenever the tops begin to round up, so as to keep the cakes flat. It will take fifteen or twenty minutes to bake. The muffins should be about two inches thick and as large as a saucer. Tear apart, toast and serve very hot with butter or syrup. They may be kept a week, toasting whenever wanted for use.

MRS. RICHARD C. STEVENS.

Breakfast Gems

Will Make One Dozen.

¾ cup of milk
Butter size of an egg
1 teaspoonful baking pow-
der

1 tablespoonful sugar
1 cup flour
2 eggs
Pinch of salt

Drop into heated and well greased pans and bake about fifteen minutes in quick oven. Serve *hot.*

MRS. LATIMER.

Chocolate Gems

2 tablespoonfuls butter, adding carefully 1 cup sugar; stir in ½ cup water, 1½ cups flour; beat thoroughly; add 2 teaspoonfuls of cocoa. 1 teaspoonful vanilla and 2 eggs beaten to a stiff froth. Before adding eggs add 1 teaspoonful baking powder. Pour this into greased gem pans and bake in moderate oven twenty minutes. By permission of

MRS. S. T. RORER and THE HOUSEHOLD NEWS CO.

Pop-Overs

2 eggs
1 cup flour

1 cup milk
½ teaspoonful salt

Beat eggs well, stir in a little of the milk, then a little of the flour, alternating until all is used; add the salt. Beat thoroughly just before baking. Bake in a quick oven about twenty minutes. The secret of good popovers is the vigorous beating.

MRS. WINFIELD R. SMITH.

Cream Waffles

Take 1 pint of thick cream, stir in 1 teaspoonful of soda and flour, sufficient to make a thin batter; beat 2 eggs and stir in. Bake, and butter before sending to table.

MRS. HATFIELD.

WEBB'S Extracts are triple strength. Use them.

Waffles

1 pint flour
½ teaspoonful salt
3 eggs
1¼ cups milk

1 teaspoonful baking powder
1 teaspoonful of butter, melted

Mix in order given. Add the beaten yolks of eggs to milk. then the melted butter. and whites of eggs last.

H. VAUGHAN HOWELL.

Rice Cakes

1 cup cold boiled rice
1 teaspoonful salt
3 eggs

1 pint hot milk
1 teaspoonful baking powder

Stir rice and milk together till smooth, then add salt and eggs. well beaten; stir slowly into this enough flour to make a thin batter. and fry as you would griddle cakes.

H. VAUGHAN HOWELL.

Mary's Pancakes

1 pint sour milk
1 saltspoonful salt

1 pint (*scant*) flour
½ teaspoonful soda

Mix the milk. flour and salt the night before using. In the morning beat well. and just before cooking. add the soda dissolved in a little boiling water. Beat well again. An egg may be added if desired.

MRS. WINFIELD R. SMITH.

Profile House Griddle Cakes

6 eggs. yolks and whites beaten separately
1 quart sour milk
2 teaspoonfuls soda
Piece of butter size of an egg
Flour to make a thin batter like rich cream.

WEBB'S Ground Spices are perfectly pure.

Buckwheat Cakes

1 pint of buckwheat
2 tablespoonfuls of corn meal
2 tablespoonfuls of wheat flour
2 tablespoonfuls of fresh yeast

Mix in a stiff batter about 9 o'clock at night; set in a warm place to rise; mix with lukewarm water. Next morning add ½ teaspoonful of soda in a cup of milk; stir into the batter thinning it sufficiently to use; salt to taste. This will serve four persons.

MRS. F. A. BUCK.

Mr. and Mrs. S. Merrill Allerton

invite you to be present

at the marriage of their daughter

Hattie Lois

to

Mr. Walter Allison Williams

Tuesday evening, June sixth

eighteen hundred and ninety-six

eight o'clock

at Saint Mark's Church

Fifth Avenue

Seattle

Mrs. A. B. Curtiss

Wednesdays

Miss Sadie Friend

HOUSEHOLD ECONOMY

"For nothing lovelier can be found in woman than to study household good."

No one can entirely solve for someone else, if they ever do for themselves, the difficult problem of household economy, but when it has passed into a proverb, that "A French family can live on what an American family throws away." it is time for us to give the subject more attention. The economical management of the household is not accomplished without "eternal vigilance" on the part of the mistress, and the woman who delegates to a servant duties that belong to the mistress only, and who does not *personally* supervise every department of her household, can never hope to be a good manager.

Hoping that they may be found useful. we give the following suggestions. for the care of food and a few ways of utilizing the "left-overs":

Muffins left from breakfast may be split into halves and toasted for lunch.

Cold mashed potatoes may be saved for croquettes or potato puff. One cupful makes six croquettes.

Small pieces of plain or puff paste trimmed from pies or patties may be used for cheese sticks.

Fat from stock, suet from chops and steaks should be saved. tried out, clarified and strained into the drip-

USE Knox's Sparkling Gelatin.
C. C.—10   (145)

ping pail for use in frying. It is preferable to lard.

Save every scrap of bread for crumbs to use for breading croquettes, chops, scollop dishes, etc.

It is well to have two kinds of crumbs, using the white ones for the outside of fried articles, as they give a better color. To prepare the crumbs dry them slowly on the shelf of the range. When dry, roll, sift and place them in glass preserve jars until wanted.

When an egg is opened for the white alone, drop the yolk carefully into a cup, cover the cup with a wet cloth, and keep it in the ice box until wanted. When whites are left over make a small angel cake, or cover any dessert with meringue.

Oatmeal, hominy, cracked wheat and other cereals which are left over can be added next day to the fresh supply, for they are improved by long boiling.

Any of the cereals make good pancakes, or a small amount added to the ordinary pancake batter improves it. It can also be moulded and used for fried mush.

Sour milk can be used for cottage cheese, and makes good biscuits or pancakes.

When fruits show signs of deterioration stew them at once instead of letting them decay.

Grate cheese which becomes dry, and use for pies or soup; or it can be served with crackers, or bottled and kept for future use.

Lard is hot when a blue smoke rises from it.

To freshen stale crackers put them into a hot oven for a few minutes.

To prevent flour from lumping, add a little salt before mixing with milk or water.

Chop the tough ends of steak very fine, season and form them into balls or cakes.

Everything good too small to utilize in other ways should be put into the soup kettle—the French woman's stronghold—and should be boiled up, in winter, twice a week, and in summer every day. A spoonful of gravy or rice, any kind of vegetables, the bones from roasts,

TRY Sioux Corn Starch for puddings.

steaks, chops or poultry, the tough end of a steak, the trimmings from roasts, steaks and chops, which will be sent with the meat if asked for, all should go into that invaluable soup kettle, and will give a stock far richer in flavor and more nutritious than if prepared in the usual manner. It will, of course, not do for clear soups, but for thick soups, or tomato, bean or vegetable soups, sauces, minces, scollops, meat pies and the like, it is most excellent.

The coarse stalks and roots of celery make a good vegetable when cut in pieces and boiled, or they make a good cream of celery soup.

The leaves are valuable in the soup kettle for flavor; also are useful for garnishing.

To Clean Currants

Add one cup of flour to every quart of currants and rub them well between the hands. This will free them from stems and stones. Then turn them into a colander and shake until the stems have passed through. Now put them in a pan of cold water, thoroughly drain and wash a number of times. Spread on boards or flat dishes and stand in a warm place to dry.

To Make a Pastry Bag

Fold a piece of very strong muslin (one foot square) from two opposite corners; fell the edges tightly together, thus forming a triangular bag. Cut off the point to make an opening large enough to insert a tin pastry tube. It is better to have two or three pastry bags, each fitting their respective tubes.

To Use the Pastry Bag

Put the tin tubes into the bag and fit it into the opening. Fill the bag with the mixture, close the top of the bag, give it a twist and hold it tightly with the

GERMEA—The Delightful Breakfast Dish.

right hand.   Put the point of the tube close to the place where the mixture is to be spread; press with the left hand, and guide the mixture into any shape desired, eclaires, lady fingers, etc.

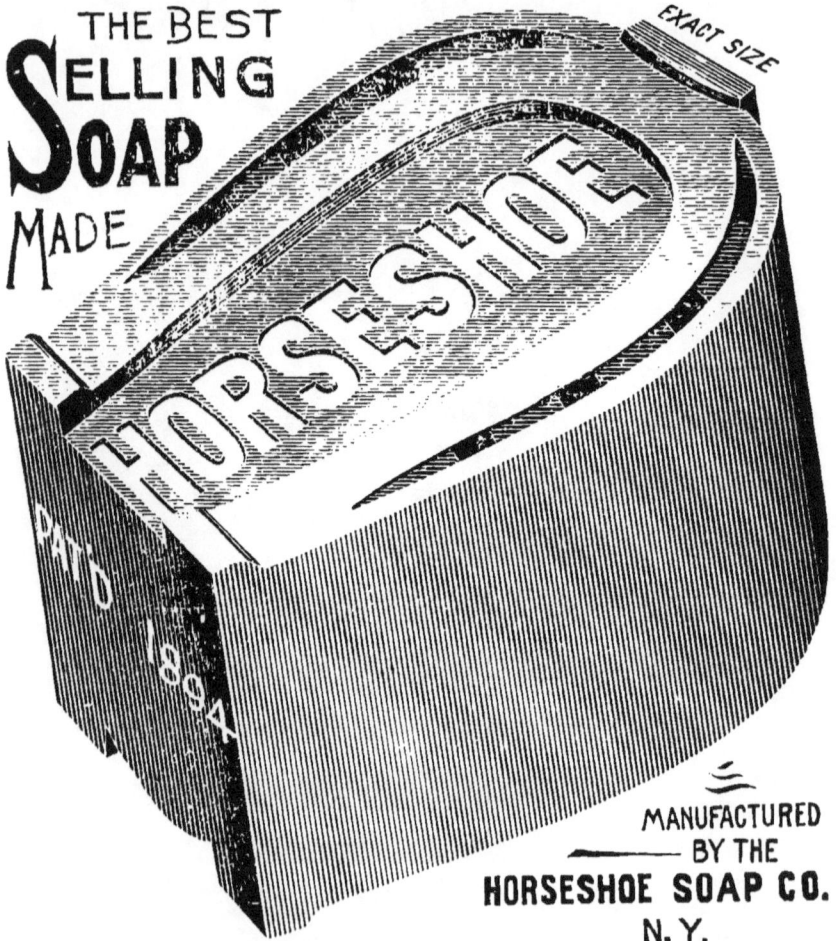

PASTRY

Puff Paste

1 pound of flour   1 pound of butter
1 teaspoonful of salt   1 yolk of egg
1 cup of cold water

Take flour and salt and ½ pound of butter; rub together till real fine, then put the yolk of egg in a cup, beat it well and fill the cup with cold water, add to the flour and butter, and mix well. Take out on moulding board and work smooth. Roll out quite thin; take the other half of butter, cut in very thin slices, spread over the dough, dust with flour, then fold over from four sides, roll out again and fold; and repeat twice more. Cut in any shape, either strips or tarts, brush with egg, and bake in quick oven.

L. M. THEDINGA.

French Chopped Paste

1 pint of flour   1 cup of butter
1 teaspoonful of salt   ½ cup of water (almost)
1 teaspoonful of sugar   Yolk of 1 egg
Juice of 1 lemon (small)

Put the flour, salt, sugar and butter into a chopping

bowl and chop until the butter is in bits the size of small peas. Put the egg into a cup, beat well, add lemon and water enough to make a small half cup. Continue chopping, adding the water gradually, until mixed. No more water than is absolutely necessary should be used, the quantity depending somewhat upon the flour. Turn out onto the board, roll into a thick sheet, roll up and put on the ice if possible, or stand in a cool place, for an hour or so; cut from the end and roll out as desired. This must either be handled *as little* as possible, or rolled and folded like puff paste. No *middle* course is possible. Materials, utensils and room should be cold.

MRS. RICHARD C. STEVENS.

Mince Meat No. 1

3 pounds meat after it is boiled
4 pounds raisins
3 pounds currants
2 pounds sugar
1 quart cider
1 teaspoonful allspice
1 teaspoonful cloves
Rind of 3 lemons

2 pounds suet, chopped fine
6 pounds apples, chopped fine
1 pound citron
1 quart brandy
1 teaspoonful mace
1 teaspoonful cinnamon
2 nutmegs grated
$\frac{1}{4}$ teacupful salt

Sweeten with molasses

MRS. H C. HENRY.

English Mince Meat No. 2

1 large beef tongue, or 2 small ones, cooked and chopped
4 pounds of apples, chopped
1½ pounds of sugar
1 pound of almonds, blanched and chopped
1 teaspoonful of cloves
2 teaspoonfuls of allspice
3 or more large tumblers of sherry or Madeira

2 pounds of raisins, stoned
3 pounds of currants, washed and dried
1 pound of suet, chopped fine
½ pound of candied citron
1 teaspoonful of cinnamon
1 teaspoonful of mace
3 or more large tumblers of brandy

Mix spices well with the meat and suet, then add

JOHNSON'S Columbian Brand Pine Apples.

sugar, apples, fruit, etc., and brandy last. Mix all well
together and put away in jars for a week before using.
It should be quite wet with brandy and wine.

Mrs. A. M. BROOKS.

Mince Meat No. 3

2 pounds of beef from the neck chopped fine when *cold*
1 pound of beef suet shredded and chopped fine
7 pounds of apples, tart ones, pared, cored and chopped
2 pounds of raisins, seeded and broken in two
2 pounds of Sultana raisins well washed
1½ pounds of currants carefully washed and picked over
¾ pound of citron cut in small pieces
½ pound of lemon and orange peel cut fine
2 tablespoonfuls of cinnamon
2 tablespoonfuls of mace
1 tablespoonful of cloves
1 tablespoonful of allspice
1 tablespoonful of salt
1 tablespoonful of nutmeg
2½ pounds of brown sugar
1 pint of New Orleans molasses
1 quart of brown sherry
1 quart of brandy

Cook all but the liquors about an hour; add them the
last thing before removing from the fire. Put in deep
jar, tying over double covers.

Mrs. DOUGLAS YOUNG.

English Mince Meat No. 4

10 apples
2 cups of raisins
1 cup of mixed peel
1½ teaspoonfuls of allspice
½ teaspoonful of nutmeg
8 tablespoonfuls of brandy
2 cups of currants
1½ cups of sugar
1½ cups of chopped suet
1½ teaspoonfuls of ground cloves
½ cup of chopped almonds
Juice of 2 lemons

Chop suet alone first; then chop all together very
fine; add spices and brandy and lemon juice last. It is
much nicer if kept a few weeks before using. Mix well.

Mrs. M. P. ZINDORF.

USE Knox's Sparkling Gelatin.

Lemon Pie No. 1

6 eggs   2 lemons
6 tablespoonfuls of sugar

Make a nice pie crust and bake in a spring-form pie plate, if you have one: if not, in a deep pie plate. While baking beat the yolks of 6 eggs with 6 tablespoonfuls of sugar; gradually add the juice of 2 lemons and grated rind of one; beat all up together. Put in a double boiler and cook until begins to thicken. Remove from the fire, add the beaten whites of 6 eggs, stir them in lightly, then pour into your shell. Put into the oven until a light brown.

MRS. F. A. BUCK.

Lemon Pie No. 2

4 eggs   Grated rind and juice of 1
2 tablespoonfuls of water   lemon
          1 cup of sugar

Bake with two crusts.

MRS. M. A. KELLOGG.

Lemon Pie No. 3

1 large lemon   1 cup of milk
½ cup of sugar   2 eggs
1 tablespoonful of corn   1 teaspoonful of butter
  starch   Pastry for under crust

Bake under crust. Boil the milk; stir in corn starch and the well beaten yolks of the eggs; add the juice and grated rind of the lemon. Turn the mixture into the shell, and cover with the well beaten whites of the eggs, to which has been added a teaspoonful of sugar. Brown in the oven.

MRS. THOMAS W. PROSCH.

Whipped Cream Pie

Make a rich cream pie, and let get very cold. At serving time cover thickly with whipped cream, flavored. If you like you can dust the top lightly with sifted macaroon crumbs and it will look like a meringue browned in the oven.

Mrs. FRANK MANLEY, Tacoma, Wash.

English Apple Pie

Very Nice.

Line the *side* of a baking dish with pastry, leaving the *bottom of it bare.* Invert a small cup in the center of the dish and place around it the apple cut in little squares. Season with sugar to taste, a little allspice and a tablespoonful of sherry. Add a cup of cold water, and put on the top crust. Bake until a straw proves the apple quite tender. In serving, raise a piece of the top crust and slip a knife under the cup. All the juice will be under the cup.

Mary's Apple Custard Pie

1 cup of stewed apples
½ cup of sugar
1 egg, yolk and white separated
Flavoring (lemon is good)

Stew the apples without sugar. Press them through a sieve, add beaten yolk and beat the mixture thoroughly; then add sugar and flavoring. Bake crust first, then fill with the mixture. Put whites on the top.

Mrs. WINFIELD R. SMITH.

Pumpkin Pie

2 cups of strained pump-
kin
1 cup of sugar
½ nutmeg
3 eggs
3 cups of milk
1 teaspoonful of cinnamon
Pinch of salt

Steam the pumpkin after cutting it in pieces, then strain and while warm add the milk, sugar, eggs and spices in the order named, having the eggs well beaten. Put in pan with under crust only. This quantity will make two good deep pies in nine-inch pans.

Mrs. BOWDEN.

JOHNSON'S Columbian Brand Pine Apples.

Cocoanut Pie

½ cup of grated cocoanut   1 pint of sweet milk
Yolks of 3 eggs   Whites of 2 eggs
Butter size of hickory nut   1 tablespoonful of sugar
         ½ saltspoonful of salt

Beat yolks, add sugar, cocoanut and salt, then stir in the milk, add butter and bake as custard pie. Put whites on the top.

                        MRS. WINFIELD R. SMITH.

Pineapple Pie

1 can of grated pineapple or 2 tablespoonfuls of butter
   1 pineapple grated   1 cup of sweet cream
½ cup of sugar   Yolks of 3 eggs

Put in pan lined with rich crust and bake. Beat whites with ½ cup of sugar for meringue.

                        MRS. CHARLOTTE B. CHURCH.

Delicious Filling for Pie

1 cup of raisins, stoned   1 cup of boiling water
   and chopped   1 cup of sugar
3 teaspoonfuls of corn   Juice of 1 lemon
   starch

Washington Pie

Will Make Two Pies.

Cake.

1 large cup of sugar   1 large cup of flour
3 tablespoonfuls of milk   3 eggs.
2 teaspoonfuls of baking   Vanilla flavoring
   powder

Filling.

1 pint of milk   ½ cup of sugar
1 egg   1 tablespoonful of corn
½ pound of blanched al-   starch
   monds   Vanilla flavoring
         A dust of salt

Mix sugar and yolks of eggs together, add milk,

USE Knox's Sparkling Gelatin.

sifted flour, whites of eggs beaten stiff, vanilla, last of all baking powder. Bake in two large jelly tins in moderate oven.

Filling.

Mix milk, sugar and corn starch together; add egg well beaten. Cook in double cooker to the consistency of custard. When cool add vanilla and blanched almonds chopped fine.

Split open each cake with sharp heated knife and fill with the custard. Make a méringue flavored with almond. Spread over smoothly, then dot the top with small mounds of méringue with an almond in each mound. Brown in oven.

MRS. A. F. McEWAN.

Almond Tarts

Yolks of 3 eggs   ¼ pound of sugar
½ pound of almonds (blanched)

Beat to a cream the eggs and sugar, adding the almonds, which have been blanched and pounded to a paste. Bake in tart tins, which have been lined with puff paste, ten minutes.

MRS. C. P. DAM.

Chess Cakes

Will Make One Dozen.

1 cup of sugar
¼ cup of butter
1½ cups of raisins, seeded, chopped fine
1 cup of English walnuts, chopped fine
1 whole and yolk of 2 eggs

Beat butter and sugar to a cream, then add the eggs, raisins and nuts. Mix all thoroughly together. Bake in patty tins in pie crust.

MRS. JOHN ROCKWELL McVAY.

USE Knox's Sparkling Gelatin.

DESSERTS

"If you could make a pudding wi' thinking o' the batter, it 'ud be easy getting dinner."—*George Eliot.*

English Plum Pudding No. 1

2 pounds of raisins
¼ pound of citron
¼ pound of orange peel
1½ pounds of sugar
3 lemons
1 pound of almonds
1 teaspoonful of cloves
1 teaspoonful of mace

1 pound of currants
¼ pound of lemon peel
1½ pounds of suet
10 eggs
½ pint of brandy
1 pound of bread crumbs
1 teaspoonful of cinnamon
1 nutmeg

¼ pound of flour

This pudding must be boiled ten hours.

MRS. NUTT.

English Plum Pudding No. 2

1 pound of suet
1 pound of currants
¾ pound of bread crumbs
8 eggs
2 ounces candied peel
Cloves and ginger
1 teaspoonful of soda, dissolved in a wineglass of brandy

1 pound of stoned raisins
¾ pound of flour
½ pound of dark sugar
½ pint of milk or water
½ nutmeg
1 teaspoonful of salt

Boil five hours or longer. Serve with brandy sauce.

ADA E. MALTBY.

JOHNSON'S Columbian Brand Pine Apples.

(159)

Plum Pudding No. 3

1 egg	1 cup of black molasses
1 cup of suet	1 cup of sweet milk
2 cups of raisins, stoned	1 cup of currants
1 teaspoonful of cloves	2 teaspoonfuls of cinnamon
3 even cups of flour	1 teaspoonful of soda

Steam four hours.

MRS. E. P. FERRY.

Plum Pudding, With Ice Cream, No. 4

Make the plum pudding as usual and turn out onto a flat dish. Pour over it a wineglass of brandy and send to the table burning. Have a brick of ice cream frozen very hard, and on each slice of the hot pudding lay a slice of the cream. Delicious.

MRS. FRANK MITCHELL.

Lowell Pudding

Will Serve Eight Persons.

4 cups of flour	1½ cups of suet, minced fine
1 cup of brown sugar	
1½ cups of sweet milk	2 heaping cups of fruits (raisins, currants, figs and citron minced)
1 teaspoonful of salt	
1 teaspoonful of soda	
½ teaspoonful each of mace and nutmeg	¼ teaspoonful each of cinnamon and cloves
Allspice and ginger	

Mix all well together before adding milk and spice. Boil in well buttered mould three hours.

MRS. WEBSTER BROWN.

Christmas Pudding

Very Nice.

1 pint and 3 gills of flour	½ pint of sweet milk
½ pint of suet, chopped	½ pint of raisins
½ pint of molasses	¾ teaspoonful of soda

Mix well together, adding the soda dissolved in a

GERMEA—The Delightful Breakfast Dish.

little of the milk before putting in all the flour. Steam in a mould three hours. Serve with wine sauce. This pudding may be made richer by increasing the quantity of raisins and adding a little chopped citron.

Mrs. CALVIN VILAS.

Black Pudding

1 pint of flour	1 cup of warm water
2 cups of molasses or syrup	1 teaspoonful of soda
1 tablespoonful of allspice	1 tablespoonful of cinna-
1 saltspoonful of cloves	mon
2 cups of currants	1 cup of raisins, slightly
A small piece of citron,	chopped
chopped	

Steam four hours.

Sauce.

1 cup of butter }
2 cups of sugar } rubbed to a cream
2 eggs well beaten

Steam for half an hour, stirring often. Flavor with brandy, sherry or vanilla. Will serve twelve persons.

Mrs. M. F. BACKUS.

Suet Pudding No. 1

Will Serve Eight Persons.

1 cup of suet	1 cup of molasses
1 cup of milk	2 cups of flour
1 cup of raisins	1 cup of bread crumbs
1 teaspoonful of soda in the molasses	1 teaspoonful each of cinnamon, cloves and allspice
1 teaspoonful of salt	

Steam three hours: chop suet fine; add molasses, milk, bread crumbs, salt and spices; add flour and the raisins; mix well. Put into greased mould and steam. Serve with creamy sauce.

Mrs. LEWIS H. SULLIVAN.

TRY Sioux Corn Starch for puddings.
C. C.—11

Suet Pudding No. 2

3 cups of flour	1 cup of molasses
1 cup of milk	1 cup of chopped suet
1 teaspoonful of salt	1 teaspoonful of soda
	1 cup of raisins

Place the sifted flour in a bowl and add the other ingredients, stirring well; add the soda wet in a little of the milk; then the fruit last. Pour all into a covered buttered pudding mould and boil two and one-half hours. Serve with plum pudding sauce. Candied orange and lemon peel, currants and citron may be mixed with the raisins.

Mrs. S. W. R. DALLY.

Steamed Graham Pudding

Will Serve Twelve Persons.

2 cups of Graham flour	1 cup of milk
1 cup of molasses	1 cup of raisins
1 egg	1 teaspoonful of soda
½ teaspoonful of cloves	½ teaspoonful of cinnamon
A little nutmeg	A pinch of salt

Put the flour in a basin, then add the other ingredients. Mix thoroughly. Flour the raisins. Steam three hours.

Sauce.

1 cup of sugar	½ cup of butter
	1 glass of wine

Stir well together and boil fifteen minutes in a farina kettle.

Mrs. M. F. BACKUS.

Graham Pudding

½ cup of molasses	3 eggs
½ cup of melted butter	½ cup of sweet milk
½ teaspoonful of cinnamon	½ teaspoonful of allspice
½ teaspoonful of nutmeg	2 cups of graham flour
1 teaspoonful of soda in molasses	A little salt

TRY Sioux Corn Starch for puddings.

Steam two hours and a half. Serve with a liquid sauce.

GERTRUDE B. CARPENTER, Cleveland, Ohio.

Bachelor's Pudding

4 ounces grated bread	4 ounces currants
4 ounces apples	2 ounces sugar
3 eggs	½ teaspoonful nutmeg
½ teaspoonful lemon essence	

Pare, core and mince the apples very finely, sufficient when minced to make four ounces; add to these the currants, the grated bread and sugar; whisk the eggs, beat these up with the remaining ingredients, and when all is well mixed, put in a buttered dish, tie down with a cloth and boil for three hours.

Mrs. O. T. O. NUTT.

Baked Indian Pudding

3 pints milk	3 gills molasses
Butter size of an egg	10 heaping tablespoonfuls meal

Scald the meal with the milk, then stir in the butter and molasses. Bake four to five hours.

Mrs. S. W. CLARK.

Kentucky Roll

1 pint flour	Butter size of a duck egg
1 teaspoonful salt	1 teaspoonful baking powder

Milk enough to make a dough which can be rolled like biscuit; cover the sheet of dough with berries or any small fruit, and roll like jelly cake. Place in a pan, and pour over 1 cup of water and 1 cup of sugar. Bake in a moderate oven half an hour and serve with whipped cream.

Mrs. BONE.

GERMEA—The Delightful Breakfast Dish.

Roly Poly Pudding

1 cup jam	1 cup suet
2 cups flour	1 teaspoonful baking powder
Salt	

Chop suet fine, mix with flour and baking powder; add enough water to make stiff paste, roll very thin. Spread on the jam, roll paste, and tie in floured cloth, previously wrung out of very hot water. Tie ends securely, leaving room to swell; put in kettle of boiling water and boil fast for two hours. The same paste can be used with currants or raisins and served with sweet sauce, but do not roll the paste.

MRS. BONE.

Peach Cobbler

Fill a shallow pudding dish with ripe peeled peaches, leaving in the pits to increase the flavor; half fill the dish with cold water, sweeten to taste and cover with a rich pie crust. Bake in a moderate oven and serve either hot or cold, with cream.

MRS. O. T. O. NUTT.

Blackberry Pudding

1 egg, well beaten	½ cup milk
1 cup flour	1 heaping teaspoonful baking powder
1 small tablespoonful sugar	
Stewed blackberries	

Fill a dish half full of hot stewed blackberries, sweetened; make a batter of the preceding ingredients and drop by spoonfuls on top of the berries. Steam for twenty minutes, putting a cloth under the lid of the steamer. Serve with cream.

MRS. FRANK MITCHELL.

Fig Pudding No. 1

1 cup of molasses	1 pint of figs chopped
1 cup of suet chopped fine	½ nutmeg
1 cup of milk	1 teaspoonful of cinnamon
3¼ cups of flour	1 teaspoonful of soda
	2 eggs

Steam four hours.

MRS. GREGORY.

Fig Pudding No. 2

½ pound of figs	¼ pound of bread crumbs
1 teacup of milk	2½ ounces of sugar
3 ounces of butter	2 eggs

Chop the figs fine. Beat the butter, sugar and eggs together ; add milk. crumbs and figs. Steam three hours.

MRS. HATFIELD.

To Cook Italian Prunes

There is as much in the preparation of the prunes *before* cooking as in the quality of the prunes. Whenever this is borne in mind, a nice dish of first class prunes is pleasing to the eye and delicious to the taste. Soak the prunes for twelve hours in water enough to cover them. Put them in this same water over a slow fire to cook. adding a little sugar if not sweet enough for your taste. Let them *simmer* slowly until well cooked. This slow cooking will expand them more than the water has done. and does not destroy the flavor.

Another way is equally as good. Wash your prunes nicely, as in the first process. put in a porcelain-lined stew pan or kettle. pour over them enough cold water to cover them. Set them on the back of the cooking range. which is supposed to have fire in it, and let them stay there, heating through slowly. until nearly ready

JOHNSON'S Columbian Brand Pine Apples.

to serve.   At the last moment bring them forward to
the hot portion of the range and let them boil up
quickly.   Some prefer this method to the first.   Slow
heat and the soaking process, to make the fruit expand,
brings out all the flavor, and is the secret of disfavor
or popularity.

PACIFIC TREE AND VINE.

Prune Whip

½ cup of best prunes, after they are stewed, drained and
    put through a sieve
Whites of 5 eggs
3 tablespoonfuls of sugar

Beat the eggs very light, add the sugar and prunes
and beat again.   Bake half an hour in a moderately
quick oven.   Serve hot with whipped cream.

MRS. J. D. LOWMAN.

Prune Float

Boil prunes until they are so tender they will fall to
pieces.   Sweeten them and squeeze through a fine sieve.
Whip cream until stiff, make a round mound of whipped
cream about the size of a tart, put a tablespoonful of the
prune substance in the center and serve cold.

MRS. NATHANIEL WALDO EMERSON, Boston.

Prune Jelly

Stew prunes until perfectly tender, and squeeze out
the juice; add gelatine (dissolved) in the proportion of
half a box to 3 cups of juice.   Sweeten to taste.   Very
nice for invalids and little children.

MRS. NATHANIEL·WALDO EMERSON, Boston.

Stuffed Prunes

Wash 2 pounds of nice prunes, cover with cold water
and soak over night.   Next morning drain, saving the

water. Remove the stones without spoiling the shape of the prunes. Put an almond in each place from which a stone was taken; the almonds must be blanched and slightly roasted. Add to the water 1 teaspoonful vanilla sugar, or a tiny bit of vanilla bean, and a half cup of sugar; bring to a boil and skim. Boil two minutes, add prunes; when hot lift carefully and put aside to cool. A tablespoonful of soaked gelatine may be added when the prunes are hot. This will give a creamy, clear sauce. By permission of

MRS. S. T. RORER and THE HOUSEHOLD NEWS CO.

Prune Pudding No. 1

Stew 1 pound of prunes without sugar; drain off the juice, remove the pits and chop fine. Beat the whites of 4 eggs very stiff, adding gradually 1 cup of sugar, beating all the time; stir into the chopped prunes; bake twenty minutes. Serve cold with whipped cream, which may be flavored with wine.

MRS. RICHARD C. STEVENS.

Prune Pudding No. 2

1 cup full stewed and stoned prunes	1 pint of milk
	¾ cup sugar
1 tablespoonful cornstarch	3 eggs
1 tablespoonful butter	

Let the milk come to a boil, then add cornstarch, sugar, eggs, and butter, mixed with a little cold milk; chop prunes, put in a buttered dish and pour the mixture over. Bake twenty minutes and serve with whipped cream.

MRS. C. E. BURNSIDE.

TRY Sioux Corn Starch for puddings.

Date Pudding

Will Serve Six Persons.

1 coffee cup brown sugar
1 coffee cup fine bread
    crumbs
3 eggs
½ teaspoonful salt

1 coffee cup suet, minced
    fine
¾ pounds dates, stoned and
    chopped
½ glass brandy, good measure
2 teaspoonfuls cinnamon

Steam in buttered mould two hours. This needs no wetting but the eggs and brandy.

MRS. WEBSTER BROWN.

Batter Fruit Pudding

1 cup fruit
1 egg
1 cup sweet milk
2 cups flour
A little grated nutmeg

1 cup sugar
2 tablespoonfuls melted but-
    ter
3 teaspoonfuls baking pow-
    der

Stir the butter, sugar and egg together, add the milk, baking powder in the flour, and lastly the fruit dredged with flour. Any sort of acid fruit, fresh or preserved, may be used, as plums or peaches. Bake about twenty-five minutes in a moderate oven and serve with

Sauce.

1 cup sugar
½ cup butter, rubbed to a cream
White of 1 egg, beaten light

Just before serving beat in 1 cup of the fruit juice, heated.

MRS. A. W. ENGLE

Chocolate Pudding

Scald 1 quart milk
Beat the yolks of 6 eggs
5 tablespoonfuls sugar

Grate 4 tablespoonfuls of
    chocolate
1 teaspoonful cornstarch

Add to milk, bake half an hour, cool and frost with chocolate. Frosting made as follows:

4 tablespoonfuls sugar   4 tablespoonfuls chocolate
White of 1 egg

GERMEA—The Delightful Breakfast Dish.

Dutch Pie

1 pint of flour	1 egg
1 cup of milk	1 teaspoonful of cream of
½ teaspoonful of soda	tartar
2 tablespoonfuls of melted	A little salt
butter	

Mix like a batter, pour into a pudding dish and stick quartered apples thickly through it. Sprinkle with sugar and bake in a moderate oven about half an hour. Serve with hot sauce.

MISS MALTBY.

Baked Apples

Pare, core and cut in thin slices the apples, sprinkle sugar between each layer and bake. They will be candied and excellent.

MRS. A. J. FISKEN.

Apple Scallop

Pare and core four good-sized tart apples and cut them into slices. Put a layer of bread crumbs into the bottom of a pudding dish, then a layer of apples, then a layer of chopped English walnuts, then a sprinkling of sugar, then crumbs again, and so continue until the dish is filled, having the last layer crumbs. Pour over half a cup of water, or, if you have it, sweet cider, and bake half an hour. Serve *hot*, plain or with sugar.

By permission of

MRS. S. T. RORER and THE HOUSEHOLD NEWS CO.

Apple Float

3 apples, very tart	1 egg
1 cup of granulated sugar	

Bake the apples with skin on and without water. When done scrape out the pulp, mix well with the sugar and let get cold. Beat to stiff froth the white of 1 egg, add to apples and beat for nearly half an hour.

JOHNSON'S Columbian Brand Pine Apples.

Serve with soft custard. Looks like a mound of snow, and tastes fine.

Mrs. JOSEPH SHIPPEN.

Apple Dessert

Wash and core 8 red tart apples and put them in a kettle of boiling water. Boil till you can put a straw through them. Take off and let stand a few moments, then peel off the skin. Make a syrup of 1 cup of sugar, a little water, juice of 2 oranges and boil till thick. Pour over the apples and let stand till cold before serving.

GERTRUDE CARPENTER, Cleveland, Ohio.

Apple Pudding

Will Serve Four Persons.

Take four apples, pare and quarter; put in a small pudding dish; sprinkle sugar and nutmeg to taste; then pour over the whole the yolks of 2 eggs well beaten with 3 tablespoonfuls of water and bake until tender. Beat the whites of the 2 eggs to a stiff froth and cover the pudding just before serving, which may be either hot or cold.

Mrs. J. K. BROWN.

Apple Trifle

3 pints apples (pared, cored   ½ pint water
and quartered)   1 cup sugar
Grating of nutmeg   3 pints whipped cream

Place the water and apples in stewpan and boil until tender; then add sugar and nutmeg and cook for ten minutes. Set away to cool. At serving time put apples in deep glass dish and heap the whipped cream on top. Very delicate and good.

Mrs. C. P. DAM.

TRY Sioux Corn Starch for puddings.

Roxbury Pudding

Cover the bottom of a pudding dish with strained apple sauce. sweeten and season with vanilla. Make a custard of the yolks of 5 eggs. 1 pint of milk, and grated rind of 1 lemon, and a small pinch of salt. Cook in double boiler until smooth, pour over the apple, set in a warm oven till the custard hardens slightly, beat the whites of the eggs to a stiff froth, and add almost a pound of powdered sugar. Pour this over the custard already baked. and set in the oven long enough to harden. Serve cold.

Mrs. LOUISE A. THOMPSON.

Baked Pears

Put no water into the pan in which the pears are baked, unless the oven is very hot. Make a syrup of sugar and water and pour over the pears while they are hot. Serve with cream.

Mrs. C. E. SHEPARD.

Walled Peaches

Cut off the top of a loaf of stale sponge cake, scoop out the inside. leaving enough for a substantial wall; fill with canned peaches, sprinkle with pulverized sugar, and heap with whipped cream.

Mrs. L. H. GRAY.

Orange Pudding No. 1

2 cups bread crumbs soaked in ½ pint milk
2 oranges, juice and grated rind
2 eggs, the yolks beaten into the crumbs. the whites beaten and put in last
1 cup of sugar
A little citron cut in fine strips, and a pinch of salt

Stir all the ingredients together with 1 pint of milk; bake in moderate oven until done, but not watery. Serve cold with sweetened whipped cream.

Mrs. J. C. HAINES.

TRY Sioux Corn Starch for puddings.

Orange Pudding No. 2

1 cup of stale bread crumbs	1½ cups of milk
2 eggs, yolks and whites	Grated rind of 1 and juice
¼ cup of sugar	of 2 small oranges

Soak the crumbs in the milk until soft and beat to a pulp. Mix with this the orange rind and juice, the beaten yolks and sugar, and lastly the whites whipped very stiff. Bake in a pudding dish, or in custard cups set in a pan of hot water, in a moderate oven, about fifteen or twenty minutes. Serve with

Golden Sauce.

1 cup of powdered sugar	¼ cup of cream
4 tablespoonfuls of wine	¼ cup of butter

Yolks of 2 eggs

Cream the butter and sugar and add, one at a time, the unbeaten yolks; beat until very light; then add the wine and cream, a little at a time and alternating them, beating constantly. When all are mixed, place the bowl in a pan of hot water over the fire and stir just three minutes; it will curdle if left too long. Use cold. Vanilla, lemon or orange juice may be used instead of the wine.

Mrs. HELEN M. HUNT.

Raisin Puffs

2 eggs	¼ cup of butter
2 tablespoonfuls of sugar	1 cup of sweet milk
1 cup of seeded raisins, chopped fine and floured	2 cups of flour
	3 teaspoonfuls of baking powder

Steam in cups one hour, and serve with lemon sauce.

ANNA BEACH.

Snow Balls

Beat the yolks of 3 eggs light, then add gradually 1 cup of sugar, beating all the time. When very light

add 2 tablespoonfuls of milk, 1 cup of flour and beat
again. Beat the whites of the eggs to a stiff froth, add
quickly to the batter with 1 rounded teaspoonful of
baking powder. Fill buttered cups two-thirds full and
steam twenty minutes. Roll in powdered sugar and
serve at once with hard sauce. By permission of

Mrs. S. T. RORER and ARNOLD & CO.

Sponge Pudding No. 1

¼ cup of sugar   1 tablespoonful of butter
2 eggs, beaten separately ¼ cup of milk
1 teaspoonful of baking 1 cup of flour
 powder

Steam in mould three-fourths of an hour.

Sauce.

¼ cup of brown sugar 2 tablespoonfuls of syrup
1 small cup of water 1 tablespoonful of butter
Cinnamon, nutmeg and lemon

Boil till thick.

MISS HOPKINS.

Sponge Pudding No. 2

¼ cup of sugar   ¼ cup of butter
½ (generous) cup of flour Yolks of 5 eggs
1 pint of boiled milk Whites of 5 eggs

Mix the sugar and flour, wet with a little cold milk
and stir into the boiling milk. Cook until it thickens
and is smooth; add the butter, and when well mixed,
stir it into the well-beaten yolks of the eggs; then add
the whites beaten stiff. Bake in cups or a shallow dish,
in a hot oven. Place the dish in a pan of hot water
while in the oven. Serve with wine sauce.

Mrs. C. E. SHEPARD (from Mrs. Lincoln).

TRY Sioux Corn Starch for puddings.

Banana Puffs

Will Serve Six Persons.

1 cup of sugar   ¼ cup of water
1 cup of flour   3 eggs
1 teaspoonful of baking   3 bananas, sliced
     powder

Stir the bananas into the batter, half fill buttered cups and steam one hour. Serve with liquid sauce or clear cream.

MRS. RICHARD C. STEVENS.

Swiss Pudding

Will Serve Six Persons.

1 cup fine bread crumbs   2 cups milk
3 eggs   1 tablespoonful melted but-
½ teaspoonful salt   ter
¼ saltspoonful pepper   ½ pound cheese, grated

Soak the crumbs in the milk, add other ingredients, cover with dry crumbs, and bake in quick oven till browned.

MRS. WEBSTER BROWN.
(From Mrs. Lincoln's Peerless Cook Book.)

Tapioca Cream

Will Serve Six Persons.

3 tablespoonfuls pearl tapi-   1 quart rich milk
   oca   3 eggs
⅔ cup sugar   1 pinch salt
     Any flavor desired

Cover the tapioca with cold water and let stand three hours, or over night. Place the milk in a rice boiler, and when it has reached the boiling point, stir in the tapioca. As soon as the latter becomes clear, add the yolks, beaten to a cream with the sugar and thinned with a little cold milk. Stir this in carefully and keep stirring until a thin custard is formed; then pour into a buttered dish, cover with a meringue made of the beaten whites, and brown in the oven. Serve cold with cream and sugar.

MRS. C. P. DAM.

GERMEA—The Delightful Breakfast Dish.

Tapioca Cream No. 2

2 tablespoonfuls tapioca   Yolks of 12 eggs
1 pint rich milk

Put the milk on the stove to heat, beat the yolks of
the eggs, sweeten and flavor to taste; add the tapioca,
which has been previously soaked; add this mixture to
the boiling milk and cook till it thickens (must not boil),
stirring constantly. Pour into a custard dish; make a
meringue, spread over the top and brown lightly. Serve
cold. A good way to use the yolks of eggs after making angel cake.

MRS. M. A. KELLOGG.

Rice Dessert

¼ pound rice boiled in 1 quart   1 teaspoonful butter
fresh milk   1 tablespoonful vanilla
1 tablespoonful gelatine   Sugar
1 cup almonds   1 quart whipped cream

Boil the rice until very tender, but preserve the
grain. Before it is cold add the gelatine (dissolved) and
butter. When very cold add the almonds blanched and
chopped very fine; then add vanilla and whipped cream.
Pour in dish and serve very cold.

MRS. M. A. KELLOGG.

Raw Rice Pudding

2 quarts rich sweet milk   ¾ cup rice
1 cup sugar   ½ teaspoonful salt
½ nutmeg, grated

Wash the rice, drain off the water and add the milk
and other ingredients. Bake about two hours in a slow
oven, stirring two or three times the first hour. Serve
cold.

MRS. R. W. EMMONS.

Rice Pudding

Put 2 tablespoonfuls of raw rice and 2 tablespoonfuls of sugar and 1 quart of *new* milk into an earthenware dish and set on the back of the range. where it will keep *hot*, but *not boil*, for two or three hours, stirring from the bottom as often as every fifteen minutes. Add salt and a little nutmeg, vanilla or seeded raisins. Put into a buttered pudding dish and bake till it is creamy and browned over the top. Stir two or three times after putting in the oven. If the oven is too hot and the pudding thickens too much stir in a little fresh milk.

MRS. RICHARD C. STEVENS.

Stuffed Bananas

Turn back a section of skin from 6 bananas, scoop out the inside and press through fruit press. Pour 1 tablespoonful of cold water onto 1 tablespoonful of gelatine, and when well softened add 1 tablespoonful of hot water. Whip 1 cup of cream. add the banana pulp, the gelatine and a little powdered sugar. Fill the banana skins. replace the section of skin and place on ice for several hours.

ADELAIDE M. BLACKWELL.

Snow Pudding

¼ box gelatine	¼ cup cold water
1 cup boiling water	1 cup sugar
¼ cup lemon juice	Whites of 3 eggs

Custard

Yolks of 3 eggs	3 tablespoonfuls sugar
½ saltspoonful salt	1 pint hot milk
¼ teaspoonful vanilla	

Pour the cold water over the gelatine; after a few minutes pour on the hot water; add the sugar and lemon juice and allow it to boil. Put in wet moulds. When serving put the custard around it. and over this the beaten whites. sweetened.

H. ALICE HOWELL.

JOHNSON'S Columbian Brand Pine Apples.

Lemon Honey

| 1 pound sugar | ¼ pound butter |
| 6 eggs | Juice and rind of 3 lemons |

Beat the eggs well, cream the butter and add the other ingredients. Cook like custard in a double boiler. This will keep several weeks and can be used for cheese cakes or pies. If it is to be used at once, a couple of the whites of the eggs may be left out for frosting.

MISS MALTBY.

Floating Island

Will Serve Eight People.

| 1 quart milk | 5 eggs |
| 1 tablespoonful sugar | Flavoring |

Put the milk on in the double boiler and when it boils add the yolks of the eggs well beaten, and the sugar. Stir well until the mixture thickens and then add the flavoring. Pour into a mould and remove to a cool place. When cool pour it into the dish in which it is to be served and beat the whites of the eggs to a stiff froth and drop on the top with bits of jelly. This also makes a very nice and wholesome dish for the sick.

MRS. N. H. LATIMER.

Lemon Sponge

1 box gelatine	1 pint cold water
½ pint boiling water	2 cups sugar
Juice of 3 lemons	Whites of 3 eggs

Soak gelatine in the cold water for fifteen minutes; add boiling water, sugar and lemon juice. When this is cool before it sets add the beaten whites and beat well fifteen minutes, or until the mixture thickens, then turn into mould. Serve with cream.

MRS. J. R. ANDERSON.

JOHNSON'S Columbian Brand Pine Apples.
C. C.-12

Lemon Foam

4 eggs   4 tablespoonfuls sugar
Juice of 2 and grated rind of ½ lemon

Beat the yolks of the eggs and the sugar together,
put in a double boiler and cook until thick; remove from
the fire, add lemon and the whites of the eggs beaten
stiff. Serve in glasses.

MRS. FRANK MITCHELL.
(Mrs. Hinckley's Portland Cooking Class.)

Chocolate Bread Pudding

10 tablespoonfuls of bread   6 tablespoonfuls of grated
  crumbs   chocolate
1 pint of sweet milk   4 eggs
              1 cup of sugar

Put crumbs, milk, sugar and chocolate together on
stove. When boiling, add yolks of eggs and let thicken
like custard and pour into a pudding dish. Beat whites
stiff with sugar, put in oven on a sheet of manilla paper
and brown; then slip carefully off on the pudding.

MISS NANCY BREWER.

Chocolate Custard

Will Serve Six Persons.

Stir into 1 quart of milk, 3 bars of chocolate grated,
sweeten and flavor with vanilla. Let it boil up once or
twice, take from fire and cool, beat yolks of 4 eggs and
stir in, then the whites beaten to a stiff froth, pour
in pudding dish and bake fifteen or twenty minutes. To
be eaten warm.

MRS. WEBSTER BROWN.

Chocolate Blanc Mange.

Will Serve Six Persons.

1 quart of milk   ½ box of gelatine
3 tablespoonfuls of grated   1 pint of cream whipped
  chocolate

Dissolve the gelatine in a little of the milk, heat the

USE Knox's Sparkling Gelatine.

rest, stir in dissolved gelatine, 1 teaspoonful of vanilla. and sugar to make quite sweet; pour out, and when *set* but *not hard* stir in the whipped cream; put in moulds and set on ice or in very cold place. This is delicious.

Mrs. WEBSTER BROWN.

Chocolate Cream

Will Serve Six.

½ box of gelatine
1 cup of white sugar
½ cup of grated chocolate
1 pint of milk
½ pint of cream
1 teaspoonful of vanilla

Soak the gelatine in the warm water one hour; add to this the grated chocolate, sugar and milk. Stir all together and cook five minutes in a double boiler. Then add the cream and boil one minute. Flavor with vanilla and pour into a mould to cool. Serve with whipped cream.

Mrs. G. W. BOARDMAN.

Orange Cream

1 pint of cream
A little of the grated rind
Yolks of 3 eggs
Juice of 3 oranges
1 cup of sugar
1 ounce of gelatine

Soak the gelatine in half a cup of cold water. Grate the rind and squeeze the juice of the oranges. Take half the cream and put in a double boiler. Add the beaten yolks and sugar; stir, and when it begins to thicken add the gelatine. When it has cooled a little add the orange juice and rind, beat and add remainder of cream. Put in moulds and serve with whipped cream.

Mrs. S. L. CRAWFORD.

Corn Starch Pudding

Will Serve Six People.

1 pint of sweet milk
3 tablespoonfuls of corn starch
Whites of 3 eggs
3 tablespoonfuls of sugar
A little salt

Put milk in a pan and set in a kettle of hot water.

USE Knox's Sparkling Gelatine.

When the milk boils add the sugar, then the corn starch dissolved in a little cold milk, and the whites of the eggs whipped to a stiff froth. Beat the mixture and let it cook a few minutes, then flavor with lemon, pour in a mould and set on the ice. This can be made with water instead of milk, in which case add another tablespoonful of corn starch, a walnut of butter and flavor with the juice of a large lemon.

Sauce.

One pint of milk, 3 tablespoonfuls of sugar, the beaten yolks of 3 eggs thinned by adding 1 tablespoonful of milk. Boil, and stir till it thickens, flavor with 2 teaspoonfuls of vanilla, and set to cool. In serving, put the moulded pudding in a deep dish and pour the custard over it, or it can be served with whipped cream.

ANNA BEACH.

Lemon Pudding

Mix 3 large tablespoonfuls of corn starch in cold water to dissolve it. Pour on 3 cups of boiling water, stirring all the time over the fire. Add 2 cups of sugar, 2 eggs beaten separately, rind and juice of 2 lemons. Bake about five minutes. Serve cold with clear cream.

MRS. FRANK BEACH.

Sponge Whips

2 eggs, beaten separately	1 cup sugar
¼ cup milk	3 dessert spoonfuls butter
1½ cups flour	1 teaspoonful cream tartar
½ teaspoonful soda	½ teaspoonful salt

Flavor with lemon

Bake in small round tins. Take off center of tops and take out enough of the cake to fill in 1 tablespoonful of whipped cream; put back covers and frost them.

Fruit Jelly

This is a nice way to use up fruit juice of any kind that is left, or orange juice may be used. Always add the juice of one or two lemons, according to size. Use ¼ box of gelatine to 1 quart. The amount of sugar required depends upon the juice and fruit used.

Sweeten the juice if necessary and add the dissolved gelatine. Let it stand until it begins to thicken; stir in raisins, grapes, small pieces of bananas, thin slices of orange, preserved fruit of any kind, candied fruit, and halves of English walnuts. Any combination may be chosen. Serve with whipped cream.

MRS. WINFIELD R. SMITH.

Fruit Salad No. 1

Equal quantities of canned pineapple, oranges and bananas, cut in small dice-shaped pieces. To be served with a spoonful of powdered sugar on the side of each plate.

MISS HOPKINS.

Fruit Salad No. 2

¾ box gelatine
6 figs
9 dates
½ pint boiling water

2 lemons
2 oranges
10 nuts of any kind
2 cups sugar

½ pint cold water

Soak the gelatine in the cold water for one hour; then add the boiling water, the juice of the lemons and the sugar. Strain and let stand till it begins to thicken. Stir in all of the fruit cut into small pieces and let it harden. Pour into a mould.

MRS. FRED RICE ROWELL.

Orange Charlotte

¼ box gelatine
¼ cup boiling water
Juice of 1½ lemons

¼ cup cold water
1 cup sugar
1 cup orange juice and pulp

Whites of 3 eggs

Soak the gelatine in cold water until soft. Pour in the boiling water, add the sugar and lemon juice, also

USE Knox's Sparkling Gelatine.

orange juice and pulp with a little of the grated rind; strain and cool in a pan of ice water. Beat white of eggs stiff, and when the jelly begins to harden beat until light, then add the whites and beat together until stiff enough to drop. Pour into a mould and let stand for a couple of hours. Serve with soft custard made from the yolks of the eggs.

Mrs. B. F. BUSH.

Charlotte Russe

1 quart of good cream	½ pound of lady fingers
¾ cup of powdered sugar	½ box of gelatine
½ gill of sherry (if you use wine)	1 teaspoonful of vanilla

Cover the gelatine with cold water, and let it soak for a half-hour. Whip the cream and lay it on a sieve to drain. Line two plain two-quart moulds with the lady fingers. Now turn the cream into a large basin and place it in a pan of cracked ice; add to the soaked gelatine just enough boiling water to dissolve it. Now add the sugar carefully to the cream, then the vanilla and wine, and last, strain in the gelatine. Commence to stir immediately; stir from the sides and bottom of the basin until it begins to thicken, then pour into the moulds and set away on the ice to harden.

Mrs. S. T. RORER and ARNOLD & CO.

Parisian Charlotte

¼ box of gelatine	1 quart of cream
1 cup of grated cocoanut	¼ pound of stale lady fin-
¼ pound of macaroons	gers
4 eggs	2 tablespoonfuls of sugar

Cover the gelatine with cold water and let it soak a half hour. Whip one-half the cream, and stand it away until wanted. Put the remaining half to boil in a farina boiler. Beat the eggs and sugar together until light (do not separate the eggs), stir into the boiling milk, and stir one minute until it thickens; add the gelatine, take from the fire, add a teaspoonful of vanilla and the lady fingers, macaroons and cocoanut, and turn into a basin. Now place the basin in a pan of cracked ice, and stir *continually* until it just begins to thicken; then add the whipped cream, and stir very carefully until thoroughly mixed. Wet a fancy mould with cold water, turn in the mixture and stand on the ice to harden.

Or, cut the center out of a one-pound, stale sponge cake, leaving a bottom and sides about a half inch thick, and pour the mixture into this instead of the mould. Serve with Montrose sauce.

MRS. S. T. RORER and ARNOLD & CO.

Cocoanut Charlotte

Grate 1 cocoanut, pour over it 1 pint of boiling water. Stir well. When cool, wring it in a cheese cloth and set this water, or milk away until cold. Cover ½ box of gelatine, with ½ cup of cold water. Whip 1 pint of cream, skim the cocoanut cream, from the top of the milk and add it to the gelatine; add ½ cup of the water also, and stir over the fire a moment till the gelatine is dissolved. Add to the whipped cream ⅔ cup of powdered sugar; then the gelatine and cocoanut cream; stir it at once and stir continually until it begins to thicken. Turn in a mould and stand away to harden. When ready to serve, turn out and garnish with preserved chestnuts. Pour over the chestnut syrup as a sauce. This is both good and sightly. By permission of

MRS. S. T. RORER and THE HOUSEHOLD NEWS CO.

Banana Cream

Take 5 large bananas, skin and mash them to a pulp, together with 5 ounces of sugar. Beat ½ pint of cream to a stiff froth, add the bananas, ¼ wineglass of brandy, and the juice of 2 lemons, and the thin yellow grated rind of 1 lemon; then ¼ ounce of gelatine (which has

USE Knox's Sparkling Gelatine.

stood for an hour in a little cold water) dissolved in little hot water; stir into the mixture; beat for a few minutes, fill a mould and set on ice for four or five hours.

MRS. J. C. HAINES.

Dorchester Club Pudding

1 cup of hot milk	1 teaspoonful of salt
½ cup of stale sponge cake crumbs	1 cup of grated apple
	2 eggs
½ cup of whipped cream	1 lemon (juice)
2 teaspoonfuls of powdered sugar	¼ cup of sugar

Soak the cake in the hot milk until soft. Beat the yolks, add sugar, salt, grated rind and juice of half the lemon, and stir this into the milk. Whip the cream. Grate the apple quickly into the mixture, add the cream and turn into a buttered pudding dish and bake about half an hour or until it puffs all over. When slightly cooled cover with a meringue, made of the whites of the eggs, powdered sugar and lemon, and brown in the oven.

MRS. LINCOLN (in the American Kitchen Magazine).

Peach Snowballs

¼ box Knox's gelatine   Whites of 3 eggs
Juice and rind of 1 lemon   Small pinch salt
Flavor with vanilla

Cover the gelatine with cold water; when soft add boiling water to make a full pint or a little more; strain it on a platter; when cool break into it the whites of the eggs and beat until it begins to stiffen. Add a little sugar, lemon juice and grated rind, salt and vanilla, also about half a pint of canned peaches, pineapple or other fruit, reduced to a smooth pulp through the colander. Have the fruit very sweet. Beat all together until stiff and foamy, then mould in café or egg cups. Set them aside to harden. Serve with whipped cream.

USE Knox's Sparkling Gelatine.

Ruby Cream

½ pint tapioca   1½ pints water
Rind and juice of 1 lemon   4 ounces sugar
½ pint currant jelly

Soak tapioca in ½ pint cold water over night; *simmer* the soaked tapioca and lemon rind cut in pieces in 1 pint water until clear; skim out rind and stir in the sugar and jelly and lemon juice; *simmer* a few minutes and pour into dish for serving. Just before serving make a snow of sweetened whipped cream or a meringue made with the whites of 4 eggs and powdered sugar, and pour over the tapioca cream.

         Mrs. CORWIN S. SHANK.

Lemon Snow

1 box Knox's granulated   1½ quarts cold water
   gelatine   4 lemons (rind and juice)
1 pound sugar   Whites of 4 eggs

Soak gelatine in the cold water, then dissolve over fire together with the lemons and sugar. Boil two or three minutes; strain and let stand until it begins to set. Then whip in the well-beaten whites of eggs until all is about the consistency of sponge. Serve with whipped cream or a thin custard.

         Mrs. CORWIN S. SHANK.

Fruit Glacé

Pour over 1 teacupful granulated sugar ½ pint hot water, let it boil without stirring a few moments; cut oranges into eighths and dip each piece into the syrup; lay on a dish to cool. Take English walnuts and treat the same way. When cool pile the nuts in the center of a pretty dish and lay the oranges around them.

         Mrs. LOUISE A. THOMPSON.

USE Knox's Sparkling Gelatine.

Vanity Pudding

Will Serve Eight Persons.

Whites of 6 eggs   6 tablespoonfuls powdered
Jelly or fruit   sugar

Beat eggs to a very stiff froth; add gradually the sugar, beating not less than thirty minutes. Put in 2 tablespoonfuls of preserved peaches or small fruits and beat ten minutes longer; set on ice or in a cool place. Serve with rich cream.

MRS. EDWARD WHEELER.

Angels Pudding

4 ounces sugar   2 ounces butter
4 ounces sifted flour   4 eggs (whites only)
1 pint thick sweet cream

Beat sugar and butter to a cream; add flour, then cream, and last the whites of eggs beaten very light. Flavor with vanilla. Bake in tartpans and cover with a stiff meringue.

MRS. J. D. LOWMAN.

Spanish Cream No. 1

1 pint milk   ¼ box gelatine
2 eggs (yolks and whites)   ½ cup sugar
Vanilla

Pour the milk over the gelatine and let stand an hour; strain, put on the stove and let come to a boil; stir in the beaten yolks of the eggs and the sugar; cook one minute. Take from the stove and add the whites whipped stiff; flavor, pour into moulds. Serve with whipped cream.

MRS. HELEN M. HUNT.

Spanish Cream No. 2

4 eggs   ½ box gelatine
1 pint milk   1 cup sugar
1 teaspoonful vanilla

Soak gelatine in the milk, then put on stove and heat

boiling hot; add beaten yolks of egg; then pour through
the whites of eggs beaten to stiff froth.

Mrs. H. R. CLISE.

Omelette Souffle

Will Serve Six or Eight Persons.

Whites of 9 eggs   Yolks of 2 eggs
2 tablespoonfuls powdered   6 macaroons crumbled fine
   sugar   1 teaspoonful vanilla

Beat the yolks very light; add the sugar, stirring
them together very thoroughly; then add vanilla. Beat
the whites very light, and very carefully and lightly add
the beaten yolks and sugar, a little at a time. Have
ready a cold plate, onto which pile the mixture, a little
at a time. but quickly, sprinkling each spoonful with the
macaroons. Make the pile high and dome-shaped.
Bake in a moderate oven about fifteen minutes.

Mrs. J. D. LOWMAN.

White and Gold Custard

5 eggs   1 quart new milk
      Sugar, salt, flavoring

Take 1 pint of the milk, the whites of the eggs
slightly beaten, about 2 tablespoonfuls of sugar, salt
and vanilla; mix and strain into a buttered pudding
mould, and bake very carefully. Set the mould into a
deep pan of hot water, which should *never boil.* Test
by cutting into the center with a silver knife, as for any
custard. Set aside to cool, and it is better made the day
before using. Make a soft custard with the yolks of
the eggs and the remaining pint of milk, and when thoroughly cold, flavor with vanilla or sherry. Turn the
baked custard into a glass dish and pour the soft custard around it.

Mrs. RICHARD C. STEVENS.

Virginia Caramel Custard

1 quart milk   ¼ pound sugar
5 eggs   Pinch of salt
   Flavor rosewater or almond, 1 dessert spoonful

Separate the whites from the yolks of the eggs; beat sugar and yolks together, add the well-beaten whites and mix with the milk, flavor and pour into a buttered mould or tin; set immediately into a pan of boiling water in a moderately hot oven. About half an hour will be required to set it firmly. When nicely browned and puffed up touch the middle with a knife blade; if it cuts as smooth there as around the sides, it is done. Be careful not to overdo. Let the custard stand until perfectly cold, turn out gently on a plate, dust thickly with sugar, place in upper part of hot oven. The sugar melts at once and browns without heating the custard.

Mrs. GEORGE HEILBRON.

Pineapple Pudding

Will Serve Six Persons.

Pour off the syrup from 1 can of sliced pineapple, add to it 1 cup of sugar; cook without stirring until it ropes. While this is cooking cut the slices of pineapple into small dice, arrange in the serving dish and pour over it the syrup. When cold put a layer of lady fingers over the pineapple and heap whipped cream on the lady fingers.

Mrs. HINCHLIFFE.

Strawberry Cream

½ box Cox's gelatine
1 pint strained strawberry juice made *very* sweet

Soak the gelatine in 1 cup of boiling water for one hour. Put the gelatine on the stove and allow it to boil until all is dissolved. Add strawberry juice and 1 pint of stiff whipped cream, beating all well together with

an egg-beater. Stand on ice over night. Turn out the
mould on a platter and pour over it stiffly whipped
cream, sweetened and flavored with the strawberry
juice, and strew the whole thickly with ripe strawberries.

Mrs. NOBLE.

Strawberry Gelatine

1 box of gelatine	1 quart of strawberries
2 lemons	1½ cups of sugar
	1 pint of boiling water

Soak the gelatine one hour in ½ cup of cold water.
Mash half the berries with ¾ cup of the sugar, add the
gelatine, the lemon juice and the remainder of the
sugar, and pour boiling water over all. Stir till the
gelatine is dissolved and strain into a mould, which
should be not more than half full. When *cold* and beginning to stiffen add the remainder of the berries whole.
Put on ice for twelve hours or more and serve with
whipped cream.

Peaches, raspberries or blackberries can be prepared in the same manner, varying amount of sugar
according to acid in the fruit.

Mrs. M. P. BENTON.

Raspberry Cream

¼ box of gelatine	½ cup of cold water
½ cup of boiling water	1 cup of sugar
1 pint of cream (whipped)	1 pint of raspberry juice

Soak the gelatine one hour in the cold water, then
put it with the sugar and boiling water in the double
boiler over the fire and stir until thoroughly dissolved.
Add the raspberry juice, strain and set in a cool place.
When it has begun to form stir in the whipped cream.
Turn into the mould and set on ice to harden.

Mrs. W. H. DE WOLF.

USE Knox's Sparkling Gelatine.

Croquante of Peaches

Will Serve Eight Persons.

18 nice ripe peaches   1 pound of sugar
1 pint of small strawberries   ½ pint of water
The recipe for Charlotte Russe

Boil the sugar and water together until it is brittle when dropped in cold water; that is. when it begins to boil up in large bubbles, take a little of it on a spoon and drop it into cold water; if it snaps in breaking, it is sufficiently boiled. Take it from the fire immediately. Rub a plain two-quart mould with melted butter or oil. Have ready the peaches pared. cut into halves and stoned, the strawberries stemmed. Put a piece of peach on a wooden skewer, dip it in the syrup, then dip a berry in the syrup, and place in the center of the peach where the stone was taken out, then press it against the side of the mould, and so continue until the mould is lined, then stand away in a cold place to harden. When hard. fill with Charlotte Russe, and stand in a cold place for an hour or two. When ready to serve, put a plate over the mould, turn it upside down, wipe the outside of the mould with a warm cloth, then carefully lift it off. This dish is both beautiful and good.

By permission of

MRS. S. T. RORER and ARNOLD & CO.

Croquantes of raspberries, strawberries or oranges may be prepared in the same manner.

Little Creams of Chestnuts

Drain the syrup from one bottle of German preserved chestnuts; whip 1 pint of cream; put it in a pan; stand this in another of cracked ice; add the syrup. a teaspoonful of vanilla and ¼ box of gelatine that has been soaked in ¼ cup of water. for half an hour; then dissolve *over* hot water. Begin at once to stir. and stir till it thickens. Turn into individual moulds, and stand

USE Knox's Sparkling Gelatine.

aside to harden, and get *very* cold. Bake a sheet of sponge cake and when ready to serve the dessert cut into stars or rounds about two inches larger than the moulds; place them on the serving dishes, cover with currant jelly and stand a mould in the center of each. Press the chestnuts through a colander; and cover the creams closely with these pressings. If done carefully they look like long pieces of boiled spaghetti neatly twined around. The remaining quantity may be softened with a little cream, and flavored with vanilla or sherry and poured in the dish as a sauce.

By permission of

Mrs. S. T. RORER and THE HOUSEHOLD NEWS.

Cream Glacé

Will Serve Five Persons.

Whites of 3 eggs
6 level tablespoonfuls granulated sugar

Beat whites to stiff froth; add the sugar gradually. Drop on greased brown paper, and bake in slow oven, to brown in about ten minutes and left in oven to cool off for three-quarters of an hour. Can be served in two ways: First, puncture the top and fill with whipped cream. Second, crush in bottom, fill with ice-cream and put two together, concealing the ice cream.

Mrs ROBERT PALMER.

Cream Puffs

This Makes Fifteen Puffs.

1 cup hot water   ½ cup butter

Boil the water and butter together and stir in 1 cup of dry flour while boiling. When cool add 3 eggs not beaten; mix well. Drop by tablespoonfuls on buttered tins. Bake in a quick oven twenty minutes.

Filling.

1 cup milk   ½ cup sugar
1 egg   3 tablespoonfuls flour

Beat eggs and sugar together, add the flour and stir

into the milk while boiling.   Flavor when cool.

Mrs. A. W. ENGLE.

Coffee Jelly

Soak ½ box in a little cold water; pour over it 1 pint of boiling coffee; sweeten to taste. Stir till all is dissolved; strain and mould. Serve very cold with whipped cream.

Mrs. M. A. KELLOGG.

Wine Jelly

Uncooked.

½ box gelatine	¼ cup cold water
1 pint boiling water	Juice of 1 lemon
1 cup sugar	1 cup sherry wine

Soak the gelatine in the cold water about fifteen minutes or until soft; add the boiling water, lemon juice, sugar and wine. Stir well, strain through a napkin into a shallow dish; keep in a cool place or in ice water until hard. When ready to serve break up lightly with a fork. If you wish to mould it add only ⅔ of a pint of boiling water.

If you wish to mould fruit into it (candied cherries are especially nice), pour a layer of the jelly into the mould, let it harden, then put in a layer of fruit, then another layer of jelly, and so on until the mould is full. During the process keep the unused jelly where it will remain in a liquid state.

Mrs. CHARLES E. SHEPARD.

Kisses

Whites of 2 eggs beaten stiff. Stir into this powdered sugar all it will contain. Blanch some almonds, and chop them fine. Mix with the above. Drop on a buttered pan and bake a light brown.

Mrs. M. A. KELLOGG.

Tipsy Cake

Will Serve Ten or Twelve Persons.

1 dozen lady fingers	1 pint of milk
1 dozen macaroons	3 eggs
1½ dozen blanched almonds	1 teaspoonful of corn
½ cup of brandy	starch
½ cup of sherry	3 tablespoonfuls of sugar
½ pint of firm raspberry jam	2 teaspoonfuls of vanilla
½ pint of thick cream to	2 tablespoonfuls of pow-
whip	dered sugar

Mix the sherry and brandy, split the lady fingers, dip 12 halves one by one quickly in the liquor and spread them on the bottom of a deep glass dish, *completely* covering the bottom, in each piece stick half of a blanched almond. Then treat the macaroons in the same way and place a layer of them on the lady fingers and finish with another layer of lady fingers, using almonds in each layer. Make the upper layer of lady fingers very even and spread the raspberry jam smoothly over them.

Make a soft boiled custard thus: Bring the milk to a boil (reserving 2 tablespoonfuls to mix with the corn starch); add the sugar; let boil up again. Stir the corn starch into the 2 tablespoonfuls of milk; stir this into the well beaten eggs and add slowly to the boiling milk. Let it come *just* to a boil, stirring constantly. Remove from the fire and when cool add 1 teaspoonful of vanilla. When *cold* put it spoonful by spoonful on the jam, making the top smooth. Set in a cold place for an hour. Have the cream very cold, whip very stiff, put in the powdered sugar and 1 teaspoonful of vanilla and heap on the custard, making a trifle higher in the center. Serve very cold.

MRS. J. McB. SMITH, Victoria.

To Make a Trifle

For the Whip.

1 pint of cream	3 ounces of pounded sugar
A small glass of cherry or	Whites of 2 eggs
raisin wine	

For the Trifle.

A custard made with 8 eggs to a pint of milk
6 small sponge cakes or 6 slices of sponge cake
12 macaroons
2 dozen ratafias
2 ounces of sweet almonds
Grated rind of 1 lemon
A layer of raspberry or strawberry jam
½ pint of sherry or sweet wine
6 tablespoonfuls of brandy

The whip to lay over the top of the trifle should be made the day before it is required, as the flavor is better, and it is much more solid than when prepared the same day.

Put into a large bowl the pounded sugar, the whites of the eggs which should be beaten to a stiff froth, the wine and the cream. Whisk these ingredients well in a cool place, and take off the froth with a skimmer as fast as it rises and put it on a sieve to drain; continue the whisking until there is sufficient of the whip, which must be put away in a cool place to drain.

The next day place the sponge cake, macaroons and ratafias in layers in the trifle dish; pour over them the wine mixed with the brandy, and should the proportion of wine not be found sufficient add a little more, as the cakes should be well soaked. Over the cake put grated lemon rind and sweet almonds, blanched and cut into strips, and a layer of jam.

Make the custard with the eggs and milk; let this cool a little, then pour it over the cake, etc. Heap the whip lightly in a mound over the top and garnish if desired with strips of currant jelly or crystallized sweet meats.

MRS. A. F. McEWAN (from Mrs. Beetan's English Cook Book).

Superior Short Cake

1 egg
2 teaspoonfuls of sugar
1½ teaspoonfuls of baking powder
½ cup of milk
1 tablespoonful of butter
2 cups of flour
A little salt

Nice with warm apple sauce and cream.

MRS. JAMES CURTIS.

PUDDING SAUCES

Rich Cream Sauce

1 pint of water	3 tablespoonfuls of flour
½ cup of butter	2 cupfuls of sugar
2 eggs	½ nutmeg

½ pint of sherry or brandy

Beat the butter and sugar to a cream; add the eggs, well beaten, then the nutmeg. Heat the brandy as hot as possible without boiling; bring the water to a boil in another vessel, and stir in the flour (rubbed smooth with a little cold water), and cook it well for about two minutes. Mix well the ingredients off the fire.

MRS. LEWIS H. SULLIVAN.

Cream Sauce

½ cup of powdered sugar   4 tablespoonfuls of cream
2 tablespoonfuls of sherry

Beat butter and sugar until *very light and creamy*, then add the wine and cream gradually. Beat very thoroughly. At serving time place the bowl over the teakettle and stir from the bottom, until it begins to look smooth, then take from the fire and beat till all is very smooth and creamy. The heat of the bowl is sufficient after the mixture begins to get smooth. This sauce must not stand after heating.

MRS. RICHARD C. STEVENS.

Ice Cream Sauce

1 cup of butter	2 cups of powdered sugar
Yolk of 1 egg	2 tablespoonfuls of sherry

Beat the butter to a cream, then add gradually the powdered sugar and the yolk of egg, with the sherry last. Serve on a glass dish and cover with the following when prepared:

Whites of 2 eggs　　　　　Sugar to thicken
½ teaspoonful of lemon ex-　1 teaspoonful of vanilla
　tract

Whip the whites to a stiff froth and add enough sugar to thicken. Flavor with the lemon and vanilla and cover the first part of sauce with it. Set away in a cool place until it stiffens.

　　　　　　　　Mrs. FRANK C. SHARP, Tacoma.

Foam Sauce

½ cup of butter　　　　　1 cup of powdered sugar
White of 1 egg　　　　　½ cup of boiling water
　　3 tablespoonfuls of brandy or lemon juice

Beat the butter to a cream, gradually add sugar, then white of egg unbeaten, and water a little at a time. Cook about two minutes until smooth.

　　　　　　　　Mrs. GEORGE NEWLANDS.

Pudding Sauce

1 cup of sugar　　　　　1 egg
4 tablespoonfuls of boiling　1 wineglass of wine
　milk

Beat the sugar and eggs together until white, stir in the milk and add the wine.

　　　　　　　　Mrs. C. E. SHEPARD.

Maple Sugar Sauce

¼ pound of maple sugar　　½ cup of water
1 lemon　　　　　　　Whites of 2 eggs
　　　　　1 cup of cream

Grate the sugar, add the water and boil until it hairs. Add the juice of the lemon. Beat whites of eggs stiff, and gradually add the syrup.

　　　　　　　　Mrs. WINFIELD R. SMITH.

Hard Sauce

¼ cup of butter   1 cup of powdered sugar
1 teaspoonful of vanilla or   Whites of 2 eggs
    1 tablespoonful of brandy

Beat the butter to a cream, add gradually the sugar, and beat till very light; add the whites one at a time, and beat all till very light and frothy, then add gradually the flavoring and beat again. Heap on a small dish, sprinkle lightly with grated nutmeg and stand on the ice to harden. Fairy or Nuns Butter is made by substituting sherry for the brandy. By permission of

Mrs. S. T. RORER and ARNOLD & CO., Pub.

Fruit Sauce

Put 1 cup of boiling water into a saucepan, add ¼ cup of any tart marmalade, and the juice of a lemon. Bring to a boil, thicken with arrowroot, about a tablespoonful, and sweeten to taste. Let it cook until clear, about five minutes, and pour it over the white of an egg, beaten to a stiff froth. Serve immediately.

Mrs. RICHARD C. STEVENS.

Laura's Pudding Sauce

1 egg   2 tablespoonfuls of sugar
      Vanilla

Beat the white and yolk of the egg separately, add sugar to yolk and thoroughly beat, then add vanilla and then the white. Beat all together thoroughly and serve *at once.*

Mrs. L. G. BANNARD.

Sauce for Suet Pudding

Beat the yolks of 4 eggs and 1 cup of sugar very light. Beat the whites of the eggs very stiff, add to the yolks and sugar and beat again.

Mrs. GEORGE OSGOOD, Tacoma.

French Pudding Sauce

4 ounces of butter   ½ ounce of brown sugar
Yolk of 1 egg   1 gill of wine
Nutmeg

Beat butter to a cream, stir in sugar, add yolk and wine. Place on stove, stirring until it *simmers*. Grate nutmeg over it before sending to the table.

THE HOME COOK BOOK.

Lemon Sauce

1 cup of sugar   1 egg
½ cup of butter   3 tablespoonfuls of boiling
1 lemon, juice and grated   water
    rind

Cook in double boiler till thick.

MRS. ISAAC H. JENNINGS.

Sauce for a Plain Pudding

Cover 1 teacupful of sugar with ½ cup of water and boil to a syrup; add butter size of a walnut, and 2 eggs beaten light, whites and yolks together. Stir very quickly until it is the consistency of cream, flavor with brandy or sherry, and use immediately.

ICE CREAM AND ICES

"I always thought cold victuals nice—
My choice would be vanilla ice."
—*Holmes*

Foundations for Ice Cream

The two principal foundations for ice creams are Philadelphia and Neapolitan, and nearly all the principal creams may be made from these by varying the flavoring, with the addition of fruits (fresh, candied or preserved), nuts, small cakes, wines, etc., and by various methods of moulding and combining a bewildering variety of delicious ice creams may be made.

Philadelphia Ice Cream is made with pure cream. To a quart of cream, *scalded* not boiled, add a cup of sugar; stir till dissolved, add the flavoring, strain and freeze. Or, whip the cream, let stand a few minutes, skim off the whipped part, put sugar and flavoring with the unwhipped part, which has been scalded, and when partly frozen add the whipped cream and finish freezing. This will give a larger quantity when frozen, and it will be very light and delicate. If fruits are to be used it is better to scald the cream, as that will prevent curdling. A quicker way is to use the cream without either scalding or whipping, but the ice cream will not be so rich or delicate.

Neapolitan Ice Cream is made by adding eggs, in the proportion of four to a quart of cream. The cream should be scalded, the eggs thoroughly beaten, sepa-

rately, the sugar added, then the hot cream and the
mixture cooked like soft custard. Or the custard may
be made with the yolks alone, and the stiffly beaten
whites added when the cream is partly frozen. Flavorings should be added when the custard has cooled.

Vanilla, Lemon, Fruit Creams and Bisque

For *vanilla* ice cream, add about 2 tablespoonfuls of
vanilla extract, according to strength to either of the
above foundations.

For *lemon* ice cream, mix about 2 tablespoonfuls of
lemon juice with a half cup of the sugar, stir into the
mixture, strain and freeze.

For *fruit* creams, add about a pint of strained fruit
juice, mash a quart of fresh fruit to a pulp, press
through a sieve and add to the prepared cream. More
or less sugar must be added according to the acidity of
the fruit, and in almost all instances the juice of a lemon
is an improvement.

For *bisque* ice cream, add about a cupful of any kind
of fine dried sweet crumbs, preferably macaroons, lady
fingers or fancy wafers. Flavor the cream with almond, vanilla or caramel, not too strong, and after adding the crumbs a slight flavoring of sherry may be
added to advantage.

MRS. RICHARD C. STEVENS.

Peach, Chocolate, and Baked Apple

For Peach Ice Cream—To a quart of plain ice cream
add about a dozen peaches. Mash half of them to a
pulp, and cut half of them in quite small pieces.
Sweeten to taste and add to the cream.

For Chocolate Ice Cream— To a quart of ice cream use
two bars of sweetened chocolate. Melt the chocolate
in a little milk or water and add to the cream. Vanilla
is the best flavoring with chocolate.

For Baked Apple Ice Cream—To a quart of cream use
from 4 to 8 apples, according to size. Bake well and
mash through a sieve. Sweeten to taste and add to the
cream. This is delicious.

MRS. WINFIELD R. SMITH.

Caramel Cream No. 1

To 1 quart of boiling milk add a very small piece of butter and 1 cup of burnt sugar, into which 1 good tablespoonful of flour has been mixed smoothly. Boil a moment to thicken and remove from the fire. When perfectly cold, add 3 pints cream, and vanilla to taste, and freeze; if not sweet enough, add plain sugar (too much of the burnt sugar will make it bitter).

Mrs. H. C. HENRY.

Caramel Ice Cream No. 2

1 gallon cream   4 teacups powdered sugar
5 tablespoonfuls caramel

For the caramel, put in a saucepan 1 teacup brown sugar and ½ cup of water; stew over a hot fire until it burns. When cold put into the mixture of cream, and freeze.

Mrs. A. J. FISKEN.

Banana Ice Cream

Make a custard with 1½ pints milk and 4 eggs; sweeten to taste and flavor with vanilla; set away to cool. When the custard is partly frozen, add 1 pint of cream which has been whipped stiff, and 4 bananas mashed fine. When all is frozen sufficiently, remove dasher and pack until needed.

Mrs. MAURICE McMICKEN.

Strawberry Ice Cream

Will Serve Six Persons.

1 pint cream   1 quart berries
Sugar

Mash the berries and add sugar to make quite sweet; then add the cream and freeze.

Mrs. WINFIELD R. SMITH.

Lemon Cream

2 quarts cream   4 lemons
1 pound powdered sugar

Add the sugar to 1 pint of the cream, then the grated

rind and juice of the lemons; beat well and add to the remainder of the cream; strain and freeze.

Mrs. RIPLEY.

Coffee Ice Cream

3 pints cream   1 cup black coffee, very
2 cups sugar   strong and clear
     2 tablespoonfuls arrowroot wet up with cold milk

Heat half the cream nearly to boiling, stir in the sugar, and when this is melted, the coffee, then the arrowroot. Boil all together five minutes, stirring constantly. When cool, beat up very light, whipping in the rest of the cream by degrees; then freeze.

Mrs. C. J. SMITH.

Bisque

    1 pint cream, whipped
    1 cup sugar beaten with yolks of 3 eggs

Beat whites separately; flavor, and beat all together. Put in mould and cover with ice and salt; pack and let stand until frozen.

ISABEL JONES.

Chocolate Mousse

Whip 1 quart of cream to a stiff froth and place in a bowl in a basin of ice. Grate 1 ounce of chocolate, add 3 tablespoonfuls of powdered sugar and 1 tablespoonful of boiling water. Stir over a hot fire till perfectly smooth, then add 6 tablespoonfuls of the whipped cream and set aside to cool. When cold add dish of whipped cream, taking care not to get any of the liquid cream at the bottom, if there is any. Stir in gently 1 cup of powdered sugar, pack in a mousse tin and put a strip of buttered muslin around the edge. In packing a mousse put a layer of fine ice, then a thick one of salt, till the mould is covered, and freeze from four to six hours. Serve on very cold plates.

Mrs. FRANK MITCHELL.

Strawberry Mousse

Wash 1 quart of strawberries, press through a sieve, add powdered sugar to taste and set on ice till very cold. Add 1 pint of whipped cream, turn into a mould and freeze as above.

MRS. FRANK MITCHELL.
(From Mrs. Hinckley's Portland Cooking Class.)

Foundation For All Ices

Will Serve Ten People.

1 quart water
Juice of 4 lemons

1 pint or 1 pound sugar
Whites of 2 eggs

Dissolve sugar in 1 quart of boiling water, add lemon juice, let cool, then freeze; when *half* frozen add the whites, beaten stiff. To make raspberry, strawberry, pineapple or plum ice add to the above 1 pint of either juice before freezing. While fresh fruit is preferable, a very good substitute for use in winter is the juice from choice canned goods, or jelly dissolved in hot water.

MRS. S. L. CRAWFORD.

Cherry Ice

1 pint of granulated sugar
1 pint of rich cherry juice
2 tablespoonfuls of pulverized sugar

1 quart of hot water
5 lemons
Whites of 2 eggs

Dissolve sugar in the hot water, add cherry juice, lemon juice and grated yellow rind of 2 lemons, and set away to cool.

While the mixture is cooling whip the whites of the eggs to a stiff froth and gradually beat the pulverized sugar with it. Freeze the cooled mixture until it begins to adhere to the sides of the freezer; then add whites of eggs and freeze until stiff. Pack in the freezer and let stand half an hour before serving.

MRS. ALEXANDER F. McEWAN.

Lemon Ginger Sherbet

Will Serve Eight Persons Bountifully.

4 lemons   1 large pint of granulated
1½ pints of boiling water   sugar
1 dessert spoonful of gela-   ½ pint of cold water
  tine

Soak the gelatine in cold water; shave off the peel
of 2 lemons, being careful to take none of the rind be-
neath the oil cells; put the parings into a bowl; add
boiling water; let stand ten or fifteen minutes; cut the
lemons in half, remove the seeds, squeeze out the juice
and add with the gelatine and sugar to the boiling
water; strain into freezer. Just after putting into
freezer add ginger extract to taste. It should be pretty
strong. When frozen, pack to ripen.

MRS. EDWIN HINCHLIFFE.

Pomegranate Sherbet

¾ tablespoonful of gelatine   ½ cup of cold water
½ cup of boiling water   1½ cups of sugar
1 lemon   6 blood-red oranges or 1
                                   pint of juice

Soak the gelatine in the cold water ten minutes, add
the boiling water and when dissolved add the sugar and
orange juice. Strain when the sugar is dissolved and
freeze.

MRS. E. A. STROUT.

Ginger Sherbet

To 1 pint of lemon ice add 3 ounces of preserved
ginger cut into small pieces, and a little of the ginger
syrup. Stir the ginger into the frozen ice and pack for
an hour or so.

MRS. WINFIELD R. SMITH.

Tutti Frutti Ice

Make an ice after the rule for lemon ice, using
peach (or raspberry) juice in place of lemon, and then

add the juice of 1 lemon. When frozen add the beaten
white of 1 egg. and 1 cup of peaches, candied cherries
and nuts cut in small pieces. Any preferred combination of fruits may be used. such as the French candied
fruits or the candied fruits and nuts, angelica, citron
and fresh oranes: or dates, figs. currants. raisins and
citron. Canned fruits may also be used in various
combinations and the canned tutti frutti.

MRS. WINFIELD R. SMITH.

Sherbet "Three of a Kind"

3 oranges	3 lemons
3 bananas	3 cups of water
3 cups of sugar	Whites of 3 eggs

Beat whites of eggs and put in freezer when the rest
is partly frozen. (Pineapple or other fruits may be
substituted.)

MRS. H. C. HENRY (from Miss Hubbard).

Milk Sherbet

Will Serve Six Persons.

3 pints of milk	$\frac{1}{2}$ pint of cream
2 cups of sugar	$\frac{1}{4}$ box of gelatine
	3 lemons

Scald the milk. adding cream and the gelatine dissolved in a little milk. Pour it over the sugar and
strain. When half frozen add juice and a little of the
rind of the lemons.

MRS. THOMAS GREEN.

Water Ice

Enough for Six Persons.

To 1 pint of cold water add the chopped peel of 4
lemons; boil. While this is boiling take 1 quart of cold
water and add the juice of the 4 lemons and 1 pint of
sugar. When the first mixture is cold add to the last
and strain. When ready to freeze add the whites of 3
eggs beaten to a froth.

MRS. DE WOLFE.

Tomato Water Ice

(From Table Talk.)

Put in a saucepan ½ can of tomatoes, 1 pint of water, the juice of 1 lemon, 3 sliced apples, ¾ cup of granulated sugar and a pinch of ground ginger. Heat slowly to the boiling point, take from the fire and rub through a sieve. Color with a little fruit red and mandarin yellow color pastes; add 4 tablespoonfuls of noyau and 2 ounces of finely chopped candied ginger and freeze. A well known *chef* also adds 4 tablespoonfuls of rum.

Claret Ice

1 quart of claret   4 oranges
4 lemons

Sweeten to taste and freeze. Excellent

MRS. H. K. L. WHITNEY.

Pineapple Ice No. 1

1 cup of grated pineapple   1 pint of sugar
1 quart of water (scant)   1 lemon
1 orange

Freeze a little, then add the whites of 2 eggs, beaten to a stiff froth.

MRS. GREGORY.

Pineapple Ice No. 2

Will Serve Twenty-five Persons.

1 quart can of grated pine-   1½ pounds of sugar
apple   Whites of 4 eggs

Boil the pineapple about fifteen minutes in 1 pint of water. When it commences to boil add the sugar. After removing from the stove add 1 quart of water. When cold add the eggs and freeze.

MRS. M. F. BACKUS.

Pineapple Sherbet

1 can grated pineapple   2 lemons, juice and pulp
1 cup sugar   1 tablespoonful gelatine
1 large cup water   White of 1 egg

Boil sugar in a little of the water; dissolve gelatine; mix ingredients together; cool and freeze. Add well-beaten white of egg when about half frozen.

Mrs. CORWIN S. SHANK.

Turkish Sherbet

Make a very thick syrup of 2 cups of sugar and ½ cup of water. While hot add the juice from a jar of preserved peaches (or any preferred fruit); add a little lemon or orange juice. When ready to serve, fill the glass half full of shaved ice and fill with the sherbet, which pours thickly.

Orange Sherbet

Will Serve Ten People.

Take 1 pint of sugar, pour over it 1 pint of boiling water and let it boil just twenty minutes (no longer); then take it off, pour into an earthen dish and add the juice of 4 oranges and 2 lemons. Set away to cool, and when ready for freezer add 1 pint cold water and the whites of 2 eggs well beaten.

Mrs. J. B. BROWN.

Lemon Sherbet

(From Table Talk.)

1 quart milk   1 pint sugar
Juice of 4 lemons

Stir together and freeze as ice cream; 1 pint of cream is an improvement.

Mint Sorbet

2 lemons   1 pint boiling water
1 cup sugar   White of 1 egg
Mint

Pare the yellow rind from the lemons, taking care to get none of the white; put this into a bowl with a good handful of mint which has been well bruised with

the sugar, add the boiling water and let stand several
hours covered close. Taste to see that the flavor of mint
is strong enough, as the stalks vary in size and strength.
Add the lemon juice and strain into the freezer and
freeze *slightly*; it should almost pour. Just before serving add the stiffly beaten white of egg and beat in well.
The glasses in which it is to be served should be well
chilled. Very nice as a substitute for mint sauce with
spring lamb.

Mrs. RICHARD C. STEVENS.

Cranberry Sorbet

1 pint of cranberry juice	1 pound of sugar
1 pint of boiling water	Juice of 1 lemon

Boil the sugar and water together for five minutes, when
cool add the juice of the cranberries and lemon, strain
and freeze ten minutes. If more sugar is required, add
it before straining and stir till dissolved. At serving
time add the white of an egg beaten stiff, and beat until
it is all light and frothy and will almost pour. Serve
in glasses, *with* roast turkey, instead of cranberry jelly
or sauce.

Mrs. RICHARD C. STEVENS.

Punch

Enough for Seventy-five People.

1 dozen bottles of Hock	2 dozen oranges
2 dozen lemons	1 pint of Santa Cruz rum
3 cans of pineapple	

To every bowlful of punch add 1 bottle of champagne, if wanted extra fine. *Good without* champagne.

Mrs. E. A. STROUT.

Punch

Pare very thin the yellow rind of 12 large lemons.
Put 2 pounds of sugar in a large bowl; squeeze over it
the juice of the lemons and add 1 quart of best rum and
½ pint of brandy; cover this mixture and let stand two

or three hours; add ½ pint of wine (sherry or Madeira).
Half an hour before the punch is to be served, boil the
yellow rind of the lemons in 1 quart of water, throwing
in 6 teaspoonfuls of the best green tea, just before taking from the fire. Strain this liquor into the punch and
add 2 quarts of boiling water.

MRS. H. C. HENRY.

"Ne Plus Ultra" Punch

For Small Punch Bowl.

Enough for Ten People.

1 quart of uncolored Japan tea (cold)
1½ wineglassfuls of Jamaica rum
½ wineglassful of Grenadine
1 pint of Reisling wine
3 wineglassfuls of brandy
½ wineglassful of Mares-chino
1 lemon (juice only)
1 small cup of sugar

Let stand not less than six hours before using.
When ready to serve add :

1 sliced orange
¼ sliced pineapple
1 pint of champagne

Serve with large lump of ice in bowl. If too strong
add cold tea.

MR. HOMER F. NORTON.

Romaine

Boil together 1 quart of water and 1 pint of sugar for
half an hour; add the juice of 6 lemons and 1 orange,
strain and set away to cool. Then prepare the following: Boil 1 gill of water and 1 of sugar eighteen minutes. While the syrup is cooking, beat the whites of 4
eggs very stiff and into these pour the hot syrup very
slowly, beating all the time, and continue to beat a few
minutes after it is all in. Set this away to cool. Place
the first mixture in the freezer and freeze by turning it
all the time for twenty minutes. Then take off the
cover, remove the beater and add 1 gill of sherry, 2
tablespoonfuls Jamaica rum and the meringue, mixing
this well with a spoon into the frozen mixture. Cover

and set away until time to serve.   Serve in punch glasses as a course between roast and entrées.

Mrs. POTTER PALMER.
(In the Columbian Exposition Cook Book.)

Christmas Punch

Boil 1 pound of sugar and 1 quart of water together for five minutes; add the grated rind of 2 lemons and 4 oranges; boil ten minutes; strain and add 1 quart of cold water and some cracked ice.   Strain in the juice of the lemons and oranges and add 1 gill of candied cherries cut in halves, 24 white grapes split, a few pieces of pineapple and 1 large banana, sliced.   Add 1 quart of claret.

Mrs. C. E. SHEPARD.

Christmas Egg-Nog

12 eggs   1 glass brandy
1 glass whiskey   3 pints cream

Beat the eggs in the punch bowl till very light; stir in as much white sugar as they will *dissolve*, and pour in the brandy *very gradually* to cook the eggs; then add the whiskey, the cream, which *may* be whipped slightly, and 1 nutmeg grated.   The nutmeg may be omitted if not liked.

Mrs. RICHARD C. STEVENS.

Bonanza Punch

Will Serve Seventy-Five Persons.

5 quarts water   4½ pounds sugar
Juice of 12 lemons   3 oranges
1 can pineapple   ½ pint gin
                1 pint white wine

Grate the rinds of 3 lemons and 2 oranges into a bowl with the juice of all; put 2 quarts water, 2 pounds sugar and juice of the pineapple on the fire and make a hot syrup of it; then pour this on the grated rinds and juices to draw the flavor.   Chop the pineapple, add to the mixture and strain all into the freezer; add remainder of sugar, water and the liquors and freeze.

MRS. RICHARD C. STEVENS.

Roman Punch

1 quart lemon ice   ½ pint brandy
½ pint Jamaica rum   1 gill sherry
Whites of 4 eggs

Have the ice frozen hard. Just before wanted for serving, stir in the liquors and beat hard. Add the stiffly beaten eggs last. The addition of ½ pint of champagne is an improvement. This must be frothy and not frozen very hard; should almost pour.

A FRENCH DINNER

The bill of fare for dinner parties as ordinarily served in England and the United States is not at all in the French style. It is the French say "à la Russe," though it is common to speak of the course dinner in this country as in the French style.

A true French bill of fare for a family, or for intimate friends is arranged as follows:

ARRANGEMENT OF A DINNER FOR EIGHT PERSONS.

First Service or Course.

Soup.   Relève.   Entrées, and Hors d'Oeuvres.

Soup, in the middle of the table. As soon as it is served, the soup tureen is to be removed and replaced by the relève, which is generally the garnished soup meat, or other piece of boiled meat.

Two or four entées, four cold hors d'oeuvres. The hors d'oeuvres are put on the table when the cloth is laid.

Second Service or Course.

Roasts.   Entremets.

The first course having been removed, the roast is placed in the center, flanked by the entremets.

Third Service or Course.

Dessert, Fruits or Light Pastries.

Entrées are defined as dishes of meat, game, fowl or fish ordinarily served with sauces.

Hors d'oeuvres are such as anchovies, sardines, olives, pickles, etc.

Entremets are composed of warm or cold dishes,

vegetables, fish, creams, cold pastry, eggs in any style, beignets, puddings, or other sugared dishes.

Dessert includes cheese, compotes, fancy cakes, confectionery.

MENU.

SOUP

Au Gourmet

HORS D'OEUVRES	ENTREES
Bouilli avec garniture de raifort	Ris au Blanc
Filets de Concombre	Escargots à la Bourguignonne
Canapé d'Anchois Salés	Filet de Sole à la Horly
Olives Radis Roses	Ragout à la Financiere

ROT

Canards au Père Douillet

ENTREMETS

Truffes à la Calonne	Croquettes de Riz
Macedoine de Legumes	Tôt fait Suisse
Beignets de Pommes à la Bourgeoise	

DESSERT

Fromage à la Crème	Darioles
Talmouses à la Façon de Saint Denis	Marrons au Caromels

Wines.

The service of wines for such a dinner as the foregoing is about as follows: Before dinner a glass of vermouth or absinthe is offered sometimes.

With the oysters, or other hors d'oeuvres Chablis, Sauterne or Barsac. After the soup Madeira or dry sherry, which is also offered after the first or second courses.

With the entrées red Bordeaux, a St. Estephe or the like.

With the second course is served the finer grades of Burgundy or Bordeaux like Beaune, Chateau Giscourt, Clos Vongeot, Chambertin, Chateau Lafite, Margant, Hermitage.

With the dessert, champagne.

MRS. ERASTUS BRAINERD.

CAKES

—

"Aye, to the leavening, but here's yet in the word hereafter the kneading, the making of the cake, the heating of the oven, and the baking. Nay, you must stay the cooling, too, or you may chance to burn your mouth."

—

Delicate Cake No. 1

½ cup butter and 2 cups sugar worked together; add 1 cup sweet milk, 2 to 2½ cups flour, 1½ teaspoonful baking powder, whites of 4 eggs. This recipe can be used for either loaf or layer cake.

LILY GUION.

Delicate Cake No. 2

Delicious.

2 cups powdered sugar	¼ cup butter
5 eggs (whites)	1 cup milk
3 cups flour	1 teaspoonful cream tartar
	¼ teaspoonful soda

Filling.

1 cup sweet cream whipped stiff
3 tablespoonfuls powdered sugar
¼ cup grated cocoanut stirred in lightly at the last
1 teaspoonful rose water

A very nice cake, but must be eaten soon after it is made.

MRS. F. A. BUCK.

(215)

Delicate Cake No. 3

1 cup cornstarch	1 cup butter
2 cups sugar	1 cup sweet milk
2 cups flour (unsifted when measured)	7 eggs (whites only)
1 teaspoonful lemon extract	2 teaspoonfuls baking powder

Rub butter and sugar to a cream, add milk, then flour and cornstarch, into which you have sifted the baking powder; then the whites of eggs, then flavoring.

Mrs. M. T. SUMMERS (White House Cook Book).

White Cake No. 1

2 cups flour	¾ cup butter
1¼ cups pulverized sugar	1 teaspoonful yeast powder
Whites of 6 eggs	

Mix butter and flour together to a smooth paste; beat eggs and sugar together, then mix and bake. Almond flavoring.

Mrs. A. M. BROOKS.

White Cake No. 2

1½ cupfuls of sugar	2½ cupfuls of sifted flour
¾ cupful of butter	Whites of 5 eggs
½ cupful of corn starch	2 teaspoonfuls of Cretata baking powder
¾ (scant) cup of milk	
1 teaspoonful of extract	

Work the sugar and butter to a cream; add the eggs beaten stiff; stir and beat until light as foam, then add ½ cup of corn starch dissolved in a little sweet milk. Stir in not quite ¾ cup of sweet milk. Put 2 teaspoonfuls of Cretata baking powder into 2½ cups of sifted flour, sift twice and add to the above. One teaspoonful of extract completes a delicious cake, which is improved by being kept three or four days.

Mrs. G. W. BOARDMAN.

Gold Cake

Yolks of 8 eggs	½ cup of milk
2 cups of sugar	3½ cups of flour
2 teaspoonfuls of baking powder	½ cup of butter (scant)

Mrs. BENTON.

Gold Cake

1½ cups of sugar
¾ cup of butter
1 small teaspoonful of soda
Yolks of 8 eggs

½ cup of milk
2½ cups of flour
2 small teaspoonfuls of cream of tartar

May be flavored with vanilla or lemon; or ½ cup of nuts and ½ cup of raisins may be used. A good spice cake is made by adding 1 tablespoonful of lemon juice, 1 tablespoonful of mixed spices and a cup of seeded raisins.

Mrs. RICHARD C. STEVENS.

Silver Cake

Whites of 8 eggs
2 level cups of sugar
½ cup of butter
Flavoring

1 cup of milk
3½ cups of flour
1 tablespoonful of baking powder

Mrs. BENTON.

Silver Cake No. 2

1 cup of butter
3½ cups of flour
½ teaspoonful of soda
Whites of 8 eggs

2 cups of sugar
1 cup of milk
1 teaspoonful of cream of tartar

Bitter almonds

Bake in sheets or layers. Also makes a loaf cake by adding candied cherries, citron, figs, angelica and a few blanched and chopped almonds.

Mrs. RICHARD C. STEVENS.

Lady Cake

Delicious.

1 cup of butter
3 cups of flour
Whites of 10 eggs
1 teaspoonful of soda

2 cups of powdered sugar
¾ cup of thin sweet cream
2 teaspoonfuls of cream of tartar in flour

In mixing put the butter and sugar together; beat until light; then add cream and about two-thirds of the whites; mix well; then add flour and beat until very light; then soda which has been dissolved in part of the cream; flavor with bitter almond; add the remainder of whites. In baking, after it has raised sufficiently, make the stove a trifle hotter so as to stiffen it quickly.

MRS. F. A. BUCK.

Bride Cake

1 pound of white sugar
½ pound butter
1 pound of flour
1 teaspoonful of baking powder

Whites of 16 eggs beaten to a stiff froth
1 teaspoonful of essence of rose

Beat sugar and butter to a cream; add eggs and beat five minutes; then add flour in which is the baking powder; then add essence. Bake in buttered tins in a moderate oven. This is a most dainty cake.

MRS. SPENCER.

Whipped Cream Cake

Make sponge cake; bake half an inch thick in jelly pans and let them get perfectly cool. Take ¼ pint of thickest cream, beat until it looks like ice cream, make very sweet and flavor with vanilla. Blanch and chop 1 pound of almonds, stir into cream, and put very thick between each layer; the top may be iced. It is a queen of cakes.

MRS. S. L. CRAWFORD.

Sponge Cake No. 1

12 eggs
Weight of 6 in flour

Weight of 9 in sugar
Juice and rind of 1 lemon

After weighing the sugar and flour, separate the eggs; beat the yolks and sugar together until *very* light; now add the juice and rind of the lemon. Beat the whites very stiff, then add to the sugar and yolks. Beat very hard; add the flour, a very little at a time; stir slowly and pour into a greased cakepan.

MRS. H. C. HENRY.

Sponge Cake No. 2

6 eggs   2 teacups sugar
2 teacups flour   1 large spoonful water
           1 large spoonful flavoring

Beat yolks light; add sugar, water and flavoring, and beat again; then add beaten whites and beat well together; then stir in flour. Bake in a moderately hot oven in long pan; frost and mark into squares.

                                 MRS. W. H. DE WOLF.

Sponge Cake No. 3

1 pint sugar   ½ tumbler cold water (small
1 pint of flour   tumbler)
              6 eggs

Beat yolks, sugar and half the water, then add remainder of water and beat again. Beat the whites stiff and add them with the flour gradually. being careful not to stir more than enough to mix thoroughly and quickly. Put in flavoring and a pinch of salt before the whites and flour.

Cream for This Cake if Baked in Layers.

Scald 1 tumbler of milk in double boiler, stir in 1 tablespoonful sugar and a pinch of salt. Wet 1 tablespoonful cornstarch with a little cold milk; add to the milk and stir till it thickens; then pour onto the beaten whites of two eggs. flavor, put between two layers.

                                 MRS. GEORGE OSGOOD, Tacoma.

Scripture Cake

1 cup of *butter*—Judges, v. 25
3 cups of *sugar*—Jeremiah. vi. 20
4 cups of *flour*—I Kings, iv, 24
2 cups of *raisins*—I Samuel, xxx, 12
1 cup of thinly sliced *melon* (citron)—Numbers, xi. 5
1 cup of *almonds*—Genesis, iii, 11
1 cup of *milk*—Judges, v. 21
6 *eggs*—Isaiah, x, 14
A pinch of *salt*—Leviticus, ii, 13
Spices to taste—I Kings, x, 10

Mix with the flour 2 tablespoonfuls of the modern ingredient called *baking powder*.

                                 MRS. J. N. GILMER.

Episcopal Cake

½ pound of flour   ½ pound of powdered sugar
4 eggs

Beat eggs for ten minutes, add sugar and beat ten minutes more; then add flour and beat ten minutes longer. Butter a mould and bake an hour or longer.

MRS. HENDERSON.

Madeira Cake

1 cup of sugar   1½ cups of flour
½ cup of butter   ½ cup of sweet milk
½ teaspoonful of soda   1 teaspoonful of cream of
2 eggs   tartar

MRS. HENDERSON.

Black Chocolate Cake

2 cups of sugar   ⅔ cup of butter
Yolks of 5 eggs   Whites of 2 eggs
½ cake of chocolate (¼ lb)   1 cup of sour milk
1 teaspoonful of soda   2½ cups of flour

Cream the butter and sugar; mix the soda with the flour; melt the chocolate over the top of the teakettle; add whites of eggs last.

Filling.

1 pound of sugar   1 cup of water
Whites of 3 eggs   ½ cake of chocolate (¼ lb)
1 cocoanut grated

Boil sugar, water and chocolate until quite thick. Pour over the beaten whites, and add the cocoanut.

MRS. SHEPARD.

"Maud S." Cake

1½ cups of coffee sugar   ½ (scant) cup of butter
½ cup of milk   ½ cup of flour
3 eggs, yolks and whites beaten separately

Rub the butter and sugar to a cream; add milk and flour, and then the eggs. Into this mixture stir a chocolate custard made as follows:

8 tablespoonfuls of Baker's chocolate, grated
5 tablespoonfuls of granulated sugar
½ cup of milk

Cook until it thickens a little and beat until cool. Stir the custard thoroughly into the cake mixture and add :

1½ cups of flour
1½ teaspoonfuls of vanilla

2 teaspoonfuls of baking powder

Bake in a moderately hot oven in three layers. Put boiled icing between the layers.

Mrs. J. D. LOWMAN.

Devil Cake

1 cup brown sugar ½ cup milk
1 cup granulated chocolate

Put together in small saucepan. set over the tea-kettle and stir until perfectly dissolved; then set aside to cool. When cool stir into the cake.

Cake.

1 cup brown sugar
½ cup milk
Yolks of 3 eggs
Vanilla

½ cup butter (small)
2 cups flour
1 teaspoonful soda, sifted
with the flour

Cream butter and sugar. add yolks of eggs whole and beat till very light and creamy; add the milk gradually, and the flour; beat thoroughly and quickly; add the chocolate and flavoring. and bake in layers or sheet. Frost with chocolate frosting. Difficult. but very good.

Mrs. RICHARD C. STEVENS.

Pork Cake

1 pound salt pork
1 cup molasses
3 eggs
1 pound raisins

½ pint water
2 cups sugar
2 teaspoonfuls soda
4½ cups flour

The pork must be chopped fine and boiled two minutes in ½ pint water. Flavor with cloves. cinnamon and nutmeg to suit the taste.

BESSIE CARKEEK.

Orange Cake

Yolks of 5 eggs, whites of 3, beaten separately	½ cup water
2 cups sugar	1 orange
3 cups flour	2 teaspoonfuls baking powder

Mix the yolks of eggs and sugar, and add the water; then the whites, with the orange juice and half the rind, grated; lastly the flour and baking powder.

Filling.

1 cup sugar	2 eggs (whites only)
1 orange	¼ cup water

Boil the water and sugar a little longer than for ordinary icing; pour slowly over the beaten whites, beating constantly. When nearly cold, add the juice of the orange and half the grated peel.

Mrs. HELEN M. HUNT.

Orange Cake No 2

2 cups brown sugar	1 cup butter
1 cup milk	4 cups flour
4 eggs beaten separately	2 teaspoonfuls baking powder
2 teaspoonfuls vanilla	

Cream butter and sugar; add yolks; then 2 cups of flour and the milk; mix well; then add balance of flour with baking powder, and last the vanilla and whites of eggs beaten to a stiff froth.

Filling.

Grate rinds of 3 oranges and 1 lemon, and to that add the juice of the fruit and 3 cups of pulverized sugar.

Mrs. R. C. WASHBURN.

Puff Cake

3 eggs	2 cups sugar
3 cups flour	1½ cups milk
Butter size of an egg	2 teaspoonfuls cream tartar

Flavor with lemon

Rub butter and sugar well together; add eggs well beaten, 1 cup of milk and 2 cups of flour. Beat light; now add the last cup of flour with the cream of tartar and lastly ½ cup of milk with soda; flavor. Bake in two tins in a quick oven. This will seem very thin, but do not add any more flour, or it will not puff as it should.

Mrs. F. A. BUCK.

Almond Cake

¼ cup of butter (scant)	1½ cups of pulverized sugar
½ cup of milk	1½ cups of flour
1½ teaspoonfuls of baking powder	½ cup of corn starch (scant)
	Whites of 8 eggs

Filling.

1 cup of cream, whipped stiff
1 tablespoonful of pulverized sugar
1 pound of almonds, blanched and chopped

Mrs. CHARLES STIMSON.

French Almond Cake

6 ounces of sweet almonds	14 eggs
3 ounces of bitter almonds	1 pound of powdered sugar
3 ounces of sifted and dried flour	12 drops of lemon extract

Blanch and dry the almonds and pound in a mortar both bitter and sweet ones, adding a little rose water occasionally. This should be done the day before making cake. Beat the yolks of eggs till thick, add sugar gradually, beating hard, and the whites of the eggs, beaten till stiff, slowly and carefully; stir in flour as lightly as possible. Bake in a quick, even, oven and cool on a sieve.

Mrs. GILBERT S. MEEM.

Cream Cake

1½ teacups of sugar	¼ cup of butter
5 eggs, beaten separately	½ cream
1 teaspoonful of baking powder	2 cups of flour

Bake in a moderate oven.

Mrs. O. T. NUTT.

Imperial Cake

1 pound of sugar	1 pound of flour
¼ pound of butter	10 eggs
1 pound of almonds,	¼ pound of citron
blanched and cut fine	½ pound of raisins
Rind and juice of 1 lemon	1 nutmeg

This is very delicious and will keep for months.

MRS. S. J. HOWELL.

Very Rich Fruit Cake No. 1

1¼ pounds brown sugar	1 pound butter
8 eggs well beaten	1 pound flour
Juice and rind 2 lemons	1 teaspoonful soda
1 teaspoonful cream tartar	1 nutmeg, grated
1 tablespoonful of ground	1 tablespoonful cinnamon
cloves	1 cup jelly or preserve syrup
2 pounds raisins, stoned	1 pound currants
and chopped	¼ pound citron, sliced

Roll fruit in flour; mix with the hands. Makes three loaves. Bake two and one-half hours in a moderate oven; paper the pans with thick paper.

MRS. M. H. YOUNG.

This is an old Massachusetts recipe, and better than wedding cake, we think.

Fruit Cake No. 2

English.

1 pound flour	1 pound sugar
1 pound butter	4 pounds raisins (stoned)
2 pounds currants	½ pint brandy
1 pound citron	12 eggs
1 ounce nutmeg	1 teaspoonful cloves
1 cup molasses	

Almond Paste for Top.

½ ounce gelatine	3 pounds powdered almonds
3 wineglasses brandy	1 pound sugar

Dissolve gelatine in ½ pint of water; add almonds and sugar, then brandy; spread on cake.

MRS. W. VAUGHAN.

Tennesse Fruit Cake

2 teacupfuls of soft, well packed butter
2½ cups brown sugar
2 pounds raisins
1 pound currants
1 pound figs
½ pound pecans
1 pint whiskey
1 tablespoonful cinnamon
1 tablespoonful nutmeg
4 level teacupsfuls sifted flour
12 eggs
1 pound citron
½ pound almonds
1 grated cocoanut
1 wineglassful brandy
1 tablespoonful allspice
1 teaspoonful cloves
1 teaspoonful ginger

Soak spices in the brandy and raisins in the whiskey all night. Cream butter and yolks of eggs, then add sugar, then flour, then fruit and almonds and pecans, then well-beaten whites of eggs, and last the cocoanut. Bake four hours.

Mrs. L. G. BANNARD.

White Fruit Cake

1 cup of butter
1½ cups of flour
1 pound of figs
1 pound of blanched almonds
2 cups of sugar
1 pound of raisins
1 pound of dates
¼ pound of chopped citron
Whites of 8 eggs
2 teaspoonfuls of baking powder

Cream the butter and sugar, then add the whites of the eggs and then the flour; add the fruit the last thing mixed with part of the flour. The fruit should be chopped very fine. This makes a very large cake and requires a long time to bake—about one and three-fourths or two hours. Bake slowly and cover with paper if it seems to brown too fast.

Mrs. ALBERT T. TIMMERMAN.

Nut Cake No. 1

Cream together ½ cup of sugar and 2 cups of butter; add ⅔ cup of sweet milk, whites of 4 eggs well beaten. 2 teaspoonfuls of baking powder, 1 teaspoonful of vanilla, 3 cups of flour and 1 cup of walnuts chopped very fine. Mix thoroughly together, and bake in loaf. This will keep well several days.

Mrs. D. B. LEWIS.

C. C. 15

Nut Cake No. 2

1 cup of sugar
1 heaping cup of flour
3 tablespoonfuls of butter
½ teaspoonful of soda

¾ cup of chopped walnuts
1 small teaspoonful of cream of tartar
2 tablespoonfuls of milk

3 eggs

MRS. GREGORY.

Caramel Cake

½ cup of butter
1½ cups of sugar
1 cup of milk

Whites of 4 eggs
2 teaspoonfuls of baking powder

2 cups of flour

Bake in layers, and bake with caramel frosting.

MRS. M. J. CARTER.

My Mother's Cup Cake

¾ cup of butter
3 cups of flour (well sifted)
1 cup of sweet milk

2½ cups of powdered sugar
4 eggs
1 small teaspoonful of soda

1 lemon, juice and grated rind

Bake slowly, as the quality of this cake depends greatly upon careful baking.

MRS. MARY M. MILLER.

Jelly Roll

Will Make Two Cakes.

12 eggs

1 pound powdered sugar
¾ pound flour

Beat the yolks, stir in the sugar, then the flour, and lastly the beaten whites. Spread to the thickness of half an inch in papered ungreased pans, and bake. When done remove from oven, turn out, moisted with hot water to remove paper, spread with jelly and roll up in a napkin or towel. Roll as quickly as possible after the cake leaves the oven.

MRS C. P. DAM.

Cheap Cake

1 cup white sugar
½ cup milk
2 eggs

Scant ½ cup butter
1½ cups flour
1 teaspoonful baking powder
½ teaspoonful flavoring extract

Beat sugar and butter to a cream, add milk, then eggs well beaten, then flour and baking powder mixed together, and last flavoring extract. Bake in ordinary cake tins in hot oven.

MRS LATIMER.

Carraway Seed Cake

½ cup butter
2 eggs
2 teaspoonfuls baking powder

1 cup sugar
2 level cups flour
Pinch salt
2 tablespoonfuls carraway seeds

Stir butter and sugar together, add the 2 beaten eggs; then add flour, with baking powder sifted through it; salt and carraway seeds. Bake in moderate oven fifty minutes.

MRS. M. P. ZINDORF.

Snow Drops

1 cup butter
1 small cup milk

2 cups sugar
3 full cups prepared flour
Whites of 5 eggs

Flavor with vanilla and nutmeg. Bake in small round tins.

MRS. HATFIELD.

Good Spice Cake No. 1

1 cup sugar
2 eggs
2 cups sifted flour
1 scant teaspoonful soda
½ teaspoonful cinnamon and nutmeg

½ cup butter
½ cup sour cream
½ cup New Orleans molasses
½ teaspoonful ginger
Grated rind of 1 lemon
1 cupful seeded raisins

MRS. J. D. CURTIS.

Spice Cake No. 2

1 egg	⅔ cup each sugar, molasses
1 cup milk	and butter
2½ cups flour (generous)	1 teaspoonful soda
1 tablespoonful lemon juice	1 teaspoonful cream tartar
or vinegar	1 cup seeded raisins
2 tablespoonfuls mixed spices	

Beat the egg thoroughly, add sugar and beat again; then add the molasses, the butter melted, but not hot; spices and milk. Sift flour, soda and cream tartar together, and mix in well; then lemon juice and the raisins well flavored. This makes two loaves in small bread tins.

MRS. RICHARD C. STEVENS.

Clove Cake

3 cups sugar	4 eggs
½ cup butter	1 teaspoonful soda
4 cups flour	1 teaspoonful cloves
	1 cup milk

MRS. S. W. CLARK.

Blackberry Cake

1 cup of sugar	4 tablespoonfuls of sour
⅔ cup of butter	milk
1½ cups of flour	4 eggs
1 cup of stewed blackber-	1 teaspoonful of soda
ries (wild berries preferred)	

Cream the butter and sugar, add the eggs well beaten, the milk and soda, then the berries and lastly the flour. Bake in a loaf forty minutes, in a moderate oven, and ice with boiled icing, or bake in two layers with icing between.

MRS. FRANK MITCHELL.

Apple Cake

1 cup of butter	3 cups of dried apples soaked
2 cups of sugar	over night, chopped fine
1 cup of milk	and stewed two hours
2 eggs	in 2 cups of molasses;
2 teaspoonfuls of soda	cooled before putting
5 cups of flour	into cake
2 cups of raisins	Spices

Beat butter and sugar to cream and add milk, in which dissolve the soda. Lastly add raisins and apples and spices of all kinds.

Mrs. C. J. SMITH.

Pound Cake

¾ cups of butter   1 cup of flour
1 cup of sugar   5 eggs

Stir butter, sugar, yolks of 5 and whites of 2 eggs together, then the 3 whites beaten stiff; add the flour last and beat till light and spongy. *No flavoring.* Bake very carefully.

Mrs. GEORGE OSGOOD, Tacoma.

Portsmouth Pound Cake

1 pound of butter   1 pound of sugar
1 pound of flour, weighed   10 eggs
  after sifting   1 teaspoonful of lemon
½ teaspoonful of mace   juice

Beat the butter to a smooth cream; add the sugar gradually; beat very light for about twenty minutes. Break in 1 egg at a time, beating five minutes between each one, until all are used. This is the best pound cake receipt, but it can be spoiled by not beating sufficiently. Bake in loaf pans lined with greased paper, in a moderate oven for fifty minutes.

Mrs. GEORGE H. HEILBRON.

Our Improved Sunshine Cake

Whites of 7 small fresh eggs   Yolks of 5 eggs
1 cup of granulated sugar   ⅔ cup of flour
¼ teaspoonful of cream of   A pinch of salt
  tartar

Sift, measure and set aside flour and sugar. Beat yolks of eggs thoroughly. Beat whites about half, add cream of tartar and beat until very, *very* stiff; stir in sugar lightly, then beaten yolks thoroughly, then add flour. Put in tube pan and in the oven at once. Will bake in thirty-five to fifty minutes.

Mrs. ROBERT PALMER.

Sunshine Cake No. 1

Whites of 11 eggs   Yolks of 6 eggs
1½ cups of fine granulated   1 cup of flour, measured
    sugar   after sifting once
1 teaspoonful of cream of   Flavoring
    tartar

Sift sugar and flour as in angel cake; whip the whites to a stiff froth and gradually sift in the sugar; add the well beaten yolks and the flour and cream of tartar, and flavoring. Mix quickly and thoroughly and bake fifty minutes in a slow oven. In making angel cake or sunshine cake use a wire egg beater. Do not stir the sugar or flour in the beaten whites, but whip them in lightly with the egg beater and the cake will never be tough.

MRS. J. D. CURTIS.

Sunshine Cake No. 2

Whites of 11 eggs   12 ounces granulated sugar
Yolks of 6 eggs   Peel of 1½ oranges (grated)
3 teaspoonfuls orange juice   6 ounces flour (sifted three
1 teaspoonful cream tartar   times)

Add the sugar to the beaten whites; beat yolks and orange peel and juice; add this to the whites, then stir in gradually the flour, into which the cream tartar has been put. Bake fifty minutes.

MRS. H. R. CLISE.

Boiled Icing

1 cup *powdered* sugar   Whites of 2 eggs
    3 tablespoonfuls boiling water

Boil sugar and water (without stirring) till it hairs, and pour in a thin stream onto beaten eggs, stirring all the time. Beat till it creams; add flavoring.

MRS. BENTON.

Soft Icing

Dissolve 1 tablespoonful of gelatine in ½ cup of boiling water, flavored with rind of lemon. Beat in 10 tablespoonfuls of powdered sugar and juice of 1 lemon.

MRS. ISAAC H. JENNINGS.

Maple Sugar Frosting

½ pound maple sugar   1 cup granulated sugar
Enough water to melt

Boil sugar till it strings from spoon, then pour over the whites of 2 eggs and beat with Dover beater. Do not stir the sugar while cooking.

Frosting

White of 1 egg (not beaten) 2 tablespoonfuls ice water
Juice of ½ lemon

Stir in powdered sugar until stiff enough to spread on cake; add ½ teaspoonful of vanilla the last thing. This receipe will do for two cakes.

MRS. H. C. HENRY.

Caramel Icing

3 cups brown sugar   1 cup milk
½ cup butter   1 tablespoonful vanilla and
                              caramel

Boil slowly until quite thick.

MRS. M. A. KELLOGG.

Caramel Frosting

1 cup of powdered sugar   1 cup of cream
½ cup of butter   1 teaspoonful of vanilla

Boil sugar, cream and butter together until it hairs, stirring only as much as will keep it from sticking; take from the fire and beat till it is thick and creamy, and will spread without running; add vanilla and spread on the cake.

MRS. RICHARD C. STEVENS.

Caramel Filling

1 cup of cream   ½ cup of butter
1 cup of brown or maple   Flavor with vanilla
  sugar

Boil until thick. Set on ice and stir until cold.

MRS B. W. BAKER.

Chocolate Filling No. 1

8 tablespoonfuls of chocolate
½ cup of milk
1½ cups of sugar

Melt chocolate and stir sugar and milk well together.
Boil ten minutes, and put on large platter and stir until
cold enough to put on cake.

MRS. W. V. RINEHART, JR.

Chocolate Filling No. 2

5 tablespoonfuls of grated chocolate, with enough
cream or milk to wet it
1 cup of sugar
1 egg, well beaten

Stir the ingredients over the fire; let them cool a few
minutes, and flavor with vanilla. Spread on cake when
cool.

MRS. LEWIS H. SULLIVAN.

Chocolate Frosting

1 cup of sugar
2 tablespoonfuls of boiling
water
1 bar of chocolate
1 egg (white only)
Vanilla

Grate the chocolate; put in a saucepan with one-third
of the sugar; add the remainder of the sugar to the
white of egg and stir, not beat, until mixed; add the
boiling water to the chocolate and sugar and boil till
smooth and glossy. Pour this gradually upon the egg
and stir till a little cool. Flavor well with vanilla and
spread on the cake. It will seem thin, but will harden.
A half cup of nuts; almonds, walnuts or pecans chopped
rather coarse, added, makes a change and is delicious.

MRS. RICHARD C. STEVENS.

Fruit Fondant Filling

Make one rule of corked fondant as for candy. (See
rule for candy.) Place half the fondant in a kettle and
heat over steam until melted, then add 1½ cups of
chopped figs, dates, seeded raisins and citron. Spread

between layers. Ice the cake with the other cup of fondant melted as above.

S. E. W.

Almond Icing

Beat the whites of 2 eggs until foamy; then sift in gradually 1 cupful of powdered sugar, beating until glossy and so firm that it can be cut with a knife. Take ½ pound of almond paste and work into it 1 or 2 whites of eggs, unbeaten, until soft enough to be mixed with the icing. Beat well together and it is ready for use.

MRS. RICHARD C. STEVENS.
(From Table Talk.)

Almond Filling

1 cup sour cream   1 cup sugar
1 cup blanched almonds chopped fine.

Marshmallow Filling No. 1

Make a boiled icing, spread on cake when warm; then cut marshmallows in halves and stick on the frosting; cover this with blanched almonds, chopped, and cover again with frosting. Ice top layer of cake.

MRS. M. J. CARTER.

Marshmallow Filling No. 2

1 pint cream, whipped stiff ½ pound marshmallows

Cut the marshmallows into small pieces and sprinkle on the cream, which is spread between the layers.

Marshmallow Filling No. 3

Make boiled frosting, and when nearly boiled, drop the marshmallows into the syrup and let them melt. Then beat into the whites of 2 eggs (which have first been beaten to a froth), and continue beating the mixture until cold; then spread between layers.

MRS. R. W. EMMONS.
(From Miss Emma Libby, Port Townsend.)

Lemon Filling

1 cup sugar	Grated rind and juice of 1
3 teaspoonfuls cornstarch	lemon

Juice of 1 orange

Grate rind of lemon, add to this the juice of lemon and orange; stir with this the cornstarch, pour in the sugar; lastly add the cup of boiling water. Boil till thick enough to spread; stir constantly to prevent burning. When cold spread between the layers of cake and sift sugar over the top.

MRS. AURELIUS K. SHAY.

Fig Filling

Chop 8 figs into small pieces; cover them with water and 2 tablespoonfuls of sugar; let *simmer* slowly on back of stove until thick like jelly. Frost the cake and spread the figs over the frosting.

LAURA K YOTT.

Ginger Cake

1 cup of molasses	½ cup of brown sugar
½ cup of butter	2 teaspoonfuls of soda in 1
2½ cups of sifted flour	cup of boiling water
1 teaspoonful each of cinnamon, cloves, allspice	2 teaspoonfuls of ginger

Add 2 well beaten eggs the last thing before baking. Put molasses, sugar, butter and spices into the mixing bowl; put soda in a cup and fill up with boiling water; pour this over first mixture; add flour; then the eggs. Bake in a moderate oven.

MRS. LEWIS H. SULLIVAN.

Ginger Bread
Excellent.

1 cup of molasses	½ cup of sugar
½ cup of butter	1 cup of hot water
2 eggs	3 cups of flour after it is
2 teaspoonfuls of soda	sifted

Ginger and spices as preferred

Mix sugar and butter together; then molasses; add eggs beaten light; then flour and water and spice. This makes enough to be baked in a good sized pan, but not too hot an *oven*.

MRS. F. A. BUCK.

Sponge Ginger Cake

1 cup of shortening, butter or lard
1 cup of sour milk or coffee
1 tablespoonful of ginger
1 teaspoonful of soda dissolved in the milk

2 cups of molasses
4 cups of flour
2 eggs
1 teaspoonful of cloves and salt

MRS. EDWARD WHEELER.

Hard Ginger Bread

1 cup of butter
1 cup of milk
¾ teaspoonful of soda

2 cups of sugar
4 cups of flour
1 tablespoonful of ginger

Beat the butter to a cream; add the sugar gradually, and when very light the ginger, the milk in which the soda has been dissolved, and finally the flour. Spread with a knife very thin on tin sheets. Bake and cut in squares while warm.

MRS. LOUISE A. THOMPSON.

Chocolate Macaroons

Whites of 5 eggs, if very large only 4
1 pound of powdered sugar
1 pound of chopped almonds
2 sticks of chocolate
1 teaspoonful of allspice
1 teaspoonful of cinnamon

Beat the whites of eggs very light, add sugar and beat stiff, then the almonds blanched and chopped fine and last of all the chocolate, allspice and cinnamon Mix all together, and bake on buttered tins.

MRS. L. H. PONTIUS.

Cocoanut Macaroons

This Will Make Eighteen Macaroons.

¾ cup of sugar	Whites of 2 eggs
1 tablespoonful of corn starch	½ package of grated cocoanut

Place the beaten whites in a bowl, add salt and beat to a stiff froth, and stir in the sugar. Place the bowl in a pan of hot water, and when the mixture is lukewarm, stir in the corn starch. Stiffen with cocoanut, drop in small bits on buttered tins and bake in slow oven until a delicate brown.

MRS. C. P. DAM.

Hickory Nut Macaroons

Will Make Seventy-Five.

Whites of 3 eggs	½ pound powdered sugar
½ pound hickory nut meats, chopped	1 tablespoonful flour

Beat the whites and sugar together, adding the sugar gradually and beating well on a platter. Add meats and flour, mixing well, and stand in a cool place about one hour to thicken; then drop on greased pan about a half teaspoonful of the mixture at a time and bake in a slow oven.

MRS. FRANK C. SHARP, Tacoma.

Fruit Pin Wheels

(From Harper's Bazaar.)

1 pint flour	1 tablespoonful sugar
½ teaspoonful salt	3 tablespoonfuls butter (generous)
2 teaspoonfuls baking powder	½ pint milk
1 cup sugar	1 cup currants

Put flour, salt, baking powder and the tablespoonful of sugar into a sieve and sift into a bowl; add 2 tablespoonfuls of the butter, wet with the milk, and roll out like biscuit, as nearly square as possible, three-quarters of an inch thick. Spread with the remaining tablespoonful of butter, which should be softened; sprinkle

with the sugar and currants and roll like jelly cake.
Cut in slices three-quarters of an inch thick, lay in a
pan without touching, and bake twelve minutes.

Mrs. T. A. MARSHALL.

Lemon Cakes

1 pound flour	½ pound butter
½ pound sugar	4 eggs
2 lemons	1 teaspoonful baking pow-
	der

Cream butter and sugar, and add the flour. Beat
whites and yolks of eggs separately, then mix and add
the grated rind and juice of the lemons. Beat thoroughly, and add to the flour, etc. Put in tin in small
rough pieces and bake in a quick oven.

Mrs. HENDERSON.

Shrewesbury Cakes

½ pound flour	½ pound butter
½ pound sifted sugar	1 egg

Rub sugar, butter and flour together; beat well and
add the yolk of the egg. Roll out very thin; cut into
squares and bake.

Mrs. HENDERSON.

Sand Tarts

1¼ pounds butter	2 pounds brown sugar
2 pounds flour	3 eggs

Cream the butter and stir in the well-beaten eggs;
add the sugar and then the flour; *mix thoroughly.* Roll
very thin and cut in diamond shape. Place in buttered
pans; moisten each one with well-beaten egg, and
dust over each tart granulated sugar made *very* brown
with cinnamon. Then place two halves of blanched
almonds on each tart. Bake quickly in a very hot oven.
Let them cool on platters before putting them in the tin
box.

Mrs. MONTGOMERY RUSSELL.

Cream Cookies

1 cup butter   2 cups sugar
4 eggs

Flour to make stiff enough to roll very thin. Flavor to taste. Bake in a quick oven.

Mrs. FRANK MITCHELL.

Excellent Cookies

2 cups of sugar   ½ cup of lard
½ cup of butter   1 cup of sweet milk
2 teaspoonfuls of baking   ½ teaspoonful of soda
   powder   ½ teaspoonful of vanilla

Make your dough as soft as possible to roll out.

Mrs. W. V. RINEHART, Jr.

Sweet Cookies

3 eggs   1 cup of butter
1½ cups of sugar   ½ cup of sweet milk
1 teaspoonful of saleratus   Flour to roll

Mrs. CARDEN.

Lemon Cookies

4 cups of sifted flour   1 cup of butter
2 cups of sugar   3 eggs whipped light
1 lemon, the juice and grated rind

Beat thoroughly each ingredient, adding after all mixed ½ teaspoonful of soda dissolved in a tablespoonful of milk. Use no other wetting. Roll and cut thin.

Mrs. THOMAS GREEN.

Small Sugar Cookies

Will Make About Forty Cookies.

1 heaping teacup of sugar   ¾ cup of butter
¼ cup of milk   2 eggs (beaten separately)
2 teaspoonfuls of baking   1 saltspoonful of salt
   powder   ½ grated nutmeg

A little more flour may be required, but care must be

taken lest the dough be too stiff. Roll thin, cut in shape, sprinkle with granulated sugar and bake in a moderate oven.

MRS. C. P. DAM.

Drop Ginger Cake

1 cup of sugar	1 cup of molasses
½ cup of lard or butter	1 cup of sour milk
2 teaspoonfuls of soda	2 eggs
1 tablespoonful of ginger	Flour to stiffen

ISABEL JONES.

Tina's Ginger Cookies

1 cup of brown sugar	1 cup of New Orleans
1 cup of butter and lard	molasses
(equal proportions)	1 tablespoonful of ginger

Boil about ten minutes, then add 1 teaspoonful of soda. When cool add 2 eggs and flour to stiffen. Roll thin and bake in quick oven.

MRS. B. F. BUSH.

Ginger Snaps

1 cup of butter and lard	1 tablespoonful of ginger
1 coffee cup of sugar	1 tablespoonful of cinna-
1 cup of molasses	mon
1 teaspoonful of cloves	½ cup of hot water
1 teaspoonful of soda	

Dissolve the soda in the hot water. Flour enough to make soft dough. Roll and bake in quick oven.

MRS. F. W. PARKER.

Ginger Wafers

1 cup of brown sugar	1 cup of cooking molasses
1 cup of butter	1 cup of flour
1 tablespoonful of ginger	

Mix thoroughly. Drop from spoon into buttered pan. Bake in moderate oven until they appear full of bubbles. Then take out on board and roll, while warm, into a hollow tube. If edges are too hard for rolling trim them off.

MRS. DAVID KELLOGG.

Nut Cookies

Will Make Three Dozen.

¼ cup butter   1 cup sugar
1 egg, well beaten   1 cup flour
½ pound English walnuts, weighed in the shells

Cream the butter and sugar; add eggs; then flour. Chop the nuts very fine and add them to the mixture. Roll out as thin as possible, and after putting in the buttered pans, flatten with a wet stamp. The bottom of a glass will answer.

Mrs. DAVID BAXTER.

Walnut Wafers

1 cup walnuts, chopped   1 cup brown sugar
2 eggs   3 tablespoonfuls flour

Do not chop the nuts too fine; put into pan in small teaspoonfuls, for it spreads. Watch carefully in baking.

Mrs. MAURICE McMICKEN.

Chocolate Wafers

1 cup brown sugar   1 cup granulated sugar
1 cup butter   1 cup grated chocolate
1 teaspoonful vanilla   2 tablespoonfuls milk
Enough flour to make stiff

Roll very thin; bake very short time. Sometimes add a little baking powder.

Mrs. B. W. BAKER.

Oatmeal Cookies

1½ cups quaker oats   ¼ cup sugar
½ cup butter, melted   1 scant cup flour
1 teaspoonful milk   1 even teaspoonful soda
1 egg   2 teaspoonfuls cream tartar
2 teaspoonfuls vanilla

Stir the sugar into the oatmeal, pour in the melted butter; add the beaten egg, the milk, the vanilla and lastly the flour, to which the soda and cream tartar must have been added, dry. Roll out, sprinkly lightly with the oats, and bake in a moderate oven.

Mrs. DONWORTH.

Cocoanut Drops

½ pound grated cocoanut   ½ pound loaf sugar
Whites of 3 eggs

Beat whites of the eggs stiff, gradually add the sugar, then the cocoanut. Drop on buttered papers and bake.

MRS. M. A. KELLOGG.

Doughnuts in Rhyme

(Ladies' Home Journal.)

One cup sugar, one cup of milk,
Two eggs beaten fine as silk;
Salt and nutmeg (lemon 'll do),
Of baking powder, teaspoonfuls two.
Lightly stir the flour in,
Roll on pie board not too thin;
Cut in diamonds, twists or rings.
Drop with care the doughy things
Into fat that swells
Evenly the spongy cells;
Watch with care the time for turning.
Fry them brown just short of burning;
Roll in sugar, serve when cool.
Price—a quarter for this rule.

MRS. M. P. ZINDORF.

Anna's Doughnuts

1 egg   ¾ cup sugar
½ cup milk   1 teaspoonful melted lard
¼ nutmeg   1 teaspoonful baking pow-
                                   der

Flour enough to admit of its being rolled out. Cut into rings and fry in boiling lard.

MRS. J. D. LOWMAN.

Yeast Doughnuts

Scald 1 quart of sweet milk and pour over ½ cup of lard and same of butter and 1½ cups of sugar. When

c. c.—16

melted stir in enough flour (about 1 quart) to make a
sponge; then add 2 tablespoonfuls of yeast and set away
for the night. In the morning work it down, adding 2
eggs. Let rise second time. Be careful not to use
too much flour. After cutting them out, let rise again.
When fried roll in powdered sugar.

MRS. JOSEPH SHIPPEN.

Doughnuts

Delicious.

1 small teacup sugar	1 cup sweet milk
2 eggs	3 generous teaspoonfuls
3 cups flour (about)	melted butter
3 teaspoonfuls baking	Salt
powder	$\frac{1}{4}$ teaspoonful nutmeg grated

Drop from spoon into boiling lard.

MRS. JOSEPH SHIPPEN.

Fried Cakes

About Three Dozen.

1 cup powdered sugar	1 piece butter size of an egg
3 teaspoonfuls baking pow-	$\frac{1}{4}$ nutmeg
der	2 eggs
1 cup milk	3$\frac{1}{2}$ cups flour (generous)
$\frac{1}{4}$ teaspoonful salt	

Beat butter, sugar and eggs together fifteen minutes;
add the milk; then the flour, with the baking powder
and salt. Mix very soft, roll out one-half inch thick,
cut with cutter with hole in the middle, and fry quickly.
Roll them in powdered sugar as needed. This will keep
them fresh much longer than if all are rolled at one
time.

MRS. RICHARD C. STEVENS.

ELEANOR MAKES MACAROONS

Light of triumph in her eyes.
Eleanor her apron ties;
As she pushes back her sleeves,
High resolve her bosom heaves.
Hasten, cook! impel the fire
To the pace of her desire;
As you hope to save your soul,
Bring a virgin casserole,
Brightest bring of silver spoons,-
Eleanor makes macroons!

Almond-blossoms, now advance
In the smile of Southern France;
Leave your sport with sun and breeze.
Think of duty, not of ease;
Fashion, 'neath their jerkins brown.
Kernels white as thistle-down,
Tiny cheeses made with cream
From the Galaxy's mid-stream,
Blanched in light of honeymoons; —
Eleanor makes macaroons!

Now for sugar,   nay, our plan
Tolerates no work of man.
Hurry, then, ye golden bees;
Fetch your clearest honey, please.
Garnered on a Yorkshire moor,
While the last larks sing and soar.
From the heather-blossoms sweet
Where sea-breeze and sunshine meet,
And the Augusts mask as Junes,—
Eleanor makes macaroons!

Next the pestle and mortar find.
Pure rock-crystal,- -these to grind
Into paste more smooth than silk,
Whiter than the milkweed's milk;
Spread it on a rose-leaf thus,
Cate to please Theocritus;
Then the fire with spices swell,
While for her completer spell,
Mystic canticles she croons,—
Eleanor makes macroons!

JAMES RUSSELL LOWELL.

HOW TO KEEP HOUSE SUCCESSFULLY WITH ONE SERVANT

The problem of how to get on with one servant at times confronts most housekeepers, and particularly young housekeepers.

To be successful, one must be systematic and must require that the work be done, as near as practicable, at the designated time. However, too much must not be demanded, and, although requiring the table to be always carefully served and the house kept in order, the housekeeper may, by a little attention to details, arrange her work so that on days when it falls heaviest her menus will consist of dishes most easily prepared and served. On such days she may assist materially by dusting and attending to minor matters, which, while not laborious, require considerable time.

In the first place it is essential to provide good utensils, of which by far the most important is a reliable stove or range. The servant should rise at least one and one-half hours before the breakfast, when much of the routine work of the house, such as building the fires, airing the rooms, taking up ashes, etc., can be done.

After the breakfast is cleared away the house should first be put in order and all of the rougher work attended to; after luncheon the lighter and neater work, such as baking, ironing, etc., can be done. This will enable the servant to be more neatly dressed to answer the door when most likely to be summoned; although at *all times* a fresh white apron must be kept in a convenient place so that it can be easily put on when she is called from the kitchen for any purpose.

Dinner being over, the kitchen should be put in order and arrangements made for the morning's breakfast. After this the servant, as far as practicable when the mistress is at home, should be free to occupy her time as she pleases. The answering of the door may then be done by some member of the family.

The manner of preparing and serving should be as follows: The table should be carefully laid in ample time and always furnished with fresh linen. Require the same care and attention when the family is alone as when guests are present, by doing which, confusion will be avoided if strangers come unexpectedly. Have everything for the proper serving of the meal in readiness and arrange conveniently the dishes required for the various courses. The first course should be placed upon the table and the water glasses filled before the dinner is announced. After serving this, the next course should be prepared for the table and kept warm, if necessary, until the first course has been removed, and each course in its turn in the same manner.

The maid should stand at the left of the host or hostess, who is serving, and take the plate on her tray, placing it from the left, directly in front of each person, Anything, such as bread, vegetables, celery, etc., should be offered from the left in such a position that it may be easily taken.

In removing a course take first the dish from which the host or hostess has been serving and then the plates, removing them from the right, one or two only at a time. Have the crumb knife used as often as required. In serving be careful to avoid unnecessary noise and haste. As the various dishes are removed they should be carefully placed on a table in the kitchen, set aside for that purpose.

Servants will not find it difficult, after a little experience, to do the work of an ordinary household in a systematic manner, having a time for everything as well as a place for everything.

A simple menu, carefully cooked and served, will be found much more appetizing and attractive than an elaborate one poorly cooked and carelessly served.

SANDWICHES

The secret of a sandwich is entirely in the manipulation. Given good bread and good butter, and the rest is largely a matter of patience. The bread must be delicately thin and crustless, the butter must be soft and evenly spread, cheese must be finely grated, and meat or fish chopped or pounded to a paste. The best bread is bakers' water bread a day old, though the loaf must not be cut before using. Brown bread being much more moist, may be used on the day of baking. Sandwiches should never be made long before serving. If, however, they must stand any length of time, their freshness is insured by wrapping them in a thick brown paper, over which a doubled napkin wrung out in cold water is folded, and setting them in a cold place.—*Harper's Bazaar.*

Cheese Sandwiches

Mix cheese (Deilcatesse or Club House) with mayonnaise or prepared mustard, and with some hard-boiled eggs chopped exceedingly fine. Put this mixture into a mortar and rub together into a paste. Spread on buttered squares of bread, or thin crackers, or best of all, thin slices of buttered toast.

MRS. NATHANIEL WALDO EMERSON, Boston.

Walnut Sandwiches

1 pound English walnuts, cut kernels in small pieces; cover with a nice mayonnaise dressing. Cut bread in

fancy shapes, round, square or triangular, and spread with mixture. Set in cool place till nearly ready to serve.

MRS. V. A. RITON.

Sardine Sandwiches

Chop the sardines very fine, and mix with Worcestershire sauce, or with mayonnaise dressing. Spread on small squares of thin bread and butter.

MRS. NATHANIEL WALDO EMERSON, Boston.

Peanut Sandwiches

Mash peanuts in a mortar to a paste, or chop as fine as possible. Thoroughly mix with Worcestershire sauce; spread on thin slices of bread and butter cut small. A good "appetizer" and nice to serve at "5 o'clock tea."

MRS. NATHANIEL WALDO EMERSON, Boston.

Oyster Sandwiches

Will Make Sixty.

Chop 1 quart of oysters very fine; season with pepper, salt, and a little nutmeg. Mix with ½ cupful melted butter, the same of rich cream, whites of 3 eggs, beaten, and 8 ordinary round crackers, powdered. Heat in double boiler until a smooth paste; set away until cold; spread between slices of buttered bread.

Roast Beef Sandwiches

Chop *rare* roast beef very finely; season with salt, pepper, a very little mustard and a dash of Worcestershire sauce. Use plenty salt.

Mixed Sandwiches

Chop fine cold ham, tongue and chicken. Mix with 1 pint of meat, ½ cup of melted butter, 1 tablespoonful of salad oil, 1 tablespoonful of mustard, yolk of 1 egg, beaten. a little pepper. Spread on lettuce leaf between slices of bread and butter.

Lobster Sandwiches

Chop the meat of a fresh or canned lobster very fine; add a few drops lemon juice, a dash of cayenne, and mix quite soft with mayonnaise. A tablespoonful of finely chopped capers, cucumber pickles or olives improves it greatly. Spread between thin buttered slices of brown or Graham bread.

Mrs. RICHARD C. STEVENS.

Salmon Sandwiches

Free cold canned salmon from all skin and bone, shred finely with a silver fork; add a squeeze of lemon juice, a little paprika and tomato catsup; mix to a paste with melted butter.

Baked Bean Sandwiches

Rub cold baked beans through a sieve; add salt and pepper to taste, and mix with mayonnaise to a smooth paste. Add finely chopped celery leaves or a little celery salt and spread between buttered brown bread.

Mrs. RICHARD C. STEVENS.

Cottage Cheese Sandwiches

Rub cottage cheese to a paste; add olives or capers, *finely minced*, and a little Worcestershire. Should be well salted. Spread between buttered white or brown bread.

Egg Sandwiches

Chop hard-boiled eggs; season with salt, cayenne and a little vinegar; mix to a paste with soft butter. Add pickles chopped fine, and a little devilled meat of any kind, or a little minced ham, tongue or chicken. Spread between slices of white bread or finger rolls.

Mrs. RICHARD C. STEVENS.

Anchovy Sandwiches

3 anchovies   4 ounces butter
1 hard-boiled egg   Salt and pepper
A little nutmeg

Bone the anchovies, and pound them with the butter, egg, salt, pepper and nutmeg. Slice bread very thin; spread with the paste and roll.—*Harper's Bazaar.*

Chicken Jelly Sandwiches

Make chicken jelly the day before wanting the sandwiches; cut in thin slices and lay between thin slices of buttered bread. The bread should be spread with softened butter before cutting.

MRS. RICHARD C. STEVENS.

American Sandwiches

Chop ½ pound of ham very fine, together with 2 chopped pickles; mustard, salt and pepper to taste. Beat 6 ounces of butter to a cream, add the chopped ham and mix well. Cut thin slices of bread, spread with the mixture, press together, cut into diamonds and garnish with parsley.—*Harper's Bazaar.*

Valentine Sandwiches

Chop together 1 cup of chicken meat, 6 button mushrooms; add salt and pepper, and ½ pint of mayonnaise dressing. Spread on thin slices of buttered bread, cut into hearts and garnish with parsley.—*Harper's Bazaar.*

All Sorts

Thin slices of fruit or pound cake between brown bread.

Lettuce leaves with mayonnaise between thin slices white bread and butter.

Tender nasturtium leaves, or cresses, in same manner.

Chestnuts, boiled, rubbed to a paste with mayonnaise.

Any nut meats, chopped, pounded and mixed with mayonnaise.

Chestnuts boiled, sprinkled with sugar and seasoned with vanilla.

Graham bread spread with crabapple jelly and preserved ginger chopped.

Raisins, figs, dates and nuts, chopped, in equal parts, or in any combination.

Veal, ham and hard-boiled eggs; equal parts chopped and seasoned with salt, cayenne and lemon; mixed with soft butter.

Salted almonds chopped and pounded.

Any jelly or jam. If tart mixed with a little finely chopped, preserved ginger, or ginger syrup.

Chicken and ham, chopped and pounded; season with salt, pepper and a little mace.

Cold roast turkey, beef, boiled tongue and ham, equal quantities, chopped and pounded; add finely minced pickles, olives and capers; mix with mayonnaise.

Cold veal and hard-boiled eggs chopped, season with salt, pepper and catsup; mix with creamed butter.

Anchovy paste.

Thin slices of rare roast beef, salted freely.

Fromage de Brie, or cream cheese, spread thinly on bread; add a little paprika.

SUGGESTIONS FOR A CHRISTMAS DINNER

"And care—well may she come at most like Christmas—once a year."

Oyster Cocktail

Spinach Soup

Celery   Radishes

Lobster Baskets

Roast Turkey   Cranberry Jelly

Moulded Potato   Asparagus

Tomato Jelly Salad

Olives   Cheese Crackers

Plum Pudding

Mince Pie

Ice Cream   Cake

Bon-Lons   Coffee

If spinach cannot be obtained, a green soup can be made from canned peas; and canned lobster, asparagus and tomatoes could be used for the other courses. Have red bon-bons in the dishes, and cut the cranberry jelly with a small heart-shaped cutter and serve individually. Frost the small cakes with red frosting (colored with beet juice), and have strawberry and pistachio ice cream. Use a center-piece embroidered in holly, or lay small twigs of holly with the berries on, to simmulate a centerpiece. In the center of the table place a mock Christmas tree about a foot high. It is convenient to put it in a flower-pot of earth. Put the smallest-size toy red candles and tiny red glass balls on the tree. Around the pot put cotton patting, pulled out fleecy and soft; tie it on with red ribbon, and sprinkle with diamond powder until it glistens like frost. Tie bows of red ribbon wherever possible in the room—for instance, around potted plants. If one has electric light, wind the chandelier with cotton batting, sprinkle with diamond powder, and decorate with the bows and holly twigs or green vines trailing down to the table. With gas it might be dangerous to use the cotton batting, but the ribbon and vines are a pretty combination. If one has silver candleabra use red candles in them and tie with red ribbon. For name cards have Christmas cards, and if desired, small souvenirs of the dinner may be hung on the dwarf tree.

PRESERVES, PICKLES, ETC

Canning

Have the jars and tops in *hot* water, and the rubbers in cold water. Cook only enough syrup at one time for one can, and by using two kettles no time is lost by having the *syrup* for the second can, cooking in one kettle, while the *fruit* for the first can cooks in the other.

For *small fruits* make a thin syrup of 1 cup of sugar to 1 cup of water to each can; put in enough fruit for the one can, allow it *just* to come to a boil, pour into the can and seal at once. Be sure the can is brimming full. If the syrup was a little short fill the can with boiling water.

For *large fruits* make a syrup of 1½ cups of sugar to 1 cup of water. When it boils put in the fruit and let it cook until *nearly* tender. Seal quickly.

In the evening screw the tops as tight as possible and again in the morning; then set in a cool dark place.

If large cans are used proportionately more syrup must be made.

Canned Peaches

Make a syrup of 1 pint of sugar and ½ pint of water to a quart of fruit. Boil syrup till clear, skimming carefully; put in the fruit, cook till tender and seal at once.

MRS. F. W. PARKER.

Tutti Frutti

Put in a two-gallon jar, 1 quart of brandy and 3 pounds of granulated sguar. As various kinds of fruit are obtained, add 1 pound of sugar for each pound of fruit. Begin with strawberries, cherries stoned, bananas, pineapple cut in pieces, etc. Keep in a cool place and stir every few days until the last of the fruit has been added. The quantity of brandy and sugar mentioned at first will bear seven or eight pounds each of fruit and extra sugar. Put in small cans or jars, or cover with a paper wet in brandy and tie a second paper over the first. This is an easy way to preserve fruit so that it will retain its natural flavor, and is delicious for tutti frutti ice cream, or for jellies or sauces.

Preserves

Pears, quinces and clingstone peaches should be first cooked in clear water until almost tender. Drain and add ¾ pound of sugar and ½ pint of water (in which fruit was cooked) to each pound of fruit. After skimming add fruit a little at a time to avoid crushing, and cook till clear. When all is cooked boil the syrup down and seal. If the fruit is not to be sealed use a pound instead of ¾ of a pound of sugar to each pound of fruit. Care should be taken to skim the syrup frequently, to keep clear.

MRS. F. W. PARKER.

Strawberry Preserves

¾ pound of sugar and ½ pint of water to each pound of fruit. Put part of the sugar over the berries at night; in the morning drain, add the remainder of the sugar and boil until quite thick; add the fruit and cook until clear. Seal when hot. Or make the syrup with the water; add the fruit and cook.

MRS. F. W. PARKER.

Currant Jelly

Pick over, but do not stem, the currants. Mash them a little; add a cup of water if necessary to keep them from burning, and cook gently (do not let them boil) until they look ragged. Put in a bag made of two thicknesses of cheesecloth and let them drip over night. Next morning strain the juice thus obtained, measure it and weigh the sugar—a pound of sugar for every pint of juice. While the juice is heating put the sugar in shallow dishes and set in the oven, stirring occasionally. Boil the juice just ten minutes, *simmering* until clear; then put in gradually the hot sugar and stir constantly until it is dissolved. As soon as it comes to a boil again remove from the fire and pour into glasses. When cold lay neatly-fitted rounds of white paper, dipped in brandy, next the jelly, taking care to exclude the air bubbles and to entirely cover it. Then paste paper covers over the tops of the cups. The currants are better for being *very* ripe. A clear day is preferable for jelly-making. Many people like a little raspberry juice mixed with the currant juice.

Mrs. CHARLES E. SHEPARD.

Crabapple Jelly

A sprig of rose geranium dipped in the crabapple jelly just before putting into glasses gives a pleasant flavor.

Mrs. T. M. DAULTON.

Orange Marmalade No. 1

12 oranges (medium size)   2 quarts water
2 lemons   9 pounds sugar

Wash the oranges clean, wipe dry and cut in thin slices (just as you would slice potatoes for frying), using peel and pulp but rejecting the seeds. Pour over them 2 quarts of cold water and boil until very tender (about an hour and half); add 9 pounds of sugar and boil an hour or a little longer.

MISS MALTBY.

Orange Marmalade No. 2

Take the juice and pulp of 12 oranges; add the grated rind of 6; put equal weight of sugar and oranges together and boil slowly to the consistency of a thick syrup. If the bitter taste is preferred, the rind of 6 oranges may be sliced in extremely thin strips and boiled until tender, changing the water several times, and then added to the boiling fruit about ten minutes before it is taken from the stove. Bottle while very hot.

MRS. BANGS.

Crystalized Orange Peel

Nice as a Confection for Teas. Receptions, Etc.

Cut oranges lengthwise, take out pulp and most of the white part. Put into a strong solution of salt and water for six days; then boil them in a quantity of water till tender and drain. Make a thin syrup of sugar and water (a pound of sugar to a quart of water); put in the peel and boil one-half hour, or until it looks clear. Have ready a thick syrup of sugar and just water enough to dissolve it; put in the rinds and boil slowly until you see the syrup candy about them. Take them out and roll one by one in granulated sugar.

MRS. GEORGE OSGOOD, Tacoma.

Pickled Peaches or Pears

Prepare a syrup in proportion of:

3 pounds sugar	1 pint vinegar
1 tablespoonful each of whole and ground cloves	4 tablespoonfuls cinnamon

to each gallon of fruit. Boil sugar, vinegar and spices five minutes. Pare the fruit, cut in halves and core. Put part at a time into the syrup and cook till a silver fork will pierce it easily. Skim out the fruit and put in a stone jar. When all the fruit is cooked, boil the syrup ten minutes longer and pour over all. In the morning drain off the syrup and cook fifteen minutes and pour over the fruit again. Repeat three mornings. The third morning thoroughly heat the fruit and boil the syrup till like maple syrup; pour over the fruit; tie the covers down with cloth; not necessary to seal.

MRS. F. W. PARKER.

Spiced Plums or Prunes

7 pounds plums	1 pint sour vinegar
4 pounds sugar	1 tablespoonful mace

2 tablespoonfuls each of cloves and cinnamon

Put sugar and vinegar on to boil; add spices, in a thin muslin bag, and boil fifteen minutes. Put in the plums and just heat through; skim them out into jars. Let the syrup boil down a few minutes longer; then pour over the plums and seal the jars.

Mrs. F. W. PARKER.

Currant Catsup No. 1

Take 2 quarts of ripe red currants, stem and put them in a stewpan with ½ pint of boiling water; let them boil ten minutes, strain through a colander. Then add ½ pint of best vinegar. 1 pound of brown sugar, 1 tablespoonful each of mace, ground cloves and cinnamon. 1 teaspoonful of allspice. Boil quickly for half an hour; bottle and seal for use. This is delicious and improves with age.

Mrs. A. W. ENGLE.

Currant Catsup No. 2

5 pints ripe currants after stripping from the stem
3 pints sugar
1 pint vinegar
1 tablespoonful each of cloves, cinnamon, allspice and
    black pepper
½ tablespoonful salt

Boil all together until sufficiently thick.

Mrs. H. C. HENRY.

Gooseberry Catsup

8 pounds berries	4 pounds sugar
1 pint vinegar	2 ounces whole cloves

2 ounces cinnamon

Boil four hours, and seal carefully.

Mrs. WINFIELD R. SMITH.

C. C.-17

Apricot Catsup

1 gallon sliced ripe apricots	2 tablespoonfuls salt
1 tablespoonful allspice	1 tablespoonful black pepper
1 pint best cider vinegar	½ teaspoonful cloves
6 red peppers	2 teaspoonfuls dry mustard

1 small onion or a tablespoonful of onion juice

Cook 2½ hours, then cool and run through a colander. Put in kettle and boil (careful not to burn), then add 1 teaspoonful of cornstarch dissolved in a little vinegar. After it comes from the stove add the cloves. or same amount of mace. Bottle.

Cucumber Catsup

3 dozen cucumbers	12 onions
½ pint salt	1 teacup mustard seed

½ teacup ground black pepper

Pare and chop cucumbers and onions very fine. sprinkle over them the salt: put the whole in a sieve or bag and let drain over night. Mix will with the mustard seed and pepper: place in jars and cover with vinegar. This is delicious with oysters. It is better if kept from the light.

MRS. EDWARD WHEELER.

Tomato Catsup

1 gallon tomato juice	1 quart vinegar
2 tablespoonfuls cloves	2 tablespoonfuls cinnamon
1 tablespoonful allspice	1 tablespoonful black pepper
1 tablespoonful red pepper	
2 tablespoonfuls salt	2 tablespoonfuls white mustard seed
¼ cup brown sugar	

Boil four hours: seal and bottle while hot.

MRS. S. W. CLARK.

Tomato Catsup No. 2

1 gallon tomatoes	1 teaspoonful cayenne
1 tablespoonful mustard seed	½ tablespoonful whole cloves
Small stick cinnamon	1 tablespoonful whole allspice

Stew and strain the tomatoes, then cook again till thick. When about half thick enough add spices tied loosely in a thin muslin bag; also 1 tablespoonful of sugar, 1 cup of strong vinegar, and salt to taste. If onions are liked they should be put in while stewing. This will not be discolored by spices, but as bright as stewed tomatoes; if liked more highly colored, like the prepared catsups, a *little* fruit red and mandarin yellow fruit paste may be used.

Mrs. RICHARD C. STEVENS.

Spiced Tomatoes

5 pounds green tomatoes	2 pounds brown sugar
1 pint best cider vinegar	½ ounce whole cloves
1 ounce stick cinnamon	¼ ounce mace

Cut the tomatoes into small pieces and boil them with the sugar, vinegar and spices (in a muslin bag) until cooked through; then remove the fruit, leaving the spices and syrup to be boiled together until the syrup is sufficiently spiced. This is then poured over the fruit, the spices being left in the syrup to further flavor it.

Mrs. S. W. R. DALLY.

Bordeaux Sauce

1 gallon green tomatoes	1 large head cabbage
1 dozen onions	4 green peppers

Chop all together; add ½ pint salt and let it stand half an hour. Then drain through a colander, placing a weight on top to press out all the juice. Put in porcelain kettle with 1 gallon of strong vinegar, ½ ounce of tumeric, ¼ ounce of celery seed, ¼ ounce of Coriander seed, ¼ pound of white mustard seed, ½ pound of brown sugar. Boil one hour. Will keep the year round if kept in a cool dark place.

Mrs. FRANK BEACH.

English Mustard Pickle

24 medium-sized cucumbers	1 quart small onions
2 cauliflowers	6 green peppers

Cut all into small pieces, put in salt and water over

night; scald in the same water. Drain them and put
into 3 quarts of boiling vinegar with 2 cups of sugar,
4 teaspoonfuls of celery seed, ½ pound of ground mustard, ¾ cup of flour, ½ ounce of tumeric. Boil all together fifteen minutes; then cool and bottle.

MRS. FRANK BEACH.

Sauce for the Goose

½ peck ripe tomatoes	1 cup chopped celery
1 cup chopped onions	1 cup brown sugar
¼ cup salt	1 nutmeg grated
1 teaspoonful ground cloves	1 teaspoonful cinnamon
1 teaspoonful white pepper	3 green peppers chopped
1 quart good vinegar	

Peel and chop the tomatoes; then drain two hours.
Mix all well together; add the vinegar and seal. No
cooking required.

MRS. L. LUDLOW MOORE.

Chili Sauce No. 1

12 large ripe tomatoes	4 peppers
2 onions	2 tablespoonfuls salt
2 tablespoonfuls sugar	1 tablespoonful cinnamon
3 cupfuls vinegar	

Peel the tomatoes, and chop fine; then add the
onions and peppers chopped *very fine*. Boil one and one-
half hours. One quart can of tomatoes may be used
with the other ingredients instead of the ripe tomatoes.

MRS. ALBERT T. TIMMERMAN.

Chili Sauce No. 2

1 peck ripe tomatoes	6 onions, medium size
5 large red peppers	1½ cups sugar
¼ cup salt	1 even teaspoonful each of
1 pint vinegar	ground allspice, cloves
	and cinnamon

After the tomatoes are cooked and strained add
spices and other ingredients. Boil gently until thick.

MRS. A. F. McEWAN.

Sweet Tomato Pickles

1 peck green tomatoes	1 teaspoonful black pepper
4 large onions	2 tablespoonfuls whole
1 cup salt	cloves
2 tablespoonfuls cinnamon	2 quarts cider vinegar
2 tablespoonfuls allspice	2 pounds sugar
1 tablespoonful ginger	

Slice the tomatoes and onions. add the salt and let stand over night. In the morning cover with cold water and drain well. Put the spices in a muslin bag and soak in the vinegar over night. In the morning add the sugar, and *simmer* two hours. Then add the tomatoes and onions and boil forty minutes.

MRS. GREGORY.

Spiced Green Tomatoes

1 peck green tomatoes. sliced
12 large onions. sliced

Leave in salt and water twenty-four hours; then drain; and add:

¼ pound mustard seed	1 ounce cloves
1 ounce cinnamon	1 ounce allspice
1 ounce whole black pepper	1½ pound sugar

Cover with vinegar and boil till transparent. Using whole spices makes the pickle look better.

MRS. A. M. BROOKS.

French Pickles

1 peck green tomatoes, sliced	6 large onions. sliced
3 quarts vinegar	1 teacup salt
¼ pound white mustard seed	2 pounds brown sugar
	2 tablespoonfuls ground allspice
2 tablespoonfuls cinnamon	2 tablespoonfuls cloves
2 tablespoonfuls ginger	2 tablespoonfuls ground mustard

Put tomatoes and onions in alternate layers. well sprinkled with salt; let stand over night. Next day drain thoroughly and boil in 1 quart of vinegar and 2 **quarts of water for** fifteen or twenty minutes; drain

,

add sugar. mustard seed and spices to the remaining 2
quarts of vinegar; throw all together. boil fifteen minutes and put in jars.

MRS. EDWARD WHEELER.

Piccalilli

1 peck green tomatoes, chopped fine
2 dozen cucumbers. peeled and chopped fine
1 small head of cabbage, chopped fine

Sprinkle salt over each and let stand over night. In
the morning drain perfectly dry; mix all together and
heat enough vinegar to cover the mixture; pour over it
and let stand over night. After draining off the vinegar in the morning add 6 or 8 chilli pepper, chopped
fine; 1 pound of white mustard seed. 1 cup of sugar, 1
tablespoonful of cloves. 1 ounce of allspice, salt to taste.
Cover with vinegar and cook several hours until tender. Put in airtight jars.

MRS. WARBASS.

Watermelon Pickle

3 pounds brown sugar   1 scant quart vinegar

Cut watermelon rinds in squares. soak in alum
water over night; in the morning drain. Put vinegar
and sugar on the stove, and when boiling add watermelon. and boil until syrup is as thick as honey and the
rinds are clear.

MISS NANCY BREWER.

Cucumber Pickle

1½ dozen old cucumbers   ¼ dozen onions (small)
1 ounce white mustard seed

Pare and slice cucumbers. leaving out the seeds;
chop. sprinkle well with salt and let stand over night;
onions the same way, separately. Next morning rinse
thoroughly in cold water. mix cucumbers, onions and
mustard seed, pouring over all enough vinegar to cover.
When in jars, cover to about the depth of one inch with
olive oil and seal.

MRS. STROUT.

Dressing for Chopped Pickles

In 3 pints of vinegar boil 1½ cups brown sugar and •
all sorts of spices to taste. Make a smooth paste of ¼
pound of mustard, ½ cup (scant) of flour, 1 ounce of
tumeric, 1 gill of olive oil, and 1 pint (scant) of cold
vinegar. Stir the mixture into the boiling vinegar till
smooth and pour hot over the pickle, which should be
previously salted and scalded in 1 pint of vinegar, and
1 pint of water, and thoroughly drained. This quantity
dressing is sufficient for two gallons of pickles.

Chow Chow

2 quarts beans	4 dozen cucumbers
2 quarts onions	2 dozen green peppers
2 quarts green tomatoes	½ dozen ears corn
1 head cabbage	2 pounds cauliflower
¼ pound mustard seed	½ pound mustard
¼ pound celery seed	4 ounces tumeric

½ bottle olive oil

Cut the vegetables into small pieces, sprinkle thickly
with salt and let stand over night. In the morning
rinse with cold water and drain. Add the whole
spices and enough vinegar to make of it a good consistency. Mix mustard and tumeric with cold vinegar and
stir in while boiling. Cook thirty or forty minutes, or
until vegetables are tender.

Mrs. S. W. CLARK.

CONFECTIONERY

"A wilderness of sweets."

Fondant

1 pint granulated sugar   ½ pint (scant) cold water

Mix well together, and put on to boil, being careful not to disturb until done. (*Never* stir it.) After ten minutes of boiling, gently try it with a fork and if it hairs, keep close watch of it, trying it in cold water until it forms a soft ball. Remove quickly from the stove, pour into an earthen bowl and set away to cool. At blood heat, a thin icing will have formed on the top, which should be gently lifted off with a wide-tined fork, in order that not a bit remain, and none of the syrup be wasted. When this is done beat hard with a fork until stiff; then take in the hands and work until smooth and creamy, not a grain should remain. This will keep for weeks in a cool place. If a quantity of fondant be made the skimmings may all be boiled over with the addition of a little water.

To insure success in making, close watch must be kept during the boiling, and quick judgment used as to the time for removing from the fire. Boiling sugar is full of whims, and is better than any barometer in forecasting the weather. Therefore *watch it!* On a windy day the syrup is likely to grain; on a damp dry it may take much longer to boil, and may even refuse to stiffen, and will need a second boiling.

These minute directions may discourage some from

attempting fondant, but with a little practice one soon learns to avoid "breakers," and becomes fascinated with the infinite possibilities for variety. Individual ingenuity will devise new kinds, so we give but a few which have already been tested.

Peppermints or Wintergreens

Take a portion of the fondant and melt again by putting it into a small bowl set in boiling water. When melted flavor with 1 or 2 drops of oil of peppermint and drop on paraffine paper. For wintergreens use oil of wintergreen and color a delicate pink.

Orange Creams

Grated rind of 1 orange   1 tablespoonful juice
Confectioners' sugar to stiffen

Roll into small balls and dip into fondant melted as for peppermints. If the fondant stiffen again with the continued heat, add a drop or two of boiling water. Use a wide-tined fork for dipping in order that the surplus fondant may fall back into the bowl. It will harden almost at once on the paraffine paper. Variety of form and color is desirable, so we suggest that these creams be made round and small, giving the coating a tint of orange.

Lemon Creams are made the same way, using lemon in place of orange. These may be moulded into oblong pieces.

Cocoanut Cream

Mix shredded cocoanut into some fondant and flavor with vanilla. Form into cones, dip in fondant and sprinkle with cocoanut.

For *Fig Creams* use chopped figs in place of cocoanut.

Nut Creams are made by using chopped nuts in place of cocoanut; flavor with almond, color green. Chopped citron, raisins, dates, raspberry jam or chocolate may be used instead.

MRS. CALVIN E. VILAS.

French Fondant

White of 1 egg and equal amount of cold water beaten briskly, 1 teaspoonful of vanilla (or any preferred flavoring) and sufficient confectioners' sugar to make it stiff enough to form into balls. Before it is quite stiff it can be divided and the various portions flavored and colored according to fancy. Those balls to be covered with chocolate should stand several hours before covering. We have found vanilla or pineapple better for walnut creams; vanilla with figs or dates. A mixture of flavorings is very nice, such as lemon and cinnamon.

Flavorings and coloring can be varied according to taste. Candied fruits cut in small pieces may be encased in the fondant or used on top of ball.

The *fruit* colorings are preferable and can be obtained at a grocers.

French fondant is the simplest way of making candy, but we much prefer the *cooked* fondant, made as above.

Chocolate Fondant for Dipping

Add 2 tablespoonfuls of grated chocolate to about 1 pound of fondant; melt the chocolate and stir the fondant into it. Nut balls and fig balls dipped in this are delicious.

Walnut Creams

Cook some fondant, flavor with pineapple or vanilla, make into balls and put half a walnut on the top.

Date Creams

Remove the stones and fill with fondant.

Stuffed Dates

Remove the stones; have ready blanched walnuts. If you leave the nuts in halves use two dates to one piece, place one date on each side of the nut and pinch together, completely covering the nut, or use one-quarter of a walnut and but one date. Roll in granulated sugar.

MRS. WINFIELD R. SMITH.

Maple Creams

1 cup water   2 cups maple sugar
Butter size of a hickory nut

Boil water and sugar until it is hard; add butter. Place candy pan in a pan of cold water and stir until it becomes a waxen substance. Make into balls and put a walnut on one side.

MRS. WINFIELD R. SMITH.

Butter Scotch

2 cups sugar   2 tablespoonfuls water
Butter size of an egg

Brown the sugar a little first, then boil without stirring until it will be crisp when dropped in cold water. Pour on buttered plates to cool.

MRS. WINFIELD R. SMITH.

Peanut Candy

2 cups confectioners' sugar   1 cup peanut meats

Put the sugar in a shallow pan to melt; when it is melted add the peanut meats, which have previously been partly broken. Pour into a buttered pan and press down quickly with a broad knife, as the mixture hardens very rapidly.

MRS. WINFIELD R. SMITH.

Peanut Caramel

1½ cups granulated sugar   1 cup chopped peanuts

Have the pan hot; pour on the sugar, stirring constantly until it is caramel, when add quickly the nuts; stir once and pour into buttered tins; mark into squares. This candy hardens very quickly, so it must be marked very soon after it is poured out.

MRS. HINCHLIFFE.

Vassar Fudgies

2 cups white sugar   ½ cup *hot* water
1 cup sweet milk   2 squares unsweetened
Butter size of small egg   chocolate
1 teaspoonful vanilla

Put sugar and water in a kettle on the back of the stove until the sugar is dissolved; then set the kettle over the fire and add the milk and the chocolate. Cook until you can make a soft ball in water. It will need to *boil* about fifteen minutes. Add the butter a few min utes before it is done, and the last thing add the vanilla. Pour into a buttered pan to cool. When *cool* but not *cold* beat vigorously with a fork until it is stiff enough to cut into squares. If this is cooked too much it will be sugary and hard.

Mrs. WINFIELD R. SMITH.

Pinochee

3 cups finest light brown	1 cup of cream
sugar	Butter size of walnut
1 tablespoonful vanilla	1 cup walnuts, broken a little

Boil sugar, cream and butter about twenty minutes until when it is dropped in a cup of cold water it can be gathered into a ball, soft but not sticky, then remove from fire and add vanilla. Put the kettle of candy into a pan of cold water and stir until it begins to grain; stir in the nuts and pour quickly into buttered pans. Cut into squares when cold. If it is stirred too long it will be too hard to mould in the pans; if on the other hand, it has been poured into the pans too soon, before it is sugared, if a fork is run through it in the pans for a few moments, it will help it grain. Milk *can* be used by adding more butter, but it is not as good, as the candy will not be as creamy. When the candy is on the stove do not stir at first, and only enough at the last to keep from burning.

MISS BOYER, Walla Walla, Wash.

Maple sugar may be used in place of brown sugar, by melting it first in a very little water, then use a little less butter, as it is rather rich, but is delicious.

Nut Candy

2 cups granulated sugar	½ cup water
¼ teaspoonful cream tartar	1 pound nuts

Boil sugar and water without stirring until it forms

soft ball. When cool stir until it creams. flavor and add nuts. Drop on waxed paper.

MRS. CHARLES E. SHEPARD.

Molasses Nut Candy

1 cup granulated sugar	4 tablespoonfuls molasses
4 tablespoonfuls water	4 tablespoonfuls vinegar
Butter size of an egg	1 pound nuts

Boil all together. except nuts, until it makes a soft ball in water. Take from fire and add nuts. Pour on buttered plates. Score before it hardens.

MRS. CHARLES E. SHEPARD.

Molasses Taffy

2 cups brown sugar	1 cup molasses
1 tablespoonful vinegar	⅓ cup water

Boil until it makes a crisp ball in cold water. Stir in ½ teaspoonful of soda. Pour on buttered plates to cool, then pull.

Pulled Sugar Candy

4 cups sugar	½ cup vinegar
¼ cup water	3 tablespoonfuls cream

Boil without stirring over a quick fire; when it begins to rope from the spoon drop a small quantity into a cup of cold water; if it hardens it is ready to be poured upon a buttered dish. Flavor with vanilla. Begin to pull as soon as it can be handled. using only the fingers.

MRS. THOMAS GREEN.

Chocolate Caramels

2 pints brown sugar	1½ squares bakers' chocolate
1 cup new milk	
Butter size of a walnut	

Boil quickly. stirring all the time. Just before removing from the fire add vanilla. Try in cold water; if brittle, it is done. Pour in buttered tins to cool. When nearly cold mark in squares.

M. E. BLUM.

Butter Scotch

1 cup molasses   1 cup sugar
½ cup butter

Boil until it hardens in water.

Mrs. V. A. RITON.

Hickory Nut Candy

2 cups sugar flavor   ½ cup water

Boil without stirring until thick enough to spin a thread. Set the dish into cold water; stir quickly until white. Stir in 1 cup hickory nuts, turn into a flat tin. When cool cut into squares.

Mrs. V. A. RITON.

Popcorn Candy

2 cups shelled corn   2 tablespoonfuls lard
2 cups molasses

Pop the corn in the lard when it is smoking hot in a deep kettle. Boil molasses until it threads; add 1 tablespoonful of butter and 1 teaspoonful of vanilla. Pour over corn, stirring constantly. Pack *tightly* the corn in a deep narrow bread tin. When cold it will slice nicely.

MISS N. BREWER.

THE SICK ROOM

A few strong instincts and a few plain rules.

Recipes for Invalid Cooking

Beef Tea—Free a pound of lean beef from fat, tendon, cartilage, bone and vessels; chop up fine; put into a pint of cold water to digest two hours. *Simmer* on range or stove three hours, but do not boil. Make up for water lost by adding cold water, so that a pint of beef tea represents one pound of beef. Press beef carefully and strain.

Beef Juice—Cut a thin, juicy steak into pieces one and one-half inches square; brown separately one and one-half minutes on each side before a hot fire; squeeze, in a hot lemon-squeezer; flavor with salt and pepper. May add to milk or pour on toast.

Mutton Broth—Lean loin of mutton, 1½ pounds, including bone; water 3 pints. Boil gently till tender, throwing in a little salt and onion according to taste. Pour out broth into basin; when cold skim off fat. Warm up as wanted.

Chicken Broth—Skin and chop up small a small chicken or half of a large fowl. Boil it, bones and all, with a blade of mace, a sprig of parsley, 1 tablespoonful of rice, and a crust of bread, in a quart of water, for an hour, skimming it from time to time. Strain through a coarse colander.

See page inside back cover.

Clam Broth—Wash thoroughly 6 large clams in shell; put in kettle with 1 cup of water; bring to boil and keep there one minute; the shells open, the water takes up the proper quantity of juice, and the broth is ready to pour off and serve hot.

Cream Soup—Take 1 quart of good stock (mutton or veal), cut 1 onion into quarters, slice 3 potatoes very thin, and put them into the stock with a small piece of mace; boil gently for an hour; then strain out the onion and mace; the potatoes should by this time have dissolved in the stock. Add 1 pint of milk, mixed with a very little corn flour to make it about as thick as cream. A little butter improves it. This soup may be made with milk instead of stock, if a little cream is used.

Apple Soup—Two cups of apple, 2 cups of water, 2 teaspoonfuls of corn starch, 1½ tablespoonfuls of sugar, 1 saltspoonful of cinnamon and a bit of salt. Stew the apple into the water until it is very soft, then mix together into a smooth paste the corn starch, sugar, salt and cinnamon with a little cold water; pour this into the apple and boil for five minutes; strain it and keep it hot until ready to serve.

Raw Meat Diet—Scrape pulp from a good steak, season to taste, smear on thin slices of bread; scar bread slightly and serve as sandwich.

Nutritious Coffee—Dissolve a little gelatine in water, put ½ ounce of freshly-ground coffee into saucepan with 1 pint of new milk, which should be nearly boiling before the coffee is added; boil both together for three minutes; clear it by pouring some of it into a cup and dashing it back again; add the gelatine, and leave it to settle for a few minutes. Beat up an egg in a breakfast cup and pour the coffee upon it; if preferred, drink without the egg.

Rum Punch—White sugar 2 teaspoonfuls, 1 egg stirred and beaten up; warm milk, large wineglassful; Jamaica rum, 2 to 4 teaspoonfuls; nutmeg.

HILL'S Maple Syrup.   "Genuine."

Champagne Whey—Boil ½ pint of milk, strain through cheese cloth; add 1 wineglass of champagne.

Toast Water—Toast 3 slices stale bread to dark brown, but do not burn. Put into pitcher, pour over them 1 quart of boiling water; cover closely and let stand on ice until cold; strain. May add wine and sugar.

Rice Water - Pick over and wash 2 tablespoonfuls of rice. Put into granite saucepan with 1 quart of boiling water; *simmer* two hours, when rice should be softened and partially dissolved; strain, add 1 saltspoonful of salt; serve warm or cold. May add sherry or port, 2 tablespoonfuls.

Barley Water— Wash 2 ounces (wineglassful) of pearl barley with cold water; boil five minutes in fresh water; throw both waters away. Pour on 2 quarts of boiling water; boil down to 1 quart. Flavor with thinly-cut lemon rind, add sugar to taste. Do not strain unless at patient's request.

Koumiss—Take ordinary beer bottle with shifting cork; put in 1 pint of milk 1-6 cake of Fleischmann's yeast, or 1 tablespoonful of fresh lager beer yeast (brewer's), ½ tablespoonful of white sugar reduced to syrup; shake well and allow to stand in refrigerator two or three days, when it may be used. It will keep there indefinitely if laid on its side. Much waste can be saved by preparing the bottles with ordinary corks wired in position and drawing off the koumiss with a champagne tap.

Wine Whey- Put 2 pints of new milk in a saucepan and stir over a clear fire until nearly boiling; then add 1 gill (2 wineglassfuls) of sherry and *simmer* a quarter of an hour, skimming off curd as it rises. Add 1 tablespoonful more sherry, and skim again, for a few minutes; strain through coarse muslin. May use 2 tablespoonfuls lemon juice instead of wine.

Junket—Take ½ pint of fresh milk, heated lukewarm.

See page inside back cover.

and 1 teaspoonful essence of pepsin and stir just enough
to mix.   Pour into custard cups, let stand until firmly
curded; serve plain or with sugar and grated nutmeg.
May add sherry.

Baked Flour Porridge—Take 1 pint of flour and pack
tightly in a small muslin bag; throw into boiling water
and boil five or six hours; cut off the outer sodden portion, grate the hard core fine; blend thoroughly with a
little milk and stir into boiling milk to the desired thickness.

Rice Jelly—Mix 1 heaping tablespoonful of rice with
cold water until it is in a smooth paste; add 1 scant pint
of boiling water, sweeten with loaf sugar; boil until
quite clear.   Flavor with lemon juice.

Egg-Nog—1 egg, 1 tablespoonful of brandy, 1 tablespoonful of sugar, scant ½ glass of milk.   Beat the white
and yolk of the egg separately; put brandy, sugar and
milk in a glass and stir thoroughly, then add the beaten
eggs and serve.

Rye Coffee

When one is not allowed coffee or tea a good substitute can be made by browning rye as coffee is browned;
then to 1 cup of rye add 1 cup of cold water.   Let it boil
slowly for ten minutes, then add 2 cups of boiling water
water and serve with sugar and cream.

Egg Broth

Beat an egg up high in a broth basin; when quite
frothy stir into it ½ pint of good mutton or veal broth,
quite hot, a little salt and serve with toast.

Tapioca

Cook over night 2 tablespoonfuls of tapioca in 2 cups
of water.   In the morning add 1 pint of milk, sugar to
taste and a pinch of salt; *simmer* until soft, stirring frequently.   When dished add 1 tablespoonful of wine and
grate over a little nutmeg.

MRS. A. J. FISKEN.

HILL'S Maple Sugar for Frostings.

Blanc Mange

Mix 1 tablespoonful of corn starch in a little cold water, add ½ pint of boiling water and boil for a few moments. Take from the fire and when cold add the well beaten white of an egg, sugar and flavoring (lemon, wine or brandy) and pour into a mould to set. Serve with a custard made with ½ cup of milk, the yolk of the egg, sugar and flavoring.

MRS. SILLITOE.

Crackers and Cream

A nicely toasted cracker, with sweet cream poured over it, is delicate and nourishing for an invalid.

MRS. A. J. FISKEN.

Iced Egg

Beat very light the yolk of 1 egg, with a tablespoonful of sugar; stir in tumblerful of very finely crushed ice; add a tablespoonful of brandy and a little grated nutmeg. Beat together and drink immediately.

MRS. A. J. FISKEN.

Beef Tea

Take 2 pounds of lean beef and cut up in pieces half an inch long. Put in a double boiler and cover with cold water for half an hour; then press with potato masher; add a pinch of salt and cook for two hours in the double boiler.

MISS MURRAY.

Chicken Jelly

Clean and disjoint a chicken, removing all the fat and cut the meat into small pieces; break the bones; lay the feet in boiling water; then remove the skin and nails. Put the meat, bones and feet into a granite saucepan, cover with cold water, heat gradually and *simmer* till the meat is tender; strain and when cold remove the fat; add salt, pepper, lemon juice and the shell and white of an egg. Put it on the stove, stirring

See page inside back cover.

well till hot.   Boil five minutes. skim and pour it
through a fine cloth.   Set aside in a mould.   Turn out
and garnish and serve with thin slices of bread and
butter.

MRS. PETERS.

Panada for a New-Born Infant

Take ½ a soda cracker or 2 tiny oyster crackers. roll
them as finely as possible; add a bit of butter the size of
a pea, sweeten to taste; add a bit of nutmeg.   Set this
upon the stove and add ½ pint of boiling water and stir
until it forms a complete jelly.   After a babe is two
months old the butter may be omitted and 2 spoonfuls
of thick cream added while it is warm.   This is the
recipe of a celebrated physician of Albany, N. Y., and
is much better than cows' milk for a young infant.

MRS. RIPLEY.

Panada

Boil 1 tablespoonful of cracker crumbs five minutes
in 1 cup of boiling water. slightly sweetened. salted and
flavored with lemon.

Food for Infants

Dissolve a pinch of Cox's gelatine in enough cold
water to cover it. then pour over it ½ pint of boiling
water; mix to a paste with a little milk. 1 teaspoonful
of arrowroot. 1 teaspoonful of granulated sugar and a
little salt.   Add this to the water and gelatine; then add
sufficient milk to make a pint in all.   Put it over the fire
and let it come to a good boil. stirring often.   It is then
ready for use.   To improve this add 1 teaspoonful of
cream.   The proportion of milk may be increased. also
the cream to 2 tablespoonfuls as the child grows older.
This food is very easily digested and is particularly
good for a baby whose digestive organs are weak.

MRS. PETERS.

HILL'S Maple Syrup.   "Genuine."

Mustard Plaster

Mix with boiling water, vinegar or white of an egg to the same consistency as when prepared for table use. If too strong, add a little flour. Spread one half of a thin muslin cloth with the prepared mustard and cover the mustard with the other half of the cloth, or put mustard on cloth and put over it a thin piece of gauze. Apply, and when removed wash the skin with a soft sponge and apply a little sweet cream or oil to the skin.

Mustard Poultice

Take 8 teaspoonfuls of flaxseed meal, flour or corn meal, 1 teaspoonful of mustard; pour on boiling water until it is of the consistency of mush; spread on cloth the same as in mustard plaster recipe, and moisten the side of the cloth next to the skin and apply warm.

Soda Mint

In 2 quarts of warm water dissolve ¼ pound of bicarbonate of soda. When cold, add ½ large tablespoonful of essence of peppermint. Cook tightly. Good for indigestion.

Cough Mixture No. 1

An English physician's prescription for a cough or weak lungs:

2 ounces honey   2 ounces cod liver oil
Juice of 2 lemons

Put altogether in a bottle and shake until thoroughly mixed. Take 1 tablespoonful directly after meals. It is an excellent remedy if persevered with.

Mrs. M. P. ZINDORF.

Cough Mixture No. 2

2 ounces juniper berries   2 sticks licorice
3 grains opium   1 pint New Orleans molasses
1 pint water

Put all but the opium in a granite vessel and let it

See page inside back cover.

simmer half the day on the back of the stove. Strain off the liquor, add the opium, boil up once and bottle. The opium is to scoth the irritation of the throat.

Mrs. DOUGLAS YOUNG (from an old sea captain).

For insomnia, a glass of very hot milk has a most soothing effect.

For burns, use a cream made of lime water and olive oil. Place the oil in a bowl and add the lime water gradually, beating with a silver fork all the time. This will make a cream which is very cooling.

Stings of insects may be relieved by the application of ammonia or common table salt, well rubbed in.

For Cold in the Head—When you first feel the cold coming on, put a teaspoonful of sugar in a glass, pour upon it six drops of camphor, stir and fill the glass half full of warm water. Stir this until the sugar is dissolved, then take a dessert spoonful every twenty minutes until relieved. This remedy is good if carefully followed.

BEVERAGES

Palace Hotel (San Francisco) Coffee Blend

40 per cent best Old Government Java
40 per cent best Costa Rica
20 per cent Mocha

MR. HOMER F. NORTON.

Coffee

Allow 1 large tablespoonful of coffee to 1 cup. Put the coffee in the pot and first cover with cold water; stand over the fire until it comes to a boil, then move back on the stove where it will just keep below the boiling point. Add to it, a little at a time. sufficient *boiling* water to make the required amount. Do not boil. It needs no clearing.

MRS. WINFIELD R. SMITH.

Chocolate

Allow for each large cup (coffee cup) of chocolate 1 tablespoonful of Ghirardelli's or Maillard's chocolate, scraped; 1 coffee cup of milk, heated; 1 teaspoonful of brandy or 1 tablespoonful of sherry; sugar to taste if the unsweetened chocolate is used. Add enough water to the chocolate to dissolve it; add the sugar, if needed, and let come to a boil; add the hot milk, and when it

See page inside back cover.

boils up again, pour into the chocolate pot onto the brandy or sherry, and if the chocolate is unflavored, a little vanilla. Serve at once.

Mrs CALVIN VILAS.

Cocoa

Cocoa   Milk   Vanilla

For each cupful wanted take 1 teaspoonful (good) of cocoa; dissolve it in enough boiling water to make it about the consistency of cream. For each spoonful of cocoa used take 1 cupful of good rich milk (one-third water may be used if preferred) and let it come to the boiling point; add the cocoa, stirring carefully, and let it boil two minutes. Sweeten to taste, usually about 1 teaspoonful of sugar to a cup of cocoa, just before removing, and when it is taken off the fire flavor with a little vanilla. This is improved by serving with whipped cream.

Mrs. CHARLES I. RILEY.

Raspberry Shrub

4 quarts raspberries   1 quart cider vinegar

Put berries and vinegar together and let stand forty-eight hours. Strain and add 1 pound of sugar to each pint of juice. Boil about ten minutes. Bottle and cork tight.

Mrs. HOMER F. NORTON.

Raspberry Vinegar

3 gallons ripe red raspberries
1 gallon cider vinegar

Crush the raspberries thoroughly to a pulp. Pour the vinegar over the crushed fruit and allow it to stand two days. Strain as for jelly; add 1 pound of sugar to each pint of juice. Allow it to come to a boil, and bottle while scalding hot. Seal the corks, and set away in a cool dark place.

Mrs. J. D. LOWMAN.

HILL'S Maple Syrup. "Genuine."

Blackberry Cordial

Squeeze blackberries enough to make a quart of juice, add to it a pound of loaf sugar and let it dissolve, heating slowly. Add to it 1 teaspoonful each of cloves, cinnamon and nutmeg. Boil all together twenty minutes. On removing from the fire add a wineglassful of brandy. Put in bottles while hot and seal. Use a teaspoonful for a glass of iced water.

MRS. WM. II DE WOLF.

Blackberry Wine

Wash the berries and pour on 1 quart of boiling water to each gallon of berries. Let the mixture stand twenty-four hours, stirring occasionally; then strain and add 2 pounds of sugar and 1 pint best rye whiskey, or ½ pint alcohol, to each gallon of juice. Cork tightly and let stand until October, when rack off and bottle.

Scotch Ginger Beer

2 gallows water   2 pounds white sugar
2 ounces ginger root   4 lemons
½ yeast cake   Whites of 2 eggs

Cut the lemons and bruise the ginger root, mixing them with the sugar and water; boil, strain and set to cool; then add the yeast. Let it stand thirty-six hours; then add the well beaten whites of the eggs. Bottle, tightly cork, and in two days it will evervesce and be ready for use.

MRS. THOMAS W. PROSCH.

See page inside back cover.

MISCELLANEOUS

"There's lots of religion in a beefsteak, if you give it to the right man at the right time."—*Jerry McAuley.*

Good Kitchen and Laundry Soap

1 bar of good laundry soap shaved thin, 3 pints of water, 2 large tablespoonfuls of salsoda and 1 of borax. Let this boil until all dissolved, then take from the stove and add 1 tablespoonful of turpentine and 1½ of ammonia.

MRS. R. C. WASHBURN.

Soft Soap

1 can Babbit's lye   3 pounds fat
2½ gallons boiling water

Dissolve the lye in the water, put in fat and cook ten hours. One hour before taking off the fire add 2 gallons more water, and after it is taken off add as much more water as you have of this mixture, which will make about nine gallons of soap.

MRS. NEUFELDER.

Meat Pickle

6 gallons water	9 pounds salt
1 quart molasses	3 ounces saltpeter
1 ounce soda	3 pounds coarse brown sugar

Boil and skim until clear and add to the meat cold. The meat should be closely packed and a weight placed on top before the pickle is added. This rule is sufficient

See page inside back cover.

for a barrel of meat and half the quantity is enough for a quarter of beef.

MRS. A. T. TIMMERMAN.

Corned Beef

Get a piece of round beef from below the hip (with the bone attached), weighing thirteen or fourteen pounds. Rub over it a mixture of 1 teaspoonful of saltpetre and 1 tablespoonful of sugar; then rub 1 large handful of salt very thoroughly into each side of it, getting into all the creases. Set away in a cool place and baste it well every day for eight days in its own liquor, being careful to turn it over each day. Boil it about six hours or until tender. Better when eaten cold, thinly sliced.

MISS COLLINS.

Caramel

1 teacup sugar   4 tablespoonfuls water

Put in a skillet over hot fire, stirring constantly until thoroughly burnt, when add enough water to make a thin syrup. Bottle. This will keep any length of time and is used for coloring soups and gravies.

MRS. EUGENE RICKSECKER.

Spinach Green

Pound a quantity of spinach in a mortar; put the pulp in a muslin bag and twist and squeeze out the juice; add a quarter of its weight in sugar, heat it till reduced one-half and bottle. This is used to color soups, ices and candies.

MRS. M. A. KELLOGG.

Roux

Not quite twice as much flour as butter; melt butter; stir in flour; stir until smooth, then add boiling water until it is as thick as boiled starch; will keep a long time and is very nice for soups. For croquettes add milk.

ISABEL JONES.

HILL'S Maple Syrup.   "Genuine."

Celery Vinegar

Soak 1 ounce of celery seed in $\frac{1}{2}$ pint of vinegar; bottle it and use to flavor soups and gravies.

THE HOME COOK BOOK.

Pure Baking Powder

9 ounces cream of tartar $4\frac{1}{2}$ ounces bicarbonate soda
$2\frac{1}{4}$ ounces flour or corn starch

Sift thoroughly several times and keep in a dry place.

C. HOWELL KIRBY.

Cleansing Fluid

$\frac{1}{2}$ ounce chloroform $\frac{1}{4}$ ounce ether
$\frac{1}{4}$ ounce oil of wintergreen 1 ounce alcohol

Shake well and add $\frac{1}{2}$ gallon of deodorized benzine. One-half this quantity makes a large bottle full. This mixture is highly inflammable and should not be used at night or near a fire. Is especially nice for cleaning gloves.

MRS. M. F. BACKUS.

How to Wash Blankets

Use warm (not hot) water and add to each gallon a tablespoonful of ammonia and the same quantity of powdered borax. Put the blankets in and rub through the hands and rinse up and down. Wring by hand. Prepare another tub of water of the same temperature in the same way. using a little less ammonia and borax; the last tub (and three are usually required) need not contain any and ought to look entirely clean when the blankets come out. Choose a bright day.

MRS. CHARLES E. SHEPARD.

To Wash Flannels

Two bars of Ivory soap. $4\frac{1}{2}$ gallons of soft water. 2 ounces of borax, ammonia enough to give a strong odor. Use a cupful of the preparation in tepid water when

See page inside back cover.

washing flannels; it will remove all dirt and the flannels will not shrink.

MRS. H. C. HENRY.

To Remove Stains

Take an ounce of hartshorn and one of salts of tartar; mix them well; add a pint of soft water and bottle for use. Keep very tightly corked always. To use, pour a little of the liquid in a saucer and wash in it white articles which are stained with ink, mildew, fruit or wine. Rinse carefully in cold water, after the stains are removed; then wash in the usual manner.

MRS. RIPLEY.

Library Paste

This will not sour and will keep indefinitely. One tablespoonful of flour mixed dry with ¼ teaspoonful of powdered alum. Mix smoothly with a teaspoonful of cold water; then set on the stove and pour in about 2 teaspoonfuls of boiling water. Cook until very thick, taking care not to let it burn. A few drops of perfume may be added. Put in a wide-mouthed bottle.

Furniture Polish

½ pint raw linseed oil　　　1 gill alcohol
1 gill strong coffee

Shake well and add 1 gill of soft water.

MRS. A. W. ENGLE.

Chilblaines

Rub thoroughly and frequently with oil of lavender; or with coarse common salt.

Coloring for Finger Nails

1 part tincture benzoine　　2 parts alcohol
Eosine to color a *deep* red

Apply with camel's hair brush, and polish.

HILL'S Maple Sugar for Frostings.

Tooth Powder

Powdered pumice with a drop or two of oil of geranium in it.

Lotion for the Skin

1 part glycerine   6 parts rose water
          ½ part tincture benzoine

This is good for sun-burn, wind-burn, or chaps. It makes a milky mixture. Keep tightly corked.

Hair Wash

1 ounce borax   ½ ounce camphor

Powder these ingredients fine; dissolve them in 1 quart of boiling water. When cool, the solution is ready for use. Dampen the hair frequently. The camphor will form into lumps after being dissolved, but the water will be sufficiently impregnated.

Mrs. ISAAC H. JENNINGS.

Cold Cream

1½ drachms white wax   1½ drachms spermaceti
          ¾ ounce oil of sweet almonds

Melt the spermaceti and wax together, add the oil; then beat up into this mixture 30 minims tincture of benzoine, 2 tablespoonfuls rose water; attar of roses or any perfume desired. Beat with a Dover egg beater until the cream thickens.

Mrs. CURTIS.

½ box of gelatine will make 1 quart of jelly. The quart, however, must include the water used in soaking and dissolving the gelatine. Always soak gelatine in cold water until perfectly soft, then pour *boiling* water upon it to dissolve it. Granulated gelatine dissolves very rapidly and needs but a few moments to soften it. On ½ box of gelatine put ½ cup cold water to soften it, and from ½ cup to 1 cup of boiling water to dissolve it.

To take the taste of onion from knives, etc., slice up a raw potato.

See page inside back cover.
c. c.—19

Mix a mustard plaster with the white of an egg to prevent blistering.

To keep silver bright rinse in hot water with household ammonia; 1 teaspoonful to 1 quart.

To take fish odor from pans, wash with strong soda water.

"*A Sweet Disposition*—Three grains common sense, 1 large heart, 1 good liver, plenty of fresh air and sunlight, 1 bushel contentment and 1 good husband. Do not bring to a boil."

Cornstarch is a good substitute for eggs in cookies and doughnuts. One tablespoonful is equal to an egg.

A very good substitute for cream in coffee may be made by pouring 1 cup of *scalded* milk onto a beaten egg and adding a bit of butter size of a pea.

To Take Grease From Cloth—Make a paste of Fuller's earth and turpentine. Rub on fabric until turpentine evaporates and a white powder remains. The latter can be brushed off, and the grease will have disappeared.

To keep glass jars from breaking when pouring in boiling fruit, wrap a cold wet cloth around the jar.

To remove tar or pitch, rub well with clean lard, afterwards wash with soap and warm water. For either hands or clothing.

In making corn bread always have the bowl you mix it in hot.

To keep fruit from raising to the top of the jar, cook in a *thick* syrup and lay the can on its side.

If a clove of garlic is kept in salad oil, it will give the hint of garlic desirable in salad, and keep the oil from getting rancid.—*Mrs. T. M. Daulton.*

HILL'S Maple Syrup. "Genuine."

Lime water is an important factor in the nursery, and no mother would neglect its use, if she realized its effect on the bones and teeth of growing children.—*Mrs. L. L. Moore.*

Strew the store room shelves with a few cloves, to drive away ants.

Ink spots, when fresh, may be removed by washing in sweet milk.

A little salt rubbed on a discolored eggspoon will remove the stains.

To take out fruit stains, stretch the stained part over a bowl and pour on boiling water.

Clean white ivory knife handles or white marble with damp salt.

Clean the outside of windows in cold weather with kerosene.

For new windows use alcohol; it cuts the putty and oil.

Put a few drops of ammonia on a moist cloth to clean windows. Vinegar is also good for the same purpose.

One lemon is usually equal to two tablespoonfuls of juice.

Meats and Their Accompaniments

With roast beef: Tomato sauce, grated horse-radish, mustard, cranberry sauce, pickles.

With roast port: Apple sauce, cranberry sauce.

With roast veal: Tomato sauce, mushroom sauce, onion sauce and cranberry sauce. Horse-radish and lemons are good.

With roast mutton: Currant jelly, caper sauce.

With boiled mutton: Onion sauce, caper sauce.

With boiled fowls: Bread sauce, onion sauce, lemon sauce, cranberry sauce, jellies, also cream sauce.

See page inside back cover.

With roast lamb: Mint sauce.

With roast turkey: Cranberry sauce, currant jelly.

With boiled turkey: Oyster sauce.

With venison or wild ducks: Cranberry sauce, currant jelly or currant jelly warmed with port wine.

With roast goose: Apple sauce, cranberry sauce, grape or currant jelly.

With boiled fresh mackerel: Stewed gooseberries.

With boiled bluefish: White cream sauce, lemon sauce.

With boiled shad: Mushroom sauce, parsley or egg sauce.

With fresh salmon: Green peas, cream sauce.

Pickels are good with all roast meats.

Spinach is the proper accompaniment to veal.

Lemon juice makes a very grateful addition to nearly all the insipid members of the fish kingdom.   Slices of lemon cut into very small dice and stirred into drawn butter and allowd to come to the boiling point, forms a very nice sauce to serve with fowls.

Serve cranberry sherbet with roast turkey.

Who Shall Be First

There are different opinions regarding the propriety of serving first the most distinguished guest — the lady at the right of the host or the hostess herself.   The custom of serving the *hostess first* which obtains so largely has its origin far back in the olden times when *poisoning* was much in vogue and it was deemed wiser and safer to observe whether the hostess partook of a dish before one tasted it oneself.

MRS. D. C. GARRETT.

The *Expert Waitress* says: There are good reasons for serving the lady of the house first, although this rule is often waived to do honor to the distinguished guest for whom luncheon or dinner is given.   In a country house several distinguished guests or dear friends are entertained at one time; to serve the hostess

HILL'S Maple Sugar for Frostings.

first and follow a regular order along the table makes no distinction. Novelties are often introduced, both in food and in service. Dishes are served before which a guest hesitates as to which fork or which spoon to use until he glances at his hostess to see which one she takes up. * * * A hostess who takes pride in having her forks made to suit special courses, like asparagus, and who has several forks laid by each plate before dinner is served, finds it necessary to take up the right one before her guests make a choice. I have in mind a dinner where the hostess delayed the tasting of a course, the absent-minded host took the wrong fork. some guests took one and some another. The butler did his best to replace the right ones: but after all his efforts. somebody had a wrong fork to the end of the dinner.

MENUS.

Which May Be Prepared for $2.00.

Cream of Celery
Boiled Salmon, Sauce Hollandaise
Cucumbers

Roast Beef   Yorkshire Pudding

Stuffed Tomatoes
Pecan Salad

Fruit Jelly   Coffee

Clear Soup
Sweetbreads in Cream
Roasted Duck, Walnut Stuffing

Rice Balls   Asparagus

Fruit Salad
Queen Pudding
Coffee

Tomato Soup
Halibut à la Crème
Panned Chicken, Cream Sauce

Peas   Chestnut Croquettse

Mayonnaise of Celery

Pineapple Ice   Cake

Coffee

Consomme Julienne
Fish Cream Cutlets, Lemon Sauce
Roast Lamb, Mint Sauce

Peas   Potato Balls

Salad of Asparagus Tips
Prune Float
Coffee

HILL'S Maple Syrup.   "Genuine."

MENUS

Which May Be Prepared for $1.00.

Oyster Bisque

Baked Salmon, Stuffed

String Beans   Potatoes

Tomato Baskets

Crackers   Cheese

Coffee

———————

Tomato Soup with Stock

Broiled Steak   Potatoes on Half Shell

Macaroni with Cheese

Apple Salad

Banana Puffs

Coffee

———————

Steamed Clams

Broiled Chops   Peas

Potato Chips

Lettuce Salad

Orange Pudding

Coffee

———————

Barley Soup

Veal Cutlets, Tomato Sauce

Escalloped Potatoes   Spinach

Beet Salad

Apple Scallop

Coffee

See page inside back cover.

UNCLASSIFIED

"Table talk to be perfect should be sincere without bigotry, differing without discord, sometimes grave, always agreeable, touching on deep points, dwelling most on reasonable ones, and letting everybody speak and be heard."—*Leigh Hunt.*

Waffles

5 eggs
1 quart flour
1½ pints new milk
3 tablespoonfuls yeast
2 teaspoonfuls salt

Beat the eggs very light, add the flour and the milk and yeast; set to rise over night. In the morning stir them down with a spoon just as you are ready to bake them. They are better baked in the oven than in waffle irons.

Mrs. GILBERT S. MEEM.

Louisiana Okra Gumbo

1 pint okra, fresh or canned
1 can Eastern oysters
1 spring chicken
1 tablespoonful lard
Onion to taste
1 teaspoonful flour

Fry the chicken, cut in joints, in the hot lard until a nice brown; add flour, brown; then onion and okra; fry a nice brown; add the drained oysters, fry all about ten minutes; then add 3 quarts boiling water, including oyster liquor. Cook until chicken is tender; season highly, not forgetting a dash of cayenne pepper. Serve as soup, but accompanied by rice cooked à la Créole, that is every grain separate.

Mrs. A. B. ALLAIN.

HILL'S Maple Sugar for Frostings.

Crab Bisque

Take 1 good pint of crabs. 1 light pint of fine bread crumbs or crackers; mix thoroughly, adding 1 tablespoonful of butter, onion to taste; season highly. Fry this mixture in hot lard ten minutes, then add 2 quarts boiling water, let boil twenty minutes and serve. Delicious soup.

MRS. A. B. ALLAIN.

French Oyster Soup

1 can Eastern oysters	1 tablespoonful lard
1 tablespoonful butter	Onion to taste
1 teaspoonful flour	1 cup milk

Make a roux by browning flour in hot lard in soup kettle; then fry the onion; then the oysters previously drained; add 2 quarts boiling water, including the oyster liquid; then the butter, season to taste and boil twenty minutes. At the last add small teacup of milk to color the soup.

MRS. A. B. ALLAIN.

Jambalaya

Take any cold meat, fowl preferred, chop rather fine, add same quantity of cooked rice, a little onion, 1 tablespoonful of butter, season highly with cayenne, and fry in hot lard or butter.

MRS. A. B. ALLAIN.

Nut Jelly Salad

In a saucepan put 3 cupfuls of English walnut meats, 2 slices of onion, 1 teaspoonful of salt, 2 blades of mace, 2 bay leaves. Cover with boiling water, and boil ten minutes, drain and drop into ice water until needed. Then dry thoroughly in a towel and with a sharp knife cut (not chop) each nut into several pieces and add enough mayonnaise to mix well together.

In a clean saucepan put 1 quart of boiling water, 4 cloves, 2 blades of mace, ¼ teaspoonful of celery seed, 1 slice of onion, 1 bay leaf, 4 slices of carrot, 2 slices of

See page inside back cover.

turnip, 2 teaspoonfuls of beef extract and *simmer* gently for thirty minutes. Season to taste. add ⅔ box of gelatine, which has been soaked in water, and stir till dissolved. Strain very carefully and add 4 tablespoonfuls of tarragon vinegar. Have ready a dozen medium sized timbale moulds dipped in cold water. Pour into them the aspic and put away until set. Then scoop out the center of each and fill with the nut mixture. Put the fragments of jelly where they will melt without heating, and when liquid put a little over the top of each mould. Keep on ice until ready to use, then turn out and serve on lettuce leaves, garnishing with mayonnaise and paprika.—*From Table Talk.*

Walnut Salad

Shell ¼ pound of English walnuts, throw them into boiling water and remove the skin, then put them into stock. add 1 slice of onion, 1 bay leaf and cook for twenty minutes; a few almond nuts may be added and a handful of pine nuts. Mix these with 2 chopped apples and mayonnaise dressing and serve on lettuce leaves. Bits of cold boiled chicken may also be mixed with the mayonnaise and apples. Pare and core the apples and cut them into dice.

MRS. S. T. RORER and THE HOUSEHOLD NEWS.

Chestnut and English Walnut Salad

Prepare the walnuts as for walnut salad. Have the chestnuts shelled and blanched; boil till they are soft and tender. Mix the walnuts and chestnuts together, pour over a French dressing and serve on lettuce leaves. Celery may be cut into small pieces and mixed with them. Apples may be used instead of the celery; garnish with mayonnaise.

MRS. S. T. RORER and THE HOUSEHOLD NEWS CO.

New England Sausage

To each pound of pork (from the ham, little more lean than fat) add 2 teaspoonfuls salt, 1 teaspoonful sage, ½ teaspoonful black pepper and ¼ teaspoonful red pepper. Mix all together thoroughly. Cut cloth for bags eight inches wide and two or three feet long; press the meat in as solidly as possible.

MRS. STROUT.

Creamed Chicken

1 chicken. about 3 pounds	1½ pounds sweetbreads
1 can mushrooms	1 pint cream
1 tablespoonful flour	2 tablespoonfuls butter

Salt and pepper

Cut the chicken, which has been previously cooked, into dice, cut the mushrooms into quarters, parboil the sweetbreads and cut like the chicken. Let the cream come to boiling point in double boiler; cream half the butter and the flour and stir into the cream; cook till it thickens and season. Butter an escallop dish, and put in chicken, sweetbreads. mushrooms and sauce in layers with sauce on top. Cover with crumbs, dot with the remaining tablespoonful of butter and bake one hour.

MRS. W. I. ADAMS.

Yellow Soup

1 quart stock	¼ cup small sago (scant)
1 quart milk	4 eggs (yolks only)

Cook the sago in the stock till clear; scald the milk and add to the cooked sago and stock; season. Beat the yolks of the eggs in the tureen and carefully pour the boiling soup over them. Beat thoroughly and serve *immediately*. Any stock may be used, but half veal and half chicken makes a very delicate soup.

MRS. W. I. ADAMS.

Raspberry Meringue

Line a pie plate with good light pastry and bake in a quick oven. While still warm, spread thickly with red raspberries. Make a meringue of the whites of 4 eggs beaten stiff with ½ cup of powdered sugar and when it is a froth stir lightly through it ½ pint of

See page inside back cover.

raspberries. Heap the meringue on top of the berries in the pie plate and brown very delicately in the oven.

MRS. W. H. DE WOLF.

Potted Herrings

Will Serve Four Persons.

1 dozen herrings   ½ teacup vinegar and water
Flour, pepper and salt

Clean thoroughly, remove roe; remove head and tail and slip out bone, sprinkle with flour, pepper and salt; roll up neatly and pack in deep dish, sprinkle over with flour, pepper and salt; pour over vinegar and water and bake thoroughly; they should show a nice brown; to be eaten cold. Use Crosse & Blackwell's malt vinegar if possible.

MRS. WEBSTER BROWN.

Potted Salmon

Take some cold boiled salmon and pound in a mortar; add pepper, salt and ground herbs, a liberal quantity of butter; mix thoroughly and pack lightly into small jars; cover with melted butter.

MRS. STILLITOE.

"Some hae meat and canna eat,
And some would eat that want it,
But we hae meat, and we can eat,
Sae let the Lord be thankit."

— *Burns.*

INDEX

HILL'S Maple Syrup. "Genuine."

See page inside back cover.

See inside page back cover.

HILL'S Maple Sugar for Frostings.

C. C.—20

See inside page back cover.

MRS. WHITEMAN

RIALTO BUILDING,
Adjoining Public Library.

Embroideries: Stamping Silks.
Lessons given.

LEE & BOWDEN

REAL ESTATE LOANS
AND FIRE INSURANCE

Rooms 1, 2, 3 Dexter Horton Bank
Building,
Seattle, - - Washington.

J. & W. HOPKINS

FLORISTS.

Dealers in Fruit Trees, Plants and
Seeds; designs a specialty; ten
greenhouses. Telephone red 1015.
618 SECOND AVENUE.
Seattle, - - - Washington.

MRS. J. W. GLASSCOCK

FASHIONABLE DRESSMAKING.

Cutting and fitting. Guarantees
satisfaction. The patronage of the
lady readers of this book especially
solicited. 307 Seneca Street.

MISS C. MacLEAN

FASHIONABLE DRESSMAKING.

Rooms 15 and 16 Holyoke Building.
Cor. First Ave. and Spring St.,
Seattle, Washington.

GEORGE N. MOORE

PHOTOGRAPHER,

Boston Block, Second Avenue and
Columbia Street,
Seattle, Washington.

Established 1870.

JAMES EGGAN

—PHOTOGRAPHER—

207 Pike Street, Seattle, Washington.

Ground Floor Studio.
High Grade Work.

MRS. C. P. WILSON

MRS. R. B. SEXTON

DRESSMAKING.

Rooms 9 and 10 Starr-Boyd Block,

Seattle, Washington.

MISS N. M. CHEASTY

Importer of

FINE MILLINERY.

Colonial Block, Second Avenue and
Columbia Street.

Seattle, Washington.

IXL DAIRY

CHOICE BUTTER.
CREAM AND MILK.

PURE ICE CREAM.
Delivered free to any part o fthe city.
1405 Second Avenue, Seattle.
Telephone Pike 48.

V. R. PEIRSON

CONTRACTOR

—AND—

BUILDER.

Send a postal to 221 Cherry St.,
and I will call on you.

EUGENE RICKSECKER

CIVIL AND TOPOGRAPHICAL
ENGINEER.

Surveys, Plans, Inspection, Examinations and Reports.

532 Burke Building, Seattle, Wash.
P. O. Box 289.

Patronize Our Advertisers.

SAINT MARK'S EXCHANGE

714 Second Avenue

OPEN EVERY SATURDAY

Home Cooking, Fancy Work

Orders taken for Cakes, Ices, Ice Creams,
Rolls, etc., and for all kinds of Fancy Work.
"CLEVER COOKING" for Sale, Price 50c.

SAINT MARK'S GUILD

—— OFFICERS ——

Mrs. WINFIELD R. SMITH, President.
Mrs. HOMER F. NORTON, Vice-President.
Mrs. EUGENE RICKSECKER, Secretary.
Mrs. MARY C. CALHOUN, Treasurer.

Meets the first Friday in each month,
in the Guild Room, at 2 P. M.

Send all orders to the Secretary, 832
Albert Street.